The Global Right Wing and the Clash of World Politics

Human rights, environmentalism, and global justice: these transnational movements today face fierce opposition from networks of conservative activists promoting contrary aims. In this groundbreaking book, Clifford Bob analyzes the clashes, proposing a new model of global policy making – and unmaking. This highlights the battle of networks, marked by exclusionary strategies, negative tactics, and dissuasive ideas. Bob first investigates the fight over gay rights, in which a coalition of religious conservatives, the "Baptist-burqa" network, confronts human rights groups at the United Nations and in such countries as Sweden, Romania, and Uganda. Next, he examines conflicts over gun control, pitting firearms enthusiasts against disarmament and safety advocates in the UN, Brazil, and elsewhere. Bob's provocative findings extend beyond the culture wars. With its critical conclusions about norms, activists, and institutions, this book will change how campaigners fight, analysts study international issues, and all of us think about global politics.

Clifford Bob is associate professor of political science at Duquesne University. His first book, *The Marketing of Rebellion: Insurgents, Media, and International Activism*, won the 2007 International Studies Association Best Book Award and was named a "Top Book of 2006" by *The Globalist*. His edited volume, *The International Struggle for New Human Rights*, was released in 2009, and he has published widely in political science, sociology, law, and policy. His scholarly interests include human rights, globalization, and nongovernmental organizations. He holds a PhD from the Massachusetts Institute of Technology, a JD from New York University, and a BA from Harvard University.

To Joan

Cambridge Studies in Contentious Politics

Editors

Mark Beissinger *Princeton University*
Jack A. Goldstone *George Mason University*
Michael Hanagan *Vassar College*
Doug McAdam *Stanford University and Center for Advanced
Study in the Behavioral Sciences*
Suzanne Staggenborg *University of Pittsburgh*
Sidney Tarrow *Cornell University*
Charles Tilly *(d. 2008) Columbia University*
Elisabeth J. Wood *Yale University*
Deborah Yashar *Princeton University*

Ronald Aminzade et al., *Silence and Voice in the Study of
Contentious Politics*
Javier Auyero, *Routine Politics and Violence in Argentina:
The Gray Zone of State Power*
Clifford Bob, *The Marketing of Rebellion: Insurgents, Media,
and International Activism*
Charles Brockett, *Political Movements and Violence in Central
America*
Christian Davenport, *Media Bias, Perspective, and State
Repression*
Gerald F. Davis, Doug McAdam, W. Richard Scott, and Mayer
N. Zald, *Social Movements and Organization Theory*
Jack A. Goldstone, editor, *States, Parties, and Social Movements*
Tamara Kay, *NAFTA and the Politics of Labor
Transnationalism*
Joseph Luders, *The Civil Rights Movement and the Logic of
Social Change*
Doug McAdam, Sidney Tarrow, and Charles Tilly, *Dynamics of
Contention*

Continued after the Index

The Global Right Wing and the Clash of World Politics

CLIFFORD BOB

Duquesne University

CAMBRIDGE
UNIVERSITY PRESS

CAMBRIDGE UNIVERSITY PRESS
Cambridge, New York, Melbourne, Madrid, Cape Town,
Singapore, São Paulo, Delhi, Tokyo, Mexico City

Cambridge University Press
32 Avenue of the Americas, New York, NY 10013-2473, USA

www.cambridge.org
Information on this title: www.cambridge.org/9780521145442

© Clifford Bob 2012

This publication is in copyright. Subject to statutory exception
and to the provisions of relevant collective licensing agreements,
no reproduction of any part may take place without the written
permission of Cambridge University Press.

First published 2012

Printed in the United States of America

A catalog record for this publication is available from the British Library.

Library of Congress Cataloging in Publication data

Bob, Clifford, 1958–
The global right wing and the clash of world politics / Clifford Bob.
    p.   cm. – (Cambridge studies in contentious politics)
Includes bibliographical references and index.
ISBN 978-0-521-19381-8 (hardback) – ISBN 978-0-521-14544-2 (paperback)
1. Non-governmental organizations – Political activity.   2. Right and left
(Political science) – History – 21st century.   3. Political activists – History –
21st century.   4. Social conflict – Political aspects.   5. Culture and
globalization.   I. Title.
JZ4841.B63   2011
320.52–dc23   2011044021

ISBN 978-0-521-19381-8 Hardback
ISBN 978-0-521-14544-2 Paperback

Additional resources for this publication at
www.cambridge.org/9780521145442

Cambridge University Press has no responsibility for the persistence or accuracy
of URLs for external or third-party Internet Web sites referred to in this
publication and does not guarantee that any content on such Web sites is, or
will remain, accurate or appropriate.

Contents

Preface

For more than twenty years, climate change has divided citizens around the world. The conflicting sides have formed broad networks. They have advanced their goals in local, national, and international institutions. They have sought to convince the public and policy makers of their contrary views. At the same time, the factions have spared no effort to attack their foes – for methodological errors, scientific misconduct, and worse. Apparent milestones, like the Kyoto Protocol or the Copenhagen Summit, have in fact been mere way stations in an ongoing war. Basic matters – from the degree of warming, to its causes, to possible remedies, to their effects – remain contested.

This protracted battle over a matter portrayed as vital to the world's survival – or the economy's prosperity – is hardly unique. In issue after issue within countries and internationally, similarly discordant stories could be told. The death penalty, poverty alleviation, nuclear power, humanitarian intervention – these and countless others involve zealous activists persistently jousting over current decisions, future policies, and past interpretations.

This book concerns such disputes, proposing a way of understanding them and their outcomes. My primary focus is transnational: nonviolent conflict crossing national borders and international institutions. In this, I focus on the important but

understudied operations of right-wing activists. Equally, I analyze their continuous clashes with human rights, environmental,
and social justice groups – not only the rivals' efforts to sway
decision makers, but also their strategic attacks on one another.
In particular, I highlight fights over gay rights and gun control
at the United Nations and in countries such as Brazil, Romania,
Sweden, and the United States.

The argument I make, however, applies more broadly, to any
number of political issues, both domestic and international, as
well as the many connections between. In the Introduction and
especially in the Conclusion, I discuss the scope of my argument.
For now, it is useful to note that I do not confine it to the left-right
rift, notwithstanding the first part of this book's title. That ideological division encompasses much, but it by no means exhausts
the sources of contention in contemporary society.

In this book, I hope to convey the fervor, invention, and antagonism I have observed. I have written it not only to advance
political science, but also to inform activists and the broader
public. The issues are too hot and the personalities too intrigu-
ing to leave to specialists alone. This has posed certain problems
for the research. For one thing, to what extent can the parties
to the conflicts be trusted to have provided me with accurate
information? This problem occurs in much political research.
But because of the emotions boiling around gay rights and gun
control, partisans invariably suspect their opposite numbers of
deceit. I have been skeptical too and have sought throughout to
base my analysis on evidence beyond what I am told or given.

As a second problem indicative of the passions involved, I have
been sucked into the vortex myself, not just as an observer, but as
an unasked-for bit player. For instance, in interviewing leaders of
Brazil's pro-gun coalition, Pela Legitima Defesa (PLD), I used my
trusty if antiquated cassette tape recorder, as I do when permitted
in all interviews. Unexpectedly, my interviewees turned the tables
and upped the ante. They trained the latest pocket-sized, tripod-
mounted, digital video-recorder on me, so that both of us would
have a record of the interview. Two days later, a description of
my visit, complete with photos, appeared on a PLD blog under

the Portuguese title, "North American Expert Visits Brazil to Learn How We Won the 2005 Referendum."

A similar thing happened when I interviewed a leader of the Romanian Alliance for Families (ARF), a group defending "traditional families." Days later, he informed me by e-mail that the group's upcoming newsletter would note my 2009 book, *The International Struggle for New Human Rights*, which, among other chapters, includes one by a prominent and openly lesbian scholar on the promotion of gay rights among human rights NGOs. A few weeks later, ARF quoted a broad passage from the book's introduction in a commentary submitted to the Parliamentary Assembly of the Council of Europe. Without meaning to and admittedly in minor ways, I have therefore been inserted into these conflicts myself – a "risk" that all social scientists investigating controversial contemporary issues face.

A final point along these lines concerns my own positions on the issues. I have sought throughout to be objective and to keep my personal views out of my work. This has been difficult. Those who promote a "scholar-activist" model might say it is a mistake. Although I take strong stances in other settings, including op-ed pieces and public blogs, I believe it is important in works that seek to advance political science to keep one's own politics out – or at least to try to do so. To do otherwise distorts reality and therefore does a disservice to the groups one supports.

For information and insights that made this book possible, I thank the many people I interviewed both in person and by telephone. For critical financial support, I thank the American Council of Learned Societies fellowship program. In addition, I thank Duquesne University, particularly its Faculty Development Fund, Presidential Scholarship, and late Dean Albert C. Labriola. Duquesne has been a wonderful setting for my scholarship and teaching during this project. I am grateful to my students with whom I shared chapters and from whom I received excellent feedback. I also thank my colleagues at the McAnulty College of Liberal Arts, especially in the political science department.

During the years that I worked on this book – even before I knew that I was doing so, or knew what I was doing – I was given the chance to present pieces that, in one form or another, have become part of it. I am grateful for invitations from: Northwestern University International Organizations and International Law Workshop; Oxford University Department of International Development; City University of New York Politics and Protest Workshop; Duke University Seminar on Global Governance and Democracy; Widener University School of Law; Indiana University School of Public and Environmental Affairs; Brown University, Watson Institute for International Studies; American Society of International Law annual meeting; University of Maryland, Contentious Politics/International Relations Workshop; Norman Patterson School of International Affairs, Carleton University; University of Pennsylvania Annenberg School for Communication; London School of Economics Centre for the Study of Global Governance; George Washington University Institute for Global and International Studies; University of Pittsburgh Social Movement Forum, Center for Latin American Studies, and International Relations Workshop; and Cornell/Syracuse Universities Workshop on Transnational Contention. For their support of me during these events, I am particularly grateful to Karen Alter, Deborah Avant, Kathy Blee, Timothy Buthe, Martha Finnemore, Kirsten A. Gronbjerg, Rodney Bruce Hall, Virginia Haufler, James Jasper, Mary Kaldor, John Markoff, David Mendeloff, Hans Peter Schmitz, Susan Sell, Andrew Strauss, and Steven M. Watt.

In addition to the helpful comments I received at all these events and at regular professional meetings, a number of individuals took the time to write critiques of my work in progress. These include Cristina Balboa, Charli Carpenter, Joerg Friedrichs, Mark Haas, Michael Hanagan, James Jasper, Kate Krimmel, Daniel Kryder, David S, Meyer, Helen Milner, Aseem Prakash, Luc Reydams, James Ron, Valerie Sperling, Andrew Strauss, Sarah Stroup, June Swinski, Sidney Tarrow, Mitchell Troup, and Elke Zuern. I am particularly grateful as well for the support of Lewis Bateman, my editor at Cambridge University Press.

Others who contributed in various ways to this book include Peter Agree, Eva Bellin, Daniel Bob, Alexander Cooley, John

Dale, Kevin DenDulk, Eileen Doherty-Sil, Patrick Doreian, Mike Edwards, Jennifer Erickson, Archon Fung, Tamar Gutner, Fen Hampson, Giuditta Hanau Santini (without deprecation), Roger Haydon, Paul Heck, Bonnie Honig, Lisa Jordan, Pamela Martin, David McBride, James Morone, Charles Myers, Sharon Erickson Nepstad, Robert Paarlberg, Martin Packer, Leigh Payne, Daniel Posner, Lawrence Rosenthal, Richard J. Samuels, Alberta Sbragia, Frank Schwartz, Rudra Sil, Joel Swanson (the "man on the street"), Stephen Van Evera, Paul Wapner, Claude Welch, and Steven Wilkinson. At risk of pretentiousness, I also pay tribute to several works of art that have been constant companions as I wrote this book: Joseph Conrad's *Nostromo: A Tale of the Seaboard*, a beautiful and brilliant study of political conflict; Gustav Mahler's First Symphony; and Ludwig van Beethoven's *Missa Solemnis*.

Any errors that remain in the book – including my inadvertent omission of any who helped me in this project over the years – are of course my responsibility. Speaking of omissions, this book includes no bibliography, although I cite all references fully in the footnotes. A full bibliography is available at the book's permanent Cambridge University Press Web site. This includes "active citations," an important new idea proposed by Andrew Moravcsik, allowing readers to view at a click all or part of many of my sources, including most importantly primary sources. This should make it easier for others to detect my errors, refine my interpretations, and advance scholarship for all.

My thankfulness to my family is greatest. I hope that my years of work on conflict helped pacify me at home, but I am not so sure. In any case, I am grateful to my children, Alex and Natalie, for keeping me from becoming too serious. In particular, I will always treasure their laughing with me about a *Planet of the Apes* movie trailer about armed apes hunting "lowly terrified humans" and at me about my misadventures failing to hike up Rio de Janeiro's Sugarloaf Mountain. I also thank my mother, Renate Bob, for deluging me with useful articles on right-wing activism from her host of left-wing listservs – and generally for being the greatest Mom one could hope for.

Most importantly, I thank my wife, Joan Miles, who gritted her teeth through my obsession with the right wing and kept on smiling, usually. Joan has been an inspiration and sometimes a prod to my work. Both were critical to my finishing this book more or less on time. Whether she likes it or not, I dedicate this work to her, with love.

I

Clashing Networks in World Politics

In the summer of 2003, a handful of beleaguered Brazilians appealed for help from a powerful American rights organization. Menaced by new government initiatives, they believed the foreign group had the expertise, power, and connections to turn back the threat. At its Fairfax, Virginia headquarters, the Americans mobilized, sending a seasoned activist to São Paulo and Rio de Janeiro. On his mission, he gathered facts, met with anxious citizens, and suggested strategies. Soon the Brazilians adopted ideas and approaches the Americans had deployed elsewhere. Ultimately this foreign support helped change the direction of Brazilian law. Meanwhile, the nongovernmental organization (NGO) was busy on other fronts. In the United States, it fought to protect vulnerable citizens at home and abroad. Lobbying Congress, working the courts, and cultivating the media, its operatives crusaded for rights and freedom. At the United Nations, its staff worked with like-minded organizations from other countries to shape international policy. Members of this global network issued press releases, attended conferences, and stressed the moral imperatives of immediate action, not least in Brazil.

In many ways, this might seem an unremarkable story from the age of globalization. Today "local" rights abuses routinely attract overseas concern. Environmental devastation in one region galvanizes action in others. Legislators in the United States and the

European Union vote on domestic policies affecting foreign societies. And NGOs use the United Nations, the world media, and the Internet to advance all manner of campaigns. This story was different, however. The Brazilians were not torture victims, and the NGO was not Human Rights Watch. Rather, Brazilian gun owners reached overseas when threatened by tough new laws, including a national referendum to ban civilian firearms sales. The NGO they tapped? America's National Rifle Association (NRA). Various factors led to the referendum's defeat, but the NRA's influence was salient. Its message – honed for decades in the United States – swept Brazilians. The right to own firearms, previously unvoiced in Brazil and absent from its constitution, became a rallying cry. The disarmament referendum, backed both by the government and a transnational gun control network, had been expected to pass handily. Instead, it failed by a 2:1 margin.

In the United States, the NRA's power on national gun issues is famous – or infamous, depending on one's perspective. Less known, the group plays an important role in other countries, at the United Nations, and in U.S. foreign policy. This gun activism and its collisions with control forces are by no means unusual. Although little noted by analysts, most global issues involve not just a single "progressive" movement promoting a cause, but also rivals fighting it. The women's movement has long faced hostility from "pro-family" NGOs. Allying with locals from Sudan to China, this "Baptist-burqa" network is a major presence at UN conferences and other global forums. On ecological concerns, NGOs such as Friends of the Earth and the Sierra Club represent only one slice of the ideological spectrum. Organizations opposing environmental regulation are equally active. More generally, networks battle over the state's role in the economy, with everything from old-age pensions to foreign aid part of a global fray.

Yet for all the frequency with which activist groups clash, scholarly and journalistic accounts have been one-sided. Most focus on movements of the political left: their development, lobbying, and protest. A particular favorite has been the antiglobalization or global justice movement, its small but colorful efforts to counter neoliberalism drawing media and academic attention. Such research is useful, but contestation over global issues cannot be reduced to battles over economic globalization itself. More important, whether because of ideological proclivities, sympathy with apparent underdogs, or sheer oversight, analysts miss key parts of the story – rival activism in civil society. To quote political scientist Mary Kaldor, despite "conservative" groups being "extremely powerful," they are "rarely mentioned" in the burgeoning study of global politics. The omission is in fact greater, however. Conflict among rival networks, whatever their ideology, is seldom examined, in favor of studies that highlight one side's efforts to persuade decison makers.[1]

Investigating conflict does more than just plug a yawning empirical hole. It helps answer critical questions in world politics: Why do only a few efforts to create international policy succeed? What explains a policy's scope and strength? These questions suggest that existing research suffers from biases because it has focused on instances in which new policy has been made. But even dynamic campaigns often end with a whimper. Resistance is not the only reason, but it plays a major role. Of course, such "failures" are simultaneously victories for opponents. Analyzing new policy, as well as its subversion and aversion, highlights this reality. In addition, it challenges received wisdom about transnational activism, including the ways in which rival networks emerge, interact, and influence.

In the dominant view, NGOs are a counterweight to state repression and corporate greed, succoring the needy and uplifting the downtrodden. Researchers and romantics have toasted transnational networks as the vanguard of an emerging "global civil society." They offer new avenues of representation. They hand stifled voices a global megaphone. They express popular

[1] Mary Kaldor, *Global Civil Society: An Answer to War* (Cambridge: Polity Press, 2003). For exceptions, see Mitchell A. Orenstein, *Privatizing Pensions: The Transnational Campaign for Social Security Reform* (Princeton, NJ: Princeton University Press, 2008); Susan K. Sell and Aseem Prakash, "Using Ideas Strategically: The Contest between Business and NGO Networks in Intellectual Property Rights," *International Studies Quarterly* 48, no. 1 (2004): 143–75.

preferences better than elected governments. In this view, environmental, human rights, and social justice NGOs democratize global governance. Few analysts, however, examine the powerful networks opposing these goals.[2]

Some might retort that the novelty of these developments explains the gap. In reality, conflict only appears new because it has for so long been overlooked. Most of the networks noted previously have existed for years – as have their clashes with competitors. Further back in history, celebrated movements fought powerful but forgotten rivals – and suffered decades of defeat. Consider the suffragists, who tangled not only with governments but also with such organizations as Britain's Women's Anti-Suffrage League and the New York State Association Opposed to Woman Suffrage. Earlier still, abolitionists in England, the United States, and elsewhere confronted pro-slavers and anti-abolitionists whose own broad-based, if repugnant, movements interacted across national borders. In the economic realm, transnational movements have battled for centuries over the relationship between markets and societies. Historian Karl Polanyi argued that modern capitalism rose through a "double movement," with promoters of laissez faire matched against workers opposed to it.[3]

In short, despite recent ballyhooing of NGOs as a force for progress, civil society has long worked at cross-purposes. Neglect of these battles does not result from latter-day blindsiding by

[2] Recent work that has begun to fill the gap includes Doris Buss and Didi Herman, *Globalizing Family Values: The Christian Right In International Politics* (Minneapolis: University of Minnesota Press, 2003); William E. DeMars, *NGOs and Transnational Networks: Wild Cards in World Politics* (London: Pluto Press, 2005); Alain Noël and Jean-Philippe Thérien, *Left and Right in Global Politics* (Cambridge: Cambridge University Press, 2008); Jackie Smith, *Social Movements for Global Democracy* (Baltimore: Johns Hopkins University Press, 2008); Steven Teles and Daniel A. Kenney, "Spreading the Word: The Diffusion of American Conservatism in Europe and Beyond," in *Growing Apart? America and Europe in the Twenty-First Century*, ed. Jeffrey Kopstein and Sven Steinmo (Cambridge: Cambridge University Press, 2007), 136–69.

[3] Polanyi, *The Great Transformation: The Political and Economic Origins of Our Time* (Boston: Beacon Press, 1957), 76, 132, 149. See also Jane Jerome Camhi, *Women against Women: American Anti-Suffragism, 1880–1920* (Brooklyn, NY: Carlson Publishing, 1994); James A. Morone, *Hellfire*

newly internationalized conservatives. Rather, it stems from analytic blinders against studying failed efforts at policy making –
or from political blindness to studying "retrograde" movements.

The Argument

In this book, I make four arguments. First, *transnational politics is ideologically diverse and conflictive.* Deploying recurrent
tactics and themes, rival networks advance their positions and
slash away at the enemy's. They influence one another's development, strategies, and outlook. Clashes attract attention and
raise an issue's profile, useful in later rounds. Confrontation ful-
fills NGOs' internal needs too. How better to galvanize staff,
activate members, and raise funds than combating a reviled foe
seeking abhorrent goals on a vital issue? Contention between
networks – not just between a single network and target states
or corporations – is therefore endemic. Nor does this only follow left-right lines. Such divisions represent an important way in
which combatants understand and promote their goals. Conflict
itself is fundamental, however, its precise orientation secondary.

Second, *the battles cut across institutions and borders.* Dueling networks range the globe, their members working in international forums and states. Indeed, the latter are central because
those in power domestically determine governmental stances on
foreign policy. Activists scramble for influence at home using
ideas, strategies, and resources from abroad. They deploy developments in one country to excite or scare constituents in another.
Low-level conflict smolders in blogs, chatrooms, op-eds, and
books. Antagonists amass intellectual phalanxes in think tanks,
university centers, and media outlets, all poised for the next flare-
up. In all this, activists know that they "work on an enormous
canvas, a canvas that encompasses the entire world."[4] So in this

---

Nation: The Politics of Sin in American History (New Haven, CT: Yale University Press, 2003), 69–82; Larry E. Tise, *Proslavery: A History of the Defense
of Slavery in America, 1701–1840* (Athens: University of Georgia Press, 1987).

[4] Austin Ruse, "Toward a Permanent United Nations Pro-Family Bloc," paper
delivered to World Congress of Families II, Geneva, Switzerland, Nov. 14–17,
1999, http://www.worldcongress.org/wcf2_spkrs/wcf2_ruse.htm.

book, I take the unusual but necessary step of examining interlocking clashes both in global institutions such as the United Nations and in particular countries.

Third, *this globalized combat influences outcomes, whether policy, nonpolicy, or "zombie" policy.* Prior analyses, mostly of successful policy making, explain it by pointing to persuasion, deliberation, or appropriateness. In this view, one faction's resonant framings or cogent arguments convince government officials and broader audiences. Policy is made and progress achieved. In fact, however, the joyful birth of a meaningful new policy is rare. More common is its strangulation, nonpolicy – or its evisceration, zombie policy, the heart and soul ripped out of whatever document painfully issues. Political combat involves a host of unsavory, negative strategies aimed at dissuasion. Opposing activists present contrary ideas packaged in equally appealing terms. More belligerently, they deny the very existence of "crises" that fire their rivals. They stoke fear about the "solutions" proposed by their enemies. They bombard their foes' reputations and rationality. Notably, too, the attacks are more than just rhetorical. Indeed they must be because framing has limited ability to change the many minds in civil society and government that are already made up. Even as each side builds its own coalition, it works to unbuild its opponents'. As it enters institutions, it strives to exclude its rivals. As it sets agendas, it toils to unset its enemy's.

Conflict between networks is not the sole explanation for the politics of "stasis" or "regress." On many issues, however, opponents wield great power. All this makes certain proposals more or less costly, feasible, or risible for the governments that establish policy. At any one time, it may be difficult to measure the precise effect of rival movements, but by shaping one another's identity and strategies, they influence outcomes. Notably, however, in bitter policy battles, most "outcomes" are at best respites in wars lasting decades. Win or lose, the combatants fight on. They adapt themselves to the changed conditions, even while undermining them. They assert their root visions in new guises or different arenas.

Finally, *global civil society is not a harmonious field of like-minded NGOs. It is a contentious arena riven by fundamental differences criss-crossing national and international borders.* One side cannot be written off as GONGOs or BONGOs, government or business-organized NGOs. All are part of global politics, even if some are its enemies, sworn to reducing advocacy NGOs to charity providers and eliminating the transnational as a vibrant political sphere. For activists, this diversity poses challenges. How can institutions such as the World Social Forum claim the mantle of global civil society when ideologically contrary voices are not present? More pragmatically, how can they achieve their goals against foes who themselves claim to represent "the people?"

For scholars, the challenge is analytic. Too much of the literature has theorized about global society narrowly, studying only its progressive purlieus. Given such a limited view, policy compromises seem possible through logical persuasion or gentle tutelage. International institutions such as the United Nations appear to enjoy significant authority, even respect. A broader lens reveals deep disagreement, however. Even leaving violent conflict aside, contending groups in democratic societies hold irreconcilable values. They see the world from incompatible perspectives. They despise their adversaries as misguided, self-interested, deceitful, or downright evil. There is limited room for the deliberation so cherished by idealists. Indeed, the combatants do not seek compromise. They long for conquest, working as passionately to thwart their foes as to advance themselves. In these clashes, the rivals deride institutions, whether domestic or international, as political creatures undeserving of deference – unless they do the activists' bidding. Given these chasms, current theories emphasizing appropriateness, learning, and jawboning need to be supplemented.[5]

[5] Michael Barnett and Martha Finnemore, *Rules for the World: International Organizations in Global Politics* (Ithaca, NY: Cornell University Press, 2004), 5, 7; Martha Finnemore, *The Purpose of Intervention: Changing Beliefs about the Use of Force* (Ithaca, NY: Cornell University Press, 2003), 141–61.

If a global civil society is indeed emerging, it is more discordant and less understood than scholars have thus far imagined. In addition, it is more rooted in domestic politics than many have realized. Contending networks seek a glimmer of the global spotlight, but all include NGOs and staffs with local addresses. Most recognize the global as reflective of the national. They therefore devote much of their energy to domestic allies fighting over state policies and power.

Definitions and Caveats

Before proceeding, it is useful to discuss the concept of transnational advocacy networks, first identified by Keck and Sikkink. United by common causes and ideas, such networks include NGOs, foundations, and broader publics, as well as officials of governments and international organizations.[6] The latter have wider concerns but are less amenable to persuasion than often believed because they already occupy partisan camps. Network constituents engage in two broad activities: supporting local groups (the "boomerang" pattern); and swaying international institutions either directly, by lobbying them or member governments, or indirectly, by shaping ideas. In reality, these activities blur, with strategies and conflicts in one realm spilling into the other. For instance, members of both the women's rights and family values networks fight one another over reproductive rights/abortion at the United Nations while aiding local clients battling similar issues.

Networks are shifting and loose-knit. It is seldom accurate to ascribe motivations or intentions to them as a whole because their members differ on particular issues. For that reason, I focus on the organizations composing them. Among these, it is possible to distinguish the more from the less powerful, notwithstanding the lack of formal hierarchy within networks. If state

---

[6] Margaret E. Keck and Kathryn Sikkink, *Activists beyond Borders: Advocacy Networks in International Politics* (Ithaca, NY: Cornell University Press, 1998), 8–10.

bureaucrats are members, they hold considerable clout because in the final analysis, governments make policy decisions. In day-to-day activities, however, dedicated advocacy groups – with their laser focus on specific issues – have greater freedom to promote ideas, concepts, approaches, and proposals that in turn influence states. Accordingly, I highlight NGOs, private organizations whose primary aims are political, social, cultural, or economic. For additional concreteness, I focus on efforts to forge or foil domestic or international law. By contrast, many scholars study norms. Their "emergence," however, is more difficult to gauge and more debatable, particularly because claims to a norm's emergence are usually refuted by opponent networks.

As noted, this book places contention at the center of analysis. One of conflict's most enduring manifestations is the left-right divide, and the cases I examine fall along those lines. I therefore use the terms in this book, not least because the antagonists themselves do so. What do they mean? Some might argue that the "right" refers to groups opposing policy change and the "left" to those promoting it. On issues such as genetically modified foods, however, free-market groups promote new methods, whereas ecology organizations seek to preserve older ones, thus turning the usual meanings of "conservative" and "progressive" on their heads. Indeed, because of their tendentious connotations, I use the latter terms sparingly, primarily to improve readability. A better alternative might be to follow Thomas Sowell's distinction between those who envision mankind as capable – or incapable – of shaping society to political ends. This division, between the "utopian" or "unconstrained" vision on one hand (the left) and the "tragic" or "constrained" on the other taps the source of many contemporary controversies.[7] It is notable, however, that placing a group in one wing for one issue may not predict its classification for another. For instance, the Catholic Church has worked with NGOs seeking gun control but also favors traditional families.

---

[7] Thomas Sowell, *A Conflict of Visions: Ideological Origins of Political Struggles*, rev. ed. (New York: Basic Books, 2007 [1987]), 9–35.

The upshot: I occasionally use the terms right and left in this book but not as watertight analytic categories. Rather, I apply them to particular groups conflicting over specific goals. At a minimum, the labels are convenient shorthand to emphasize this book's real focus: gaping splits within what is too glibly termed global civil society. It is those neglected fissures and the fusillades across them that matter most. Put another way, my focus is conflict among networks, whatever tags one attaches to them. I intend that the hypotheses I test and the conclusions I draw apply beyond the left-right divide, to nonviolent contention among any opposed networks.

Notwithstanding this broad aim, a few caveats are in order, mostly concerning the controversial ideological terms. Critics might growl that right-wing organizations cat-paw for states and therefore merit no separate analysis. Of course, some groups receive state funds, employ ex-bureaucrats, and work with governments. The same could be said for left-wing networks, however, such as the campaigns for the International Criminal Court (ICC) and the landmines treaty. Others might carp that right-wing groups front for world capital or "neoliberal globalizers." This is hardly universal, however. Critical issues such as family planning and religious belief do not implicate economic interests. In other areas, corporate views are divided, and left-wing causes enjoy business largesse. The Body Shop, Ben & Jerry's, and Reebok may have paved the way, but today even Exxon and RTZ travel this familiar road, flashing the environment and human rights as part of their corporate responsibilities – or marketing plans. In any case, foundation support for left-wing NGOs is rampant. Of course, that is true for the right too. For every Ford and Open Society Foundation, there is a Koch Family or Atlas Foundation.[8]

Is it valid to distinguish left- and right-wing movements by arguing that the former enjoy grassroots support, whereas the

---

[8] See generally DeMars, *NGOs and Transnational Networks*, 11, 148–52; Volker Heins, *Nongovernmental Organizations in International Society: Struggles over Recognition* (New York: Palgrave MacMillan, 2008), 107–12.

latter are at best Astroturf groups? The claim is hard to sustain. Few NGOs are mass organizations even if individuals, along with foundations and governments, supply their financial lifeblood. Checkbook participation – the annual contribution to an organization known more by its name than its actions – is the rule. The distinction between self-interested conservatives and principled progressives is similarly overdrawn. Most ideologies assert moral motives. Free-trade fundamentalists proclaim development and democracy as benign by-products or even ultimate goals: greed is good! In sum, right-wing groups should not be placed in a different universe from left-wing ones.[9]

There is a more fundamental criticism of studying transnational actors whatever their ideology. Hard-core realists dismiss NGOs as gnats swarming around state elephants – annoying but powerless. Radicals deride them as minions of neoliberalism or Western hegemony, unworthy of separate treatment. More nuanced treatments see them as influential only when major states do not care about issues. True, the sway of individual NGOs may be overstated, but the network concept remains a powerful way of understanding policy conflicts. This is especially the case because rival networks include groups based in particular countries. There they link to or operate as interest groups, battling one another by spreading ideas, lobbying officials, infiltrating parties, and influencing domestic and thereby international policy.

Finally, a caveat is in order about the supposed distinction between local and global actors. In fact, in Tarrow's elegant words, today's transnational advocates are "rooted cosmopolitans.[10] This book will illustrate this point, showing how rival activists, even those who glorify parochial cultures or national traditions, leap levels of the political system – or use foreign developments to advance their local causes.

---

[9] Sell and Prakash, "Using Ideas Strategically."

[10] Sidney Tarrow, *The New Transnational Activism* (Cambridge: Cambridge University Press, 2005), 35–56. See also James Ferguson, *Global Shadows: Africa in the Neoliberal World Order* (Durham, N.C.: Duke University Press 2006), 89–112.

Cases and Method

In the following chapters, I have been careful *not* to choose cases involving promulgation of a signal new policy. To do so would be to stack the analytic deck. Rather, in picking my issues – gun control and gay rights – I have simply looked for major ones on which there has been significant transnational networking and conflict. Thus these two are more typical than the issues in which broad new policy has been created. They should therefore provide a more representative view of processes and outcomes, ranging from policy to nonpolicy. The cases are diverse, spanning human rights, development, and social justice networks. Other scholars have begun to chronicle how free-market libertarians with a "'missionary spirit'" have "inject[ed] their ideas into the domestic politics of other states."[11]

Have I too stacked the deck by choosing issues unusual in that they have drawn fire? No. From development aid to pension reform, most policy issues pit opposing networks against one another. Even human rights, which some believe to be beyond politics, evinces enduring controversy. Consider battles over female genital mutilation/circumcision, sex work/trafficking, and children's/parent's rights. Dispute over their very names hints at the deep conflict over their substance. Even norms against torture, once considered the most impregnable bastion of the human rights edifice, have been breached – and by democratic states backed by civil society activists. Human rights NGOs, often seen as the epitome of probity, have themselves come under assault from opposing civil society groups. The cases examined in this book are by no means rare for their clashes of NGOs. Only my approach is unusual – giving equal empirical and explanatory weight to diversity, dissonance, and rancor.

Admittedly, my selection of cases means that I cannot draw conclusions about why some issues unleash abiding conflict whereas others – in fact, only a few – spark less. In the empirical chapters, however, the intensity of advocacy changes over time.

---

[11] Teles and Kenney, "Spreading the Word," 136. See also Orenstein, *Privatizing Pensions*.

Each study discusses a long-standing global issue, probing why activism and rival advocacy arise at particular moments. Beyond this fluctuation in development and dynamics, the outcomes of conflict vary within each case. On this basis, the Conclusion compares the cases and offers hypotheses about why some issues draw more fire than others.

Regarding methodology, the empirical chapters are based on interviews with participants in the issues, as well as my personal observation of the conflicts, including at a UN meeting and an NRA convention. In addition, to counteract my subjects' memory lapses, 20/20 hindsight, political biases, and perhaps outright lies – after all, this is politics – I have collected and analyzed primary documents from many entities. In some cases too, I tap contemporaneous journalistic reports, particularly interviews conducted with participants. Used cautiously, these varied sources provide a picture of activist thinking in something near real time. In addition, they open a window that too often remains shut: onto strategies and ideas that failed in an organization's ongoing conflict with opponents and its never-ending struggle for survival.

Plan of the Book

Chapter 2 builds on but also critiques existing theories. In it, I present hypotheses about how rival activism and ensuing conflict affect the development, dynamics, and outcomes of policy battles. As will become clear, I argue for an inclusive view of where contention occurs. Ongoing clashes roil the media and the Internet. Most disputes, however, occur in three connected spheres: national societies in which outsiders help local allies; domestic institutions debating laws with cross-border repercussions; and international institutions thrashing out global policies. Groups within conflicting networks jump the boundaries, deploying recurrent strategies to advance themselves, bolster friends, defeat rivals, and achieve or block policy.

Conservative religious groups have for years engaged in clashes over family policy. Much of their activism aims to preserve traditional families against what they decry as an onslaught of feminism, abortion, and gender politics. Chapter 3 highlights one important aspect: fighting between religious groups and human rights activists over gay/homosexual rights at the United Nations. Chapter 4 examines similar warfare in two European theaters, Sweden and Romania. There, I focus on conflict between the gay rights network and American religious advocates that have major overseas activities. Both sides back local allies. Their lawyers litigate foreign cases. They defend or implant favorable statutes. They use the results, both successes and failures, in other conflicts, including California's 2008 battle over Proposition 8.

Chapter 5 examines small arms, weapons that some see as a major source of violence and crime worldwide. Since the early 1990s, two networks concerned with such weapons have squared off in various arenas. After describing the contenders and the stakes of their global fight, I focus on conflict at the United Nations. Chapter 6 examines the way in which the rival gun networks nurtured local activism in an important country, Brazil. I analyze both the clash of these globally linked Brazilian activists and the ways in which international groups used the Brazilian case in their ongoing hostilities.

In these chapters, I focus as much on the development and dynamics of conflict as on outcomes. As noted before, new policies or nonpolicies usually lead only to pauses in political wars spanning decades and sprawling across institutions. Major policy can change the terrain, but it seldom dispatches the defeated forever. Rather they rally and regroup. Studying a single campaign in a particular arena diverts attention from this range of conflict.

The empirical chapters do not offer exhaustive accounts of the issues. My aim is to provide an accurate overview, demonstrating the utility of the model developed in Chapter 2. Nor I do seek to determine which side's arguments, claims, statistics, and figures reflect the actualities. This is not because I endorse relativism. Social construction plays a major role in building campaigns, but it does not trump reality. One or another side is right in the factual aspects of these debates, even if key parts concern values that cannot be so assessed. In this book, however, my aim is to analyze the ways in which the debates are conducted and policy outcomes sought – not to assess the validity of underlying arguments. The latter is of course crucial to developing the best policies, but I leave it to others to make such judgments.

The Conclusion compares the cases and draws out the book's scope and implications. I question views of civil society as a cohesive counter to states or corporations. The ferocity of differences suggests too that conflict, rather than persuasion and cooperation, should take pride of place in studies of global governance.

2

Making and Unmaking Policy

To reach their goals, activists work not only to persuade decision makers but also to defeat powerful networks promoting
contrary aims. These battles and their strategic anticipation influence whether a policy will be adopted. They affect where and how
those fights will be fought. They shape mobilization and the very
identity of opposing networks.

This spotlight on conflict does not simply supplement current
ways of understanding advocacy. Rather, in explaining how policy networks operate, I place contention at the heart of analysis –
as it is at the nub of politics. I devote equal attention to equally
powerful contenders whatever their ideology, and I restore the
true nature of their clashes. As Craig Murphy has written, these
involve "struggles over wealth, power, and knowledge." Or, in
Lewis Coser's more biting terms, social conflict is "a struggle
over values and claims to scarce status, power, and resources in
which the aims of the opponents are to neutralize, injure or eliminate their rivals."[1] Most scholars have highlighted the first part
of Coser's definition, downplaying the crucial, if less savory, second. Certainly, it is easier to analyze one complex phenomenon

[1] Murphy, "Global Governance: Poorly Done and Poorly Understood," *International Affairs* 75, no. 4 (2000): 789–803, 799; Lewis Coser, *The Functions
of Social Conflict* (New York: Free Press, 1964), 8.

rather than two or more colliding. A network's promotion of its own goals, however, is intertwined with struggle against its adversaries. To turn one's eyes from the clash is to miss decisive events. Of course at moments, rivals may engage in high-minded dialogue. More typically, advocates work to destroy their foes' reputations, ideas, and values. Compromises are viewed not as best possible agreements but as regrettable failures to reach maximal ends.

Missing the Clash

Analysts have broached but seldom dwelled on this contentiousness. Conventional theories view policy making as linear, involving distinct stages of problem formation, agenda setting, rulemaking, and implementation. These approaches accentuate proponents pushing ideas through institutions, downplaying opponents working at cross-purposes.

In international relations, Finnemore and Sikkink allude to the fact that proposed international norms enter "a highly contested normative space where they must compete with other norms and perceptions of interest." This key insight has been overlooked, however. As Badescu and Weiss note, "contestation is a reality that is seldom explicit in the literature." Most observers examine cohesive networks promoting "progressive" principles, skipping over groups who defend old ideals or promote antagonistic ones. Boli and Thomas even suggest that NGOs march in lockstep, enacting scripts that, while contested by other actors, are "often critical of economic and political structures, stigmatizing 'ethnocentric' (nonuniversalistic) nationalism[,] . . . 'exploitative' (inegalitarian) capitalism[,] . . . state maltreatment of citizens and corporate disregard for the sacredness of nature."[2]

[2] Martha Finnemore and Kathryn Sikkink, "International Norm Dynamics and Political Change," *International Organization* 52, no. 4 (1998): 887–917, 897; Cristina G. Badescu and Thomas G. Weiss, "Misrepresenting R2P and Advancing Norms: An Alternative Spiral?" *International Studies Review* 11, no. 4 (2010): 354–74, 365; John Boli and George M. Thomas, "World Culture in

Those who highlight contestation do so in too limited a way. Risse and Sikkink analyze the pressure repressive states face from transnational networks espousing the "central core" of "most accepted" human rights. They acknowledge government delay, obfuscation, and backlash. Their "spiral model," however, downplays the support repressive states gain from opposition societal networks, often based in liberal states: anticommunist apologists for right-wing dictatorships in the 1980s; or anti-terror defenders of waterboarding and Predator missile strikes in the 2000s. In these cases, rival networks skirmish over the priority of contrary moralities – rights versus security – or the meaning of the "same" norm – rights of the accused versus rights of the victim.[3] Similar battles envelop many issues.

Other analysts focus on conflict within networks. Cooley and Ron discuss competition among development and humanitarian NGOs as they scramble for scarce funding, members, and publicity. Some note power disparities within networks, affecting resource allocations and tactical choices. Hertel has examined these among Northern and Southern members of the labor rights network. Carpenter documents disagreements within the children's rights network in explaining why certain problems such as child soldiers gain major attention, whereas others do not.[4]

the World Polity: A Century of International Non-Governmental Organization," *American Sociological Review* 62 (1997): 171–90, 173, 182. See also Frank J. Lechner and John Boli, *World Culture: Origins and Consequences* (Malden, MA: Blackwell, 2005).

3   Thomas Risse and Kathryn Sikkink, "The Socialization of Human Rights Norms into Domestic Practices: Introduction," in *The Power of Human Rights: International Norms and Domestic Change*, ed. Thomas Risse, Stephen C. Ropp, and Kathryn Sikkink (Cambridge: Cambridge University Press, 1999), 2, 22–28; Jeane J. Kirkpatrick, *Dictatorships and Double Standards: Rationalism and Reason in Politics* (New York: Simon & Schuster: 1983); Marc A. Thiessen, *Courting Disaster: How the CIA Kept America Safe and How Barack Obama Is Inviting the Next Attack* (Washington, DC: Regnery, 2010); Alan M. Dershowitz, *Why Terrorism Works: Understanding the Threat, Responding to the Challenge* (New Haven, CT: Yale University Press, 2002).

4   Alexander Cooley and James Ron, "The NGO Scramble: Organizational Insecurity and the Political Economy of Transnational Action," *International Organization* 27, no. 1 (2002), 5–39; Shareen Hertel, *Unexpected Power:*

Unexamined, however, is the more fundamental flak that even chosen issues hit – from free-market enthusiasts who oppose development aid and promote contract rights or from religious networks that abhor the Convention on the Rights of the Child. Sell and Prakash suggest ways of filling this gap, arguing that rival NGO and business networks should be seen as "two competing interest groups driven by their respective normative ideals and material concerns." Milner has shown how economic groups vie with one another both domestically and internationally to affect global trade policy. These insights can be extended to explain how clashing networks shape the dynamics as well as the outcomes of contention. McAdam, Tarrow, and Tilly have proposed one approach, urging that analysts scrutinize varied conflicts to identify common mechanisms and processes that link into larger episodes. That endeavor is important, and I incorporate one of their processes, "polarization," by which controversy deepens differences.[5] Rather than dissecting conflict for recurrent components, however, I analyze the broader strife.

This is similar to the "countermovements" approach in political sociology and the "advocacy coalition" framework in policy studies, although neither has been applied to transnational disputes.[6] More importantly, I view powerful policy networks as

Conflict and Change among Transnational Activists (Ithaca, NY: Cornell University Press, 2006); R. Charli Carpenter, "Orphaned Again? Children Born of Wartime Rape as a Non-Issue for the Human Rights Movement," in *The International Struggle for New Human Rights*, ed. Clifford Bob (Philadelphia, PA: University of Pennsylvania Press, 2009), 14–29. See also Clifford Bob, *The Marketing of Rebellion: Insurgents, Media, and International Activism* (Cambridge: Cambridge University Press, 2005); Keck and Sikkink, *Activists beyond Borders*, 189–90.

[5] Sell and Prakash, "Using Ideas Strategically," 168; Helen V. Milner, *Interests, Institutions, and Information: Domestic Politics and International Relations* (Princeton, NJ: Princeton University Press, 1997); Doug McAdam, Sidney Tarrow, and Charles Tilly, *Dynamics of Contention* (Cambridge: Cambridge University Press, 2002), 322. For an important conflict-based approach at the interstate level, see John M. Owen, *The Clash of Ideas in World Politics: Transnational Networks, States, and Regime Change, 1510–2010* (Princeton, NJ: Princeton University Press, 2010).

[6] See, e.g., David S. Meyer and Suzanne Staggenborg, "Movements, Countermovements, and the Structure of Political Opportunity," *American Journal*

rooted in long-standing, ideologically opposed blocs rather than seeing one side as reactive or "counter." I devote equal attention to the rival networks' strategic influences on one another and on policy.

Development of Conflict

Although the foregoing approaches improve over single network studies, they are too modest. I elevate conflict and the strategies it entails to principal position. If the targets of activism are governmental institutions that set policy and attentive publics that influence them, it makes little sense to highlight only one movement or network. Critical instead are the ways competing sides grapple with one another as they strive for contrary policies across institutions. Such struggles are not the only reason for specific outcomes. Preexisting power differentials and institutional rules play a role. To clarify my position, however, I highlight contention.

At the heart of these conflicts are strategic choices or "dilemmas," as Jasper calls them.[7] The combatants must make decisions about their actions. A major influence is the expectation and reality of opposition. Of course, NGOs, international organizations, networks, and states are affected by internal tensions – not only over the right strategic moves but also over resources and power. The upshot: there is nothing determinate about the way in which conflicting groups answer these dilemmas.

Analysts are not left helpless, however. I propose a model for understanding policy activism, focusing on its development,

of Sociology 101, no. 6 (1996): 1628–60; Paul Sabatier and Christopher M. Weible, "The Advocacy Coalition Framework: Innovations and Clarifications," in *Theories of the Policy Process*, 2nd ed., ed. Paul A. Sabatier (Boulder, CO: Westview, 2007). See also Tina Fetner, *How the Religious Right Shaped Lesbian and Gay Activism* (Minneapolis: University of Minnesota Press, 2008).

7 James M. Jasper, *Getting Your Way: Strategic Dilemmas in the Real World* (Chicago: University of Chicago Press, 2006). See also Jarol B. Manheim, *Strategy in Information and Influence Campaigns: How Policy Advocates, Social Movements, Insurgent Groups, Corporations, Governments and Others Get What They Want* (New York: Routledge, 2011).

dynamics, and outcomes. That tripartite division is admittedly artificial. Even as proponents push new policy, opponents repel them, not least by promoting their own, contrary initiatives. For clarity's sake, however, I present the model in the foregoing order, highlighting recurrent dilemmas faced by the combatants and presenting related hypotheses. In addition, I outline key strategies associated with the clash of networks. These come in two overlapping but distinguishable forms deployed simultaneously: affirmative, in which each network advances its own position, albeit with an eye to opponents' reactions; and negative, in which each bashes the enemy and its ideas.

Rival Issue Entrepreneurs

Like other scholars, I assume that policy battles begin with "issue entrepreneurs," individuals and groups that "construct" social problems. That is, they politicize long-standing grievances, previously accepted conditions, or future risks, demanding action to remedy them.[8] Motivating entrepreneurs is a combination of ideological and material concerns. First, heartfelt beliefs inspire them to see an issue as a potentially tractable problem. Many scholars characterize these convictions as "principled" because issue entrepreneurs are moved in part by what they believe is ethically right.[9] Activists of contrary persuasions, however, hold the same opinion of their own goals, generating clashes of morality. Analytically, therefore, it is better to characterize their convictions as ideological – rooted in systematic social, economic, religious, or other ideas and aimed at practical political ends. In addition, entrepreneurs must concern themselves with material matters, such as maintaining their organizations and raising

---

[8] Ethan A. Nadelmann, "Global Prohibition Regimes: The Evolution of Norms in International Society," *International Organization* 44, no. 4 (1990): 479–526. See also Peter Andreas and Ethan Nadelmann, *Policing the Globe: Criminalization and Crime Control in International Relations* (Oxford: Oxford University Press, 2006).

[9] Joshua W. Busby, *Moral Movements and Foreign Policy* (Cambridge: Cambridge University Press, 2010); Keck and Sikkink, *Activists beyond Borders*, 1.

funds. These affect the number and identity of problems they choose to stump for.

Overlooked in the literature, however, is political entrepreneurship's effect on opponents. If they consider their rival's activism dangerous, they will fight it. This point may seem banal. It is worth noting, however, because so few scholars have studied these clashes, leaving the impression that transnational activism is a high-minded affair devoid of the attack machine and innocent of the gutter. Far from it. New policies challenge ideas, impinge on interests, and threaten values. An enemy's success in one realm gives it an edge in others. Nor do foes rest on their laurels, content to let politicians or institutions defend them. Instead, as one side constructs a problem, opposing entrepreneurs, motivated by their own mix of moral and material concerns, mobilize too. In turn, this clash influences decisions about the aims, allies, and arenas of struggle.

Constructing – and Deconstructing – Problems

As a general matter, entrepreneurs' beliefs about an issue's gravity affect the ways in which they construct a problem. The weightier they believe it to be, the broader they will portray it and the louder proclaim it. This basic point is affected by a strategic choice related to opponents, however. Should activists style their problem broadly and shout it from the rooftops, to embolden their base, frighten their foes, or use as a bargaining chip later? Or should they frame narrowly, attempting to reduce, delay, or avoid conflict? There is no single answer, but anticipation of the foe's reactions plays a key role. If policy entrepreneurs believe a backlash will prevent them from achieving their moral and material goals, they will constrict or even camouflage the issues. On the other hand, if they believe they can muster powerful allies, contain backlash, and demonstrate their resolve, they will frame expansively and talk openly. Problem construction therefore involves strategies of gauging opposition and cloaking against it, with foes influencing decisions from the start.

Such construction has a reciprocal effect on opponents. The more threatening the new problem, the more likely they will act against it. In this, they face a choice – whether to respond forthrightly or not, with the factors noted earlier, in particular the potential for scaring or energizing the original activists, looming large. Either way, certain strategies are typical. For one, foes attack the problem, denying its seriousness, coherence, or very existence. They also seize the offensive, constructing their own problem. Its identity? The solution offered by the original issue entrepreneur – and usually the entrepreneur himself.

Network Building – and Unbuilding

Once conflict erupts, the contenders face a choice about how to conduct it. Should they mobilize their forces further? Should they harass their foes? Or should they use quieter means – or even fold? Opposition plays a major role in this decision, inadvertently creating incentives for activists to build their own coalition.

First, because they know they will need more resources to overcome organized resistance, they compensate by expanding their own mobilization. In this, they invite the most capable allies first: those with the most clout, credibility, or celebrity, who can advance the cause and attract further support. Second, because adversaries often deny a problem's existence, opposition spurs activists to link with, fund, or fashion local allies who embody the problem's pernicious effects. Grassroots partners authenticate the issues and encourage pseudo-democratic claims: that the network represents a substantial constituency, even "the people" themselves. Authentication makes it easier to dismiss foes as denialists, a proliferating slur in recent policy wars. Third, opponents unintentionally supply each other with rich fodder for mobilization: the threat posed by the rival network. Fearmongering about foes, not just about the problem constructed by one's own network, is therefore common. How better to shock one's troops into action than emotion – and what stronger than dread of an enemy massing against us?[10]

---

[10] See, e.g., Catholic Family & Human Rights Institute (C-FAM), "They Are Coming for Our Adolescent Daughters...Help Me Stop Them," *Friday Fax* fundraising letter, Aug. 11, 2010 (author's files).

Simultaneously, activists work to unbuild the rival's network. To start, they intimidate groups from joining, accusing them of "treason!" for taking comfort or mere ideas from foreigners. They strip networks of members who believe less in the cause, flaunting high-profile defections as showing their foe's decline. More subtly, they forge organizations whose main goal is deauthenticating an opponent and its claim to speak for an entire category of persons. Some of these are Astroturf groups, with no significant constituency. Others represent a real and sincere population, but their raison d'etre is aggressive – sowing doubts about whether the foe in fact represents those it claims.

A final unbuilding strategy, tarring, is anything but subtle. Activists smear an entire network with the outlandish views, fringe tactics, or moral failings of individual members – all with the hope that guilt by association will sap the coalition as a whole. In conflict over Israel's treatment of Palestinians, Human Rights Watch was condemned in 2009 by an Israeli group, NGO Monitor, which trumpeted the revelation that a senior HRW analyst collected Nazi memorabilia. This kind of incident is common, and opposing networks bristle with units specializing in it. These mudslingers sift the enemy's every move, parse its every word, and flaunt its every faux pas – sex and money scandals, of course, but also unguarded words, unvetted allies, and unconsidered positions. From such surveillance, they gather invaluable insights, always eager for gems as precious as a foe's Nazi fetish. Nor are they shy about schadenfreude. On the contrary, they revel in every delicious moment of their enemy's torment.

As a final point, the potency of tarring suggests an important caveat to network-building strategies. Expansion, though often stimulated by opposition, is not indiscriminate. The less acceptable a potential member, the less likely it will be admitted – with acceptability referring to the candidate's goals, tactics, and identity relative to the network's as a whole. Extremity, violence, or misconduct rule out possible allies because of the realistic fear that foes will sully the entire network with its most problematic element. If an existing member becomes toxic, whether because of its actions or because of changing cultural mores, the network's core will purify itself by cleansing the newfound miscreant.

In this and other ways, rivals shape the identity of one another's networks, often deepening conflict.[11]

Activating – and Deactivating – Institutions

Opposition influences the forums activists opt to use. Institutions having easy access, available allies, and divided power holders are obvious choices.[12] In addition, the amount of civil society opposition affects an institution's political opportunities – and activists' choices. The weaker a foe in a relevant body, the more likely a network's members will enter it. Once in a favored arena, advocates will bolster and legitimate it. Conversely, they will avoid and disparage those dominated by adversaries. In the extreme, activists will invent institutions where adversaries cannot block their initiatives. In the 1990s, the International Campaign to Ban Landmines (ICBL) opted to forgo a universal agreement because an anti-ban network would have crippled or killed it. The result was the Mine Ban Treaty – a significant accomplishment but an incomplete one, omitting the United States and other big mine producers and users.

Within institutions, foes continue their onslaughts. Where their own network has clout, activists tilt the institution's rules in their favor – and against their enemies. If possible, they maneuver to exclude or expel the rival. They pack agencies with stalwarts or sympathizers. Special targets, as Busby suggests, are veto points – offices that allow their occupants to shut off the opposition. All this manipulation helps explain why international forums are not neutral but, in Barnett and Duvall's words, shot through with "institutional or systemic bias, privilege, and unequal constraints on action."[13]

---

[11] Fetner, *How the Religious Right*; McAdam, Tarrow, and Tilly, *Dynamics of Contention*, 322. Cf. Badescu and Weiss, "Misrepresenting R2P," 368.

[12] Doug McAdam, *Political Process and the Development of Black Insurgency, 1930–1970*, 2nd ed. (Chicago: University of Chicago Press, 1999 [1982]); Keck and Sikkink, *Activists beyond Borders*.

[13] Joshua W. Busby, *Moral Movements*, 61–63; Michael Barnett and Raymond Duvall, "Power in Global Governance," in *Power in Global Governance*, ed. Michael Barnett and Raymond Duvall (Cambridge: Cambridge University Press, 2005), 17.

On the other hand, activists may enter unfriendly institutions, if the arena is crucial in a larger battle. Even groups that condemn the UN as treacherous territory set up camp along the East River. In such cases, they resort to what James C. Scott, in another context, has called weapons of the weak, disrupting the other side by blocking initiatives, obstructing debates, and otherwise undermining their foes. All the while, they spare no effort to delegitimate the institution itself – as inappropriate, unrepresentative, or downright corrupt.[14]

Dynamics of Conflict

Agenda Setting – and Unsetting

A key part of policy battles involves positioning issues for debate and decision. Only a fraction of problems ever reach those stages, however. One reason is a surfeit of issues, requiring selectivity. Adversaries also unset one another's agendas. Indeed, the stronger the opposition, the less likely a network will succeed in agenda setting.

In this, rival networks dramatize their contending views simultaneously. Protests, marches, and strikes are no longer the left's preserve, if ever they were. All sides exploit "focusing events," moments when the public eye is already attuned to an issue.[15] Even as one side hypes an incident as proving the need for immediate action, however, the other works to blur it with contrary interpretations. The result is a blizzard of canned and contradictory statistical reports, expert opinions, and proposed solutions. Nor do competitors take the press for granted. Rather, they cultivate reporters, pushing for a good story – or a hatchet job on the enemy. Over the long term, they nurture journalistic ties, transforming media watchdogs into poodles who bark their trainers' praise – or pit bulls who tear at the network's foes.

---

[14] James C. Scott, *Weapons of the Weak: Everyday Forms of Peasant Resistance* (New Haven, CT: Yale University Press, 1987).

[15] John W. Kingdon, *Agendas, Alternatives, and Public Policies*, 2nd ed. (New York: HarperCollins, 1995), 94–99.

Persuasion – and Dissuasion

Notwithstanding its importance in the scholarly literature, agenda setting does not guarantee new policy. That requires substantive decisions by political leaders. Here too, foes play a central role. The stronger they are, the less likely a network will convince policy makers. This hypothesis may again seem axiomatic. Still, it has been overlooked and supplements a key idea in the literature: that "networks are more effective where they are strong and dense" as measured by the "total number and size of organizations" and the "regularity of their exchanges."[16] If, however, network thickening is in part a tactic to counter opposition – or to advance pseudo-democratic claims – greater density may not make for effectiveness. Of course, drumming up supporters may energize a network and serve internal organizational purposes. If it galvanizes the opposition, however, the outcome is anything but certain.

In addition, the hypothesis suggests the need to augment dominant analytic approaches about persuasion. These highlight activism by a single network. For Finnemore, individuals and states are "socializ[ed]" or "collectiviz[ed]" into adopting norms modeled by forward-thinking movements, international organizations, or governments. According to Haas, epistemic communities, composed of scientific authorities sharing causal beliefs and validity standards, certify proposed policies. As Busby shows, moral beacons vouch for such ideas, and entertainment figures lend them luster. Fueling empathy, victims cry out for intervention with poignant personal stories. In Price's view, advocacy networks graft new ideas onto established principles. As Risse and Sikkink argue, repressive governments are denounced as pariahs and shamed into changing policies. To convince policy makers and international audiences, activists develop appealing rhetorical frames for the ideas they promote. To facilitate agreements, international institutions foster prolonged interactions, in Finnemore's view generating "social liking," even a common Habermasian "lifeworld" among participants. Through repeated

---

[16] Keck and Sikkink, *Activists beyond Borders*, 206.

usage, proposed norms jell into "soft law," eventually calcifying into law itself.[17]

If, however, one notes the frequency with which contending networks challenge one another, these constructivist "logics" fall short. Indeed, that term's overtone of inevitability is unfortunate. At best, these are controversial strategies aimed at political advantage. Activists know this well. Hence, in many cases, they seek to avoid conflict, using concealment strategies. Framing and grafting exemplify this point, even if scholars have seldom noted these purposes. Both offer the world a simplified, prettified version of complex, even ugly realities. The hope is not just to rouse believers or convince the undecided, but also to disarm adversaries by averting their mobilization.

Other furtive strategies have this as a central aim. Activists split major issues into less threatening pieces to avoid attention and contention. They secrete their campaigns in low-level venues to evade detection and rejection. The goal is to surprise foes, as an unseen groundswell mushrooms into open support for a controversial principle. Consider the self-described "stealth" tactic proposed by the Center for Reproductive Rights (CRR): working in obscure UN agencies and treaty bodies to promote slow gains. The advantage, as CRR itself stated: "[W]e are achieving incremental recognition of values without a huge amount of scrutiny from the opposition. These lower profile victories will gradually put us in a strong position to assert a broad consensus around

---

[17] Finnemore, *Purpose of Intervention*, 27, 153–55; Peter M. Haas, "Introduction: Epistemic Communities and International Policy Coordination," *International Organization* 46, no. 1 (1992): 1–35; Busby, *Moral Movements*; Richard Price, "Reversing the Gun Sights: Transnational Civil Society Targets Landmines," *International Organization* 52, no. 3 (1998): 613–44; Risse and Sikkink, *Power of Human Rights*, 15, 26–27. See generally Thomas Risse, "Let's Argue!" Communicative Action in World Politics," *International Organization* 54, no. 1 (2000): 1–39; David A. Snow and Robert D. Benford, "Master Frames and Cycles of Protest," in *Frontiers in Social Movement Theory*, ed. Aldon D. Morris and Carol McClurg Mueller (New Haven, CT: Yale University Press, 1992), 133–55; George Lakoff, *Don't Think of an Elephant!: Know Your Values and Frame the Debate – The Essential Guide for Progressives* (White River Junction, VT: Chelsea Green, 2004).

our assertions."[18] Stealth does not always work, however. Rivals guard their issues, anxious to avoid ambush. They dig hard to uncover their enemies' stratagems, expose their schemes, and lump their innocuous bits into threatening wholes.

Shining light on a foe's treachery, however, seldom ends the encounter. Instead, activists go on the warpath. For every persuasive tactic, they deploy a dissuasive one. Consider framing. Does a resonant frame bring opponents to their knees? No. They pull out the hammer and smash it to smithereens. Such unframing holds true even for supposed master frames, such as human rights. Nor do foes bow down to proposed norms grafted to well-accepted principles. They break out the chainsaw and lop off the tender splice – or cut away at the underlying doctrine. On environmental issues, free-market think tanks ridicule the idea that the Earth has rights that might place limits on economic development. More basically, influential voices attack the concept of rights as empty, overused, and pernicious.[19]

Rivals seize the offensive. They hijack their foe's cherished frames, maneuvering them in contradictory ways. If one side depicts a problem as involving harm to bodily integrity, another will argue instead that the proposed solution threatens the same or worse. In 2011, when the UN unveiled a plan to inoculate girls against human papillomavirus, justifying it as a way of averting future cervical cancers, opponents not only claimed that this was a subterfuge for promoting minors' sexual rights. Groups such as the Catholic Family & Human Rights Institute (C-FAM) also argued that vaccination would in fact increase the incidence of

---

[18] Center for Reproductive Rights (CRR), "International Legal Program Summary of Strategic Planning through October 31, 2003," reprinted in "Documents Reveal Deceptive Practices by Abortion Lobby," *Congressional Record*, Dec. 8, 2003, E2534–47, E2538.

[19] Mary Ann Glendon, *Rights Talk: The Impoverishment of Political Discourse* (New York: Free Press, 1991). See generally Rodger A. Payne, "Persuasion, Frames and Norm Construction," *European Journal of International Relations* 7 (2001): 37–61; David A. Snow, Rens Vliegenthart, and Catherine Corrigall-Brown, "Framing the French Riots: A Comparative Study of Frame Variation," *Social Forces* 86 (2007): 385–415.

HPV and cancer.[20] To take another example, ecologists decry genetically modified seeds as "Frankenfoods," menacing health, indigenous cultures, and the environment. Proponents, on the other hand, portray them as answers to malnutrition and desertification, increasing yields with less need for water and pesticides. Such "framejacking" weakens the most resonant of frames.

Shaming faces resistance too. Foes match it blow for blow, working to disgrace the shamers themselves. In addition, they honor the scapegoat their foes debase, helping immunize the target from shaming's supposedly potent effects. To take one example, the Japanese state, ostensibly keen to polish its international image, has lost little face despite decades of opprobrium against whaling. Rather, because of the hunt's supposed centrality to national culture, its indubitable importance in key electoral districts, and its support from an international pro-whaling network, the Japanese unabashedly harpoon away.[21]

Nor does certifying one's position with moral, scientific, or entertainment figures go uncontested. Even when one network bolsters its sages' qualifications with awards and accolades, foes remain unimpressed. They decertify by attacking the experts' conclusions, credentials, ethics, and sanity. They fight back with a competing stable of wise men – their own scientific wunderkinds, moral megastars, and celebrity hangers-on – recipients of separate prizes meant to intensify their own gravity. More negatively, they yoke their foes to moral monstrosities, historical events or personages whose wickedness epitomizes the enemy's secret aims. As for victims, opposing networks deploy their own, with equally compelling but contrary messages.

[20] C-FAM, "UN Wants Billions for STD Vaccination Scheme," Friday Fax, May 5, 2011, http://www.c-fam.org/publications/id.1847/pub_detail. asp. Compare also CRR, "International Legal Program Summary," E2539 to C-FAM, "UN Committee Attacks Motherhood, Demands New 'Rights' for Women," Friday Fax, July 29, 2010, http://www.c-fam.org/publications/ pub_detail.asp?id=1673.

[21] Anders Blok, "Contesting Global Norms: Politics of Identity in Japanese Pro-Whaling Countermobilization," *Global Environmental Politics* 8, no. 2 (2008): 39–66.

To challenge a detested norm's proclaimed emergence, rivals use submergence strategies. They attack purported soft laws, arguing that proponents highlighted favorable precedents while ignoring inconvenient ones – or manipulated receptive institutions while avoiding inhospitable ones. More belligerently, they invent incompatible norms, using tactics mirroring their foes': their own conference declarations, quasi-judicial rulings, joint statements, expert opinions, and law review articles. All of this is possible because, at a deeper level, international laws' sources are contested. For some activists, only ratified treaties and conventions are sufficient. For others, the foregoing publications as well as states' customary practices count, regardless of how mixed and ambiguous these typically are. In short, validity standards in the area of normative emergence are themselves contested.[22] Rivals can therefore create two or more contradictory soft laws whose priority is difficult for neutral observers to determine. Resolution occurs only years later, if at all – after grim normative struggles from which the winning soft law tumbles forth, pummeled, torn, and wary of further wallops.

In sum, what is internationally and even domestically appropriate is difficult to ascertain. Indeed, appropriateness is too temperate a term to capture the rifts over right and wrong dividing networks. If, as in most issues, two or more opponents face off, scholars must examine the strategies all deploy. Analysts must also go beyond the rhetorical persuasion on which the literature has focused and examine the range of concrete ways that networks wrestle. Not to do so ignores the extent to which one side's efforts may be distorted, weakened, or neutralized by another's – and how both sides shape one another's demands, behavior, and identity.

---

[22] Compare Jack L. Goldsmith and Eric A. Posner, *The Limits of International Law* (Oxford: Oxford University Press, 2005) and Michael J. Glennon, *Limits of Law, Prerogatives of Power: Interventionism after Kosovo* (New York: Palgrave MacMillan, 2001), with Harold Hongju Koh, "Frankel Lecture: Bringing International Law Home," *Houston Law Review* 35 (1998): 623–82.

Outcomes of Conflict

Policy, Nonpolicy, and Zombie Policy

Ultimately, what matters is not one side's efforts alone. Rather, it is its power and effectiveness relative to those of the opposing network, as determined by the full range of conflictual interactions, both rhetorical and material. At its core is the ability of one network to squelch the other's voice, purge it from key institutions, or eradicate it as a viable political option. Of course, changing policy is harder than maintaining the status quo – and the greater the proposed change, the greater inertia's sway. It is unrealistic, however, to see one bloc as inevitably holding this advantage. Thus the strategies discussed here are crucial to understanding outcomes.

Policy change happens. More likely, however, is nonpolicy – a form of governance every bit as powerful, even if its products are invisible. When opponents cannot extinguish policy making, they can stall it. Even when delay ends, foes shape the results. In some cases, their power is such that the policies produced are little more than zombies, so devoid of content that, although inscribed on paper, they are in reality dead. For scholars, the lesson is clear. We should seek to explain not only policy, but also the ideas that might have been debated, the voices that might have been heard, and the provisions that might have been included – but for an opponent's machinations and clout.[23]

Promoting – and Demoting – Outcomes

Even after an institution acts, however, policy wars do not end – a reality missed by analysts who focus on one campaign or decision. Contenders maintain the fight whether they have "won" or "lost." Those stark terms are in fact misleading, because zombie policy is so common. Indeed, after an institution's decision, much

---

[23] Mathew Crenson, *The Un-Politics of Air Pollution: A Study of Non-Decisionmaking in the Cities* (Baltimore: Johns Hopkins University Press, 1971); John Gaventa, *Power and Powerlessness: Quiescence and Rebellion in an Appalachian Valley* (Champaign: University of Illinois Press, 1980).

of the conflict involves portraying the outcome as either a win or a loss – or sometimes both in different settings.[24]

For combatants who claim victory, a primary promotional strategy is touting the win to excite one's troops. In so doing, they declare the historical inevitability of their cause and the futility of resistance. Self-proclaimed winners universalize the decision to cover other venues and allied issues. They exploit ambiguous outcomes to bootstrap their goals. Inflating a result into a precedent, trend, or cascade is common. Aiding in implementation goes without saying. Over the longer term, activists sing the beneficent effects of their pet policies. Such demonstration effects can influence events in other places, sparking another round of policy battles.[25]

Although eager to proclaim victories, activists seldom admit defeats, even when foes heckle them as dead-enders. Whatever one terms them, networks unhappy with an outcome face a strategic choice. Should they give up the ghost or continue the fight? The first is likely only for a decisive defeat, although even then, committed members will move to related issues. The second is more common, but raises another question. Should losers minimize the defeat or confront it? When the decision results in a policy zombie or minimal change, activists may bury or ignore it. If that does not work, the network will narrow it, emphasizing its specifics and the uniqueness of the institution in which it was reached. To stymie bootstrapping, opponents cement-boot the abhorred result, casting it as an exception, not a precedent; an anomaly, not a trend; a dribble, not a cascade.

More frequently, they confront the objectionable decision. They denounce the institution, the process, and the opponents behind it. They blast the outcome as a disastrous new – or abiding old – problem. If new policy ensues, they torpedo its implementation. If all else fails, advocates twist the result into a

[24] Deborah Stone, *Policy Paradox: The Art of Political Decision Making*, rev. ed. (New York: W.W. Norton, 2001).
[25] Mark L. Haas, *The Ideological Origins of Great Power Politics, 1789-1989* (Ithaca, NY: Cornell University Press, 2005), 7.

horror story illustrating the depravity of their foes and the danger of their ideas. Demonstrating a policy's negative effects spreads fear among constituents and spurs other bouts between the fighters. Sometimes this occurs in the same arena as the original decision. When this is impossible because of the newfound winner's power there, however, the other will switch to a different institution where its prospects are brighter. The upshot of all this for both winners and losers: the struggle continues.

Conclusion

This book's core hypothesis is that opposition makes policy harder to achieve. This basic but neglected point has major implications. It influences all aspects of policy making/unmaking. It presents all sides with recurrent dilemmas. It fosters both affirmative and negative strategies.

To reemphasize, these strategies are not last resorts of activists on the skids. Nor are they ploys exclusive to one or another ideology – although each side portrays itself as virtuous victim and its rival as pernicious perpetrator. At opportune moments, all sides wield them, even if few will admit it, preferring instead to claim the high road. It is, of course, true that a network's position with regard to the status quo will influence the extent to which it uses affirmative or negative strategies, at least at the opening of a new front in a long-standing war. In pitched policy battles, however, which seldom have clear beginnings or endings, all contenders deploy these strategies as conflict unfolds. They are deployed not in spite of, but because of the antagonists' deep commitment to ethically charged if antithetical goals. For this reason, conflict is peppered with hyperbole and Manicheanism. We represent the public; they shill for the interests. We speak truth – to power; they lie – for power. We defend the good; they menace rights, lives – the very Earth itself. We are rational; they are deranged.

Admittedly, the model proposed here cannot quantify the degree to which opposition bends policy relative to other factors. The fact that its effects extend across the overlapping aspects of policy making/unmaking – and that opposing networks affect one another – underlines its importance, however. By contrast, the current literature seldom analyzes rival networks, suggesting that they have little impact and that civil society speaks with one voice against state and corporate obstruction. In the chapters that follow, I show that the model provides a more comprehensive and accurate account of the development, strategies, and outcomes of policy conflict than one-sided approaches.

3

Culture Wars Gone Global

Gay Rights versus the Baptist-Burqa Network

For Brazilian delegates, it was a matter of basic justice: all people, regardless of sexual orientation, should enjoy human rights. For traditional believers, however, the resolution Brazil introduced at the 2003 meeting of the United Nations Commission on Human Rights was nightmarish. By recognizing the concept of "sexual orientation," it would have legitimized homosexual behavior. Worlds away, in Gilbert, Utah, a midnight warning call jolted Lynn Allred awake. Allred, communications director for United Families International (UFI), a nondenominational "pro-family" NGO, made a lightning decision. She would jet to Switzerland because UFI must "show up everywhere marriage and the family [are] under assault" – or "those who oppose [them] will win by default."[1] Other Christian groups joined her, but all faced a problem. As NGOs, their influence was limited.

So the activists turned to another wing of their loose-knit network, Muslim countries including Egypt and Pakistan. Nor was this move unprecedented. In fact, this "Baptist-burqa" link

[1] Lynn Allred, "Thwarting the Anti-Family Agenda: An Eyewitness Account of the Commission on Human Rights," *Meridian Magazine*, Apr. 5, 2005, http://www.meridianmagazine.com/familywatch/040505agenda.html; UFI, "UFI Overview," http://unitedfamilies.org/default.asp?contentID=27. For the Brazilian resolution, see UN, "Human Rights and Sexual Orientation," Apr. 17, 2003, E/CN.4/2003/L.92.

had been forged long before. At the Fourth World Conference on Women in Beijing in 1995, the NGO Coalition for Women and the Family had denounced lesbian delegates for their "direct attack on the values, cultures, traditions and religious beliefs of the vast majority of the world's peoples." Hammered out of this and earlier perceived threats to traditional families, the network has endured for years. Indeed, the relationship hinges as much on cross-religious trust, toleration, and respect as on tactics. Listen to UFI's Lynn Allred idolizing a favorite delegate as Superman: "I discovered a secret about our Egyptian friend Amr Roshdy during our time in Geneva. I began to suspect that beneath his shirt and tie there was very likely a big red 'S.' In his work at the United Nations, Amr is a fearless defender of the family." Less breathlessly, the head of the Catholic Family & Human Rights Institute (C-FAM), has long urged a "permanent UN pro-family bloc": Our "victory will come" from this "potent alliance between Catholic and Muslim countries... new in the world, new to history," what "[o]ur enemies call... an un-holy alliance."[2]

Members of the "Baptist-burqa" network – a term I use interchangeably with "traditional families" network to signify this informal, multi-denominational grouping – cooperate transnationally on policy goals. In Germany in the 2000s, international advocates took to the courts to defend conservative Christians prosecuted for home-schooling their children rather than sending them to secular state institutions. In Nicaragua, overseas activists provide legal and ideological support for legislation outlawing abortions. In 2009, Scott Lively, president of California's Abiding Truth Ministries, dropped what he termed a "nuclear

[2] NGO Coalition for Women and the Family flyer quoted in International Gay and Lesbian Human Rights Commission (IGLHRC) and Center for Women's Global Leadership (CWGL), "Written Out: How Sexuality is Used to Attack Women's Organizing," rev. ed., 2005, 92, www.cwgl.rutgers.edu/globalcenter/publications/written.htm; Allred, "Thwarting"; Austin Ruse, "Toward a Permanent United Nations Pro-Family Bloc," paper delivered to World Congress of Families II, Geneva, Switzerland, Nov. 14–17, 1999, http://www.world congress.org/wcf2_spkrs/wcf2_ruse.htm

bomb against the 'gay' agenda in Uganda," speaking before rapt crowds at a Kampala church. Months later, a Ugandan politician introduced a parliamentary bill calling for life imprisonment for the "offence of homosexuality" and death for "aggravated homosexuality."[3]

Clearly, these religious groups go well beyond missionary and relief work. They leap borders and institutions to help fellow believers, and they run razor-sharp campaigns to gash secular foes. Indeed, in few of these conflicts do religious conservatives act unopposed. Rather, they face off against rival networks that deploy parallel tactics to defend the rights of women, access to abortions, and protections for homosexuality.

The latter issue is particularly important in understanding recent globalization of the culture wars. Even its name sparks controversy: Is it over sexual equality and gay rights – or sexual license and special rights? This war has taken a transnational dimension recently, although homosexuality has been part of human culture since time immemorial. In this chapter, I analyze the fight at the UN. Both sides see the international institution as "a battleground in the war between the Culture of Life and the Culture of Death," as C-FAM puts it – or a "battlefield in wars over 'culture' and sexuality," as Human Rights Watch (HRW) has it.[4] Hostile networks have grappled over whether to condemn human rights violations against homosexuals, whether to accept gay rights, and, most basically, whether sexual orientation and gender identity are legitimate concepts in international law. In the chapter, I show how this combat has affected development of the gay rights issue, the strategies each side deploys, and the

---

[3] Scott Lively, "Report from Uganda," Defend the Family International, Mar. 17, 2009, http://www.defendthefamily.com/pfrc/archives.php?id=2345952; Uganda Gazette, Bill No. 18: The Anti Homosexuality Bill, Bills Supplement No. 13 to the Uganda Gazette 47: CII, Sept. 25, 2009, http://docs.google .com/fileview?id=0Bze_0VuorCQjNjdlNTMwMjItYzMwNyooN2NiLTk 1ODYtMzhkOTA2YTNlZDZi&hl=en.

[4] C-FAM, Fundraising Letter, Jan. 14, 2009 (author's files); HRW, "Anatomy of a Backlash: Sexuality and the 'Cultural' War on Human Rights," in *Human Rights Watch World Report 2005*, New York: Human Rights Watch, 83.

zombie policies that have resulted. In the next chapter, I turn to two European theaters, Sweden and Romania, where many of the same foes spar with one another, using their victories – and the other side's defeats – to advance their agendas.

One terminological note is necessary because of the conflict's intensity. When discussing the gay network, I use "gay rights" to refer to the rights of lesbian, gay, bisexual, transgender, and intersex people, rather than "struggle with" what activist Joke Swiebel has called "the tongue-twisting abbreviation 'LGBT[I].'" To let both sides speak for themselves, however, I use the term "homosexual rights." Many religious conservatives reject not only such rights but also the very word "gay." For David Kupelian, managing editor of WorldNetDaily.com, the term's popularity results from nothing more than successful "marketing." It "masks the controversial sexual behavior involved and accentuates instead a vague but positive-sounding cultural identity [which] once meant 'happy.'" [5]

Gay Rights: Promise or Peril?

Constructing Gay Rights
In the United States and northern Europe, gay groups began public political activism in the 1960s and 1970s. Over time, they succeeded, with meager advances at first but broader ones by the end of the twentieth century. In this, activists contacted those they knew in other countries, then began working together more systematically. An International Lesbian Caucus formed at the 1975 UN Conference on Women in Mexico City and attended the 1980 Copenhagen follow-up. Marking the institutionalization of such ties, advocates established the International Lesbian and Gay Association (ILGA) in 1978, headquartered in Brussels. Twelve years later, the International Gay and Lesbian Human

[5] Swiebel, "Gay and Lesbian Rights and EU Enlargement," 2002, Eumap.org, http://www.eumap.org/journal/features/2002/april02/gaylesbeu; Kupelian, *The Marketing of Evil: How Radicals, Elitists, and Pseudo-Experts Sell Us Corruption Disguised As Freedom* (Nashville, TN: WND Books, 2005), 24.

Rights Commission (IGLHRC) was founded as a one-room office on San Francisco's Castro Street. Today, ILGA is a "community-based federation" of more than 670 NGOs in more than 110 countries, coordinating transnational advocacy and supporting national groups. IGLHRC, which works in many countries and the UN to build local partners' capacity to "challenge human rights violations," has annual revenues of more than $1.7 million and eighteen staff members in New York, Buenos Aires, and Capetown.[6]

In the 1970s and 1980s, however, the emerging international wing of the gay movement was far smaller. Most of ILGA's limited work involved activists within states, particularly in Europe. Although international opposition to homosexual rights had not yet coalesced, it was latent and powerful. Conflicts over women's rights and family planning already indicated conservative sensitivity. And battles within key countries such as the United States – where in the late 1970s, Anita Bryant's Save Our Children campaign sank new antidiscrimination laws – suggested that gay activism could stir foes internationally.[7]

Given this hostile climate, advocates publicized their problem in narrow terms, focusing on discrimination and violence. Influencing the problem's definition were the sites of early activism, primarily international women's conferences. There the problem was presented by lesbians, a strategic advantage as noted by activists Kirk and Madsen, because "straights generally have fewer and cloudier preconceptions" about them, viewing them "as less threatening and more vulnerable" than gay men. In the late 1980s, at a series of World Health Organization meetings, male homosexuals became more active. There too, they highlighted discrimination, particularly in health-related issues. In this, they used the "unwelcome 'opportunity'" of the AIDS

---

[6] ILGA, About ILGA, http://old.ilga.org/aboutilga.asp.; IGLHRC, Annual Report 2007–08, www.iglhrc.org/binary-data/ATTACHMENT/file/000/000/218–2.pdf 2.

[7] Fetner, *How the Religious Right*, xiii.

crisis, which transformed gay men into a "victimized minority legitimately deserving of . . . special protection and care."[8]

This strategic conception of the problem, however, avoided a more fundamental issue: homosexuality's status as normal or deviant. By the late 1990s, as gays made gains in key states, activists expanded the definition. It began to encompass the UN's failure both to recognize homosexuality within a spectrum of sexual orientation and gender identity and to acknowledge gay rights as human rights. In the 2000s, with further domestic advances in key states, homosexuals portrayed their problem more boldly. Now it encompassed restrictions on sexual freedom for "sexual and gender outlaws, whether they be gays and lesbians, transgenders, intersexed people, unmarried youth, commercial sex workers, or heterosexual women trying to live a 'non-traditional' social and erotic existence."[9]

Deconstructing Homosexual Rights
Even with gay advocates' narrow, early construction of the problem, foes mobilized. Initially, this opposition was ad hoc. At the UN's 1985 Nairobi women's conference, many religious NGOs attended. Their role in the troubles lesbians faced – being driven from the NGO Forum by its convenor, an ex-president of the World Council of Churches – is unclear. By the early 1990s, however, religious opposition became better organized, rooted in larger, preexisting efforts to fight family planning. The Baptist-burqa network dates at least to the 1994 Cairo Conference on Population and Development. There the Holy See reached out to Islamic delegates to block proposals that would have made abortions easier to obtain. Preserving "traditional" or "natural" families against the "gendered" family and homosexuality fits in this broader agenda. As it developed, the Baptist-burqa network

---

[8] Marshall Kirk and Hunter Madsen, *After the Ball: How America Will Conquer Its Fear and Hatred of Gays in the '90s* (New York: Doubleday, 1989), 184, xxv. See also Ara Wilson, "Lesbian Visibility and Sexual Rights at Beijing," *Signs* 22:1 (1996), 214–18, 215.

[9] Sexuality Policy Watch, "Why Sexuality," http://www.sxpolitics.org/?cat=42.

spanned governments, especially conservative Islamic, African, and Caribbean nations, as well as the Holy See, which enjoys special status at the UN.[10]

Along with the Vatican, the most focused participants are NGOs, most identified with various Christian denominations and most active in a variety of related family issues. There are too many to describe all, but two gladiators merit announcement. The Howard Center for Family, Religion and Society, founded in 1976 and based in Rockford, Illinois, is a nondenominational group defending the natural family – "the fundamental unit of society, not the individual, not the state, not the church, and not the corporation." For many years, the Center focused on research. More recently, it has used its "talents and resources to create new coalitions to promote the natural family worldwide." The result is the Howard Center's "largest project, in both time and money" – the World Congress of Families (WCF), a multiday, biennial international conference. Serving as an intellectual nerve center, the Howard Center and WCF have thousands of individual members and twenty-seven partner organizations from around the world, each of the latter paying $2,500 per year. Together, in the words of Howard Center's head Allan C. Carlson, they seek to "forge a truly international profamily movement . . . embrac[ing] all religiously grounded family morality systems around the globe, without descending into the banal."[11]

---

[10] For discussion of the Nairobi conference, see Mandana Hendessi, "Fourteen Thousand Women Meet: Report from Nairobi, July 1985," *Feminist Review* 23 (1986), 147–56; Janie Hampton, "The Soapbox in the Sun: The UN Decade of Women Conference in Kenya," *Guardian* (London), July 29, 1985, www/lexis-nexis.com/. For conservative perspectives on the Cairo meeting, see WFF, "Beijing + 5 Report: Non-Governmental Organizations: Key to Defense of Traditional Family?" Voices Online Edition 15, no. 2 (2000), http://wf-f.org/Sum2K-Anderson.html. See generally Louise Chappell, "Contesting Women's Rights: Charting the Emergence of a Transnational Conservative Counter-Network," *Global Society* 20 (2006): 491–520; DeMars, *NGOs and Transnational Networks*, 143–61.

[11] Howard Center for Family, Religion, and Society, "Frequently Asked Questions," http://www.profam.org/THC/xthc_faq.htm; Allan Carlson, "A History of "the Family" in the United Nations," presentation to UN Observer

The Catholic Family & Human Rights Institute (C-FAM), founded in 1997 by journalist Austin Ruse, is another key combatant and WCF member. Guided by "fidelity to the teachings of the Church," C-FAM's mission is "reestablishing a proper understanding of international law, protecting national sovereignty and the dignity of the human person." To achieve these goals, C-FAM "publishes and promotes scholarship" meeting this understanding. At the UN, it involves itself in everything from regular meetings to special treaty negotiations. Its participation has spanned debates on the International Criminal Court, the UN Declaration on Human Cloning, the Convention on the Rights of Persons with Disabilities, and numerous women's and development issues. In addition, C-FAM plays a watchdog role, eyeing, sizing up, and attacking its enemies and their ideas.[12]

In fights over homosexual rights, members of the traditional families network rejected their opponents' basic premises. Indeed, for religious traditionalists, UN failures to recognize sexual orientation and gay rights were not problems at all. On the contrary: the possibility of such recognition was itself a threat. More broadly, the menace extended to UN usage of terminology such as "gendered families," "gender identity," and "gender" itself. For C-FAM, such "socially radical policies" threaten the "natural structure of the family" and must be "discredit[ed]." For the Family First Foundation, a WCF offshoot, they contribute to the "single most powerful force affecting the fate and future

Training Seminar (Canada), St. John the Evangelist Church, New York, NY, June 2, 2000, http://www.profam.org/docs/acc/thc_acc_un.htm.

[12] C-FAM, "Mission Statement," http://www.c-fam.org/about-us/mission-statement.html; C-FAM, "About Us," http://www.c-fam.org/about_us/. See also Ruse, "Toward a Permanent United Nations Pro-Family Bloc." In a prior incarnation, C-FAM leader Austin Ruse worked in the "New York magazine world," including a stint with *Rolling Stone* magazine. This was topped in 1990 by a night covering "gonzo journalist" Hunter S. Thompson's self-experiments in Chivas Regal and cocaine. Years later, after Thompson killed himself with a bullet to the brain, Ruse ruefully chronicled the incident – "with this I say goodbye to Senate confirmation." Austin Ruse, "Fear and Loathing: My Night with Hunter Thompson," *National Review Online*, Feb. 22, 2005, http://www.nationalreview.com/comment/ruse200502220743.asp.

of society," worldwide "demographic winter": crashing populations and the ultimate "decline of the human family." For state
members of the Organisation of the Islamic Conference (OIC),
recognition of the sexual orientation concept "could result in a
positive discrimination [at] the expense of others' rights" and
"legitimiz[e] many deplorable acts."[13]

Building Networks

With battle joined in the late 1980s, the networks began influencing one another. Facing burgeoning opposition, activists redoubled their efforts to attract powerful allies. States were the top
prize, although time-consuming to turn. In the Nairobi dustup of
1985, the Dutch became the first at a UN conference to support
gay rights – or rather lesbian rights. The Netherlands is home
to the world's oldest publicly acknowledged homosexual organization, the Centre for Culture and Leisure (COC), founded in
1946. In the late 1980s and early 1990s, political mobilization
by national gay movements prompted countries in Europe, the
Americas, and elsewhere to take major steps toward equality. In
turn, this was reflected in their stances at UN conferences. By the
2000s, most European states favored gay rights at international
forums, with pressure from the European Union (EU) and Council of Europe playing a role in this turnaround. The EU, Council,
and major foundations such as the Ford Foundation from the
early 1990s, and the Arcus and Soros Foundations in the 2000s,
provided monetary support for gay activism as well.[14]

Beginning in the late 1970s, activists sought to expand their
network to include human rights NGOs. Special targets were
Amnesty International and later Human Rights Watch, whose

[13] C-FAM, "Mission Statement"; Family First Foundation, "Welcome," http://
www.familyfirstfoundation.org/index.html; OIC, "Response to SOGI [Sexual
Orientation and Gender Identity] Human Rights Statement, Read by Syria –
18 Dec. 2008," http://ilga.org/ilga/en/article/mkjJMT21ax.

[14] History based on Douglas Sanders, "Getting Lesbian and Gay Issues on the
International Human Rights Agenda," *Human Rights Quarterly* 18, no. 1
(1996): 67–106, 89; ARC International, "Building on the Past, Looking to
the Future," n.d. 2009 (author's files).

resources, authority, credibility, and contacts made them valuable allies. Amnesty's International Secretariat long rejected these overtures, however, claiming that issues of sexual identity were beyond its mandate. Human Rights Watch too refused to act. Only in the mid-1990s did both groups relent, but only after years of discussion, conflict, and pressure – and after the growing acceptability of homosexuality among the domestic populations that are the NGOs' primary constituencies. Since then, Human Rights Watch has moved to the frontlines of the struggle, its *2005 World Report* including a chapter, "Anatomy of a Backlash," striking back at gay rights' enemies.[15]

Those enemies sought "an injection of Christian and pro-family NGOs" into global politics. According to the traditional Catholic Women for Faith & Family (WFF), these would assist the Holy See and other friendly nations in lobbying at UN conferences. They would thereby "combat the assault of the culture of death so militantly advanced by those NGOs who currently wield so much power at the international level." If the UN treated conferences with civil society participants as a "democratic means of arriving at a 'world consensus,'" then conservatives would respond in kind. By the early 2000s, conservatives fielded their own bevy of religious, women's, and other organizations.[16]

These in turn lobbied governments in the Caribbean, Asia, and Africa. Despite cultural differences, the countries and the NGOs shared common moral beliefs. At the 2000 Beijing + 5 conference, WFF courted "non-Western" countries. They even approached nations in which, as they delicately put it, "certain tribal excesses" such as female genital mutilation, honor killings,

---

[15] HRW, "Anatomy of a Backlash." For discussion of the NGOs evolving relations with gay activists, see Stephen Hopgood, *Keepers of the Flame: Understanding Amnesty International* (Ithaca, NY: Cornell University Press, 2006), 116–21; Julie Mertus, "Applying the Gatekeeper Model of Human Rights Activism: The U.S.-Based Movement for LGBT Rights," in *International Struggle*, ed. Bob, 52–67.

[16] WFF, "Beijing + 5 Report." See also Ruse, "Toward a Permanent United Nations Pro-Family Bloc"; Chappell, "Contesting Women's Rights."

and dowry deaths provided Western rights groups with "emotional clubs to cow the delegates" into accepting gay rights. WFF "decr[ied]" the excesses too, but argued that "'solving' these familial injustices" should not "be sufficient reason to dismantle traditional families world-wide." Thus, at the Beijing + 5 Prep-Com, a "large contingent of Western women from pro-family NGOs" appealed to a "stunned" Zambian delegate: "Our own delegations . . . are promoting an agenda which is not true to our family and cultural traditions – in fact, radical women have been sent here in spite of our pleas to have a more balanced team of delegates. We look to nations such as yours to speak for us, to save us from the folly of our own governments!"[17]

In addition to using shared morality to build the traditional families network, NGOs fueled fear and resentment. Stoking nationalism was a favored tactic to attract developing countries. This occurred not only in Beijing, but also five years later at the follow-up conference where anonymous flyers stated: "If the West would stop pushing homosexual and abortion 'rights' on unwilling countries, the document would be done. Don't blame the developing countries with the courage to defend their values and their right to self-government!" As a C-FAM strategist suggests conservative NGOs build their network by using "the resentment that heavy-handed pushing of novel norms generates in much of the world."[18]

Bashing Networks

Even as they gird themselves for battle, leading members of each bloc attack one another. Consider how the International Lesbian and Gay Association has been affected by such assaults. In 1993, it obtained consultative status at the UN's Economic and Social Council (ECOSOC). This is normally a routine matter, but for the gay network it was a historic marker of international recognition. Jubilation soon turned to tribulation, however, as

---

[17] WFF, "Beijing + 5 Report."
[18] Flyer quoted in HRW, "Anatomy of a Backlash," 84–85; C-FAM, "General Assembly 'Sexual Orientation' Vote Reveals Defection by Catholic Nations," Friday Fax 13, no. 4, Jan. 7, 2010, http://www.c-fam.org/publications/id.1549/pub_detail.asp.

opponents, working with powerful U.S. Senator Jesse Helms, took to the warpath. Their battle cry, bellowed in fundraising letters and blasted on prime-time news: ILGA must be ousted from the UN because its network included a pedophilia peddler. This was the North American Man Boy Love Association (NAMBLA), pledged to "support CONSENSUAL intergenerational relationships and help educate society about the true nature of such relationships." Within months, the U.S. Congress unanimously passed a law withholding $119 million from the UN, unless the President certified that the world body granted no "official status, accreditation, or recognition" to any organization that "promotes, condones, or seeks the legalization of pedophilia, that is, the sexual abuse of children." President Bill Clinton, fresh off his bruising "Don't Ask, Don't Tell" fight, signed the bill into law.[19]

The effect on ILGA was traumatic – just as its enemies had hoped. They gloated in fundraising letters over the homosexual group's coming "bind": "If it kicks out NAMBLA, it's hypocritical, if not it supports sex between boys and men!" Unsurprisingly except perhaps to NAMBLA, ILGA chose the former – although without admitting hypocrisy. At the first public attacks, ILGA distanced itself from its long-time stalwart. It rationalized the group's membership as an oversight – although foes reveled in documents demonstrating NAMBLA's centrality to the network. More importantly, ILGA began a fractious internal debate, expelling NAMBLA and two other groups promoting pedophilia in June 1994.[20]

In addition to altering its structure, ILGA changed its rules. Within two years, it had implemented a tough, four-step screening process to ensure that no group such as NAMBLA would ever be admitted in the future. Most fundamentally, leaders of the homosexual community in the United States and internationally

---

[19] This and the next three paragraphs are based in part on Joshua Gamson, "Messages of Exclusion: Gender, Movements, and Symbolic Boundaries." *Gender and Society* 11, no. 2 (1997): 178–99; NAMBLA mission, quoted in ibid., 183 (emphasis in original); H.R. 2333 (1994). See also NAMBLA, "Who We Are," http://www.nambla.org/welcome.htm

[20] The Report, fundraising letter 1993, quoted in Gamson, "Messages of Exclusion," 183–84.

redefined the very boundaries of gay identity. Gregory King, spokesman for America's largest gay advocacy group, the Human Rights Campaign Fund, put it bluntly: "NAMBLA is not a gay organization.... They are not part of our community and we thoroughly reject their efforts to insinuate that pedophilia is an issue related to gay and lesbian civil rights." To which NAM-BLA spokesperson Bill Andriette shot back: his group represented a "main tradition" of homosexuality. Gay leaders were "rewrit[ing] history," "join[ing] the violence against and oppression of boy lovers," and "presenting their most sanitized image" to pander for respectability and UN status.[21]

Despite all ILGA's changes, the UN suspended the network anyway in September 1994. It had neglected to shed a small German group promoting decriminalization of pedophilia. Too late, ILGA reemphasized its newfound identity by tossing out the Germans. It then waited five years to reapply for ECOSOC status but was repeatedly rejected because of the earlier scandal. Tarred with the same feather, separate groups such as IGLHRC were refused ECOSOC consultative status and harried at UN conferences such as the 2001 Special Session on HIV/AIDS. For key members of the traditional families network, NAMBLA was too valuable a prey to release so soon. Only in 2006 did ECOSOC grant consultative status to ILGA-Europe, with IGLHRC gaining it in 2010.

This decades-long onslaught on ILGA's most unacceptable member – aimed at smearing and smashing the gay network as a whole – is hardly unique. In 2000, C-FAM's Austin Ruse denounced "enormous" and "very radical" American foundations that "put direct pressure on governments to change their laws and vote a certain way on UN resolutions," striking "at the heart of the family, religious faith, the nation and the Church." Such rhetoric is meant partly for internal consumption, as a

---

[21] King quoted in Gamson, "Messages of Exclusion," 179; Andriette quoted in Duncan Osborne, "Ill Will toward ILGA: The Senate Takes Aim at an International Gay Group," *The Advocate*, Mar. 8, 1994, 27. See also Kirk and Madsen, *After the Ball*, 184.

means of mobilizing the converted. In addition, it wounds the opposition, as groups such as IGLHRC acknowledge. "Sexuality baiting" – "discrediting and controlling people, organizations and political agendas through strategic use of allegations related to sexuality" – influences "how organizations choose projects and set priorities . . . how they measure goals and vision against political realities and risk." Among specific effects are self-censorship and deterrence of would-be allies. As another example, gay activists admit to being stung by the accusation that they are neo-imperialists, spreading alien practices to indigenous societies. According to the progressive think tank Political Research Associates (PRA), left-leaning churches have been reluctant to promote gay rights in Africa in part because of "liberals' sensitivity to the charge of colonialism."[22]

Facing these assaults, gay activists have not turned the other cheek. They too have worked to unbuild their enemy's network. As a long-term strategy, they support struggling gay movements in key countries. This has helped change domestic attitudes and national policies. As C-FAM laments, it has led to costly "defections" by once-reliable allies, especially Catholic-majority countries in southern Europe and Latin America. To further undermine the Baptist-burqa network, gay advocates use similar strategies in Islamic countries. ARC International, a Geneva-based NGO, has targeted Turkey because it is "in a crucial position to bridge the gap between East and West that often divides State discussions at the international level." In a more aggressive move aimed at sapping the religious network, PRA investigated and publicized the U.S. Christian right's linkages with violent anti-gay activism in Africa.[23]

---

[22] Ruse, "Joyful Warrior: An Interview with Austin Ruse," *Inside the Vatican*, June-July 2000, http://indigo.ie/~imr/otr-un.htm#Austin%20Ruse; IGLHRC and CWGL, "Written Out," 17; PRA, "Groundbreaking PRA Investigation Exposes Influence of U.S. Religious Conservatives in Promoting Homophobia in Africa," press release, n.d. 2009, http://www.publiceye.org/publications/globalizing-the-culture-wars/press-release.php.

[23] C-FAM, "General Assembly 'Sexual Orientation' Vote Reveals Defection"; ARC International, "International Experiences in the Struggle against Homophobia, Ankara, Turkey," presentation of John Fisher to KAOS GL Meeting,

At the UN, gay activists use negative tactics to exclude key foes from participation, just as ILGA was for so long kept out. Human Rights Watch has griped that foes such as C-FAM "oppose the U.N. and all international human rights mechanisms." The implication: such NGOs do not deserve UN consultative status. In related cases, this has in fact come to pass. In the early 1990s, as Peter Willetts has shown, Human Life International's (HLI) application failed because of its "hostil[ity] to a whole field of UN activity" – family planning. (Perhaps playing a role as well, HLI had run a high-profile American campaign against the UN's "Trick or Treat for UNICEF" program.) After C-FAM's UN acceptance, it too faced accusations about its close relationship to HLI. These attempts to tar C-FAM – published in a forty-page report by Catholics for a Free Choice (now Catholics for Choice) (CFC), an NGO supporting abortion, feminism, and gay rights – failed to catch fire.[24]

As a further example of such exclusionary tactics, consider CFC itself, whose application for consultative status came under attack from the Holy See in 1998. After a bruising battle, CFC gained UN accreditation. In retaliation, it launched the "See Change" campaign to strip Rome of its special UN status. Since 1964, the Holy See has been a non-member state "Permanent Observer" – a position unique to any religious organization. In this capacity, it enjoys most rights accorded member states, although it has chosen not to vote

May 17–21, 2006, http://www.arc-international.net/network-development/conference-presentations/presentation-on-un-mechanisms.htm. See also Kapya Kaoma, "The U.S. Christian Right and the Attack on Gays in Africa," *Public Eye Magazine* (PRA), Winter 2009/Spring 2010, http://www.publiceye.org/magazine/v24n4/us-christian-right-attack-on-gays-in-africa.html; Kapya Kaoma, "Globalizing the Culture Wars: U.S. Conservatives, African Churches, & Homophobia," PRA, 2009, http://www.publiceye.org/publications/globalizing-the-culture-wars/press-release.php.

[24] HRW, "Anatomy of a Backlash," 84; Peter Willetts, *The Conscience of the World: The Influence of Non-Governmental Organizations in the UN System* (Washington, DC: Brookings Institution Press, 1996), 4, 37, 60, n. 24; CFC, "Bad Faith at the UN: Drawing Back the Curtain on the Catholic Family and Human Rights Institute," 2001, http://www.catholicsforchoice.org/topics/politics/keypubs.asp.

on UN resolutions. As such, it is a cornerstone of the religious network, one whose heft rival NGOs cannot match. Unsurprisingly, therefore, the Vatican's status became a target. The See Change campaign – headlined by the slogan, "When the United Nations treats a religion as a country, we all suffer" – aims to degrade the Holy See to lowly NGO rank. Endorsed by hundreds of NGOs, the campaign has nonetheless gained little traction. Part of the reason: C-FAM rallied to the Holy See's defense, attracting support from governments and NGOs in the thousands. To date, the Holy See retains its unusual seat at the UN table. There it has been a leader on "dignity of the person" issues.[25]

In a further effort to subvert the Baptist-burqa network in the post-9/11 era, Human Rights Watch has stressed the "irony" of the "odd alliance" between Christian conservatives and repressive Muslim states. The alliance batters "the most vulnerable edge of the human rights movement" and threatens the "whole body politic." The result: "Societies are devastated. People die." More broadly, Human Rights Watch assails the network for "open[ing] space for attacking human rights principles themselves – as not universal but 'foreign,' as not protectors of diversity but threats to sovereignty, and as carriers of cultural perversion."[26]

The barbs have hurt. As the Holy See complained in 2011, "people are being attacked," "stigmatized," "vilified, and prosecuted" when they express their "moral beliefs or beliefs about human nature, which may also be expressions of religious convictions, or state opinions about scientific claims." Going further, the Vatican argued that the "attacks are violations of fundamental human rights, and cannot be justified under any circumstances."[27] Key members of the religious network have

---

[25] CFC, "It's Time for a Change – a See Change," http://www.seechange.org/; C-FAM, "Campaign in Support of the Holy See at the United Nations," Nov. 15, 2000 (author's files); DeMars, *NGOs and Transnational Networks*, 156–58.

[26] HRW, "Anatomy of a Backlash," 84, 83, 71, 88, 82, 71.

[27] Holy See, "Statement on '"Sexual Orientation,'" Mar. 24, 2011, http://www.zenit.org/article-32108?l=english.

come to understand the dangers they run in promiscuous relations with extreme voices. Whether or not they learned this from ILGA's NAMBLA crisis, they distance themselves from fringe antihomosexual activity that might sully the entire network. Of course, the definition of acceptability varies over time with broader cultural change. And in the unending war, gay advocates, like their opponents, seize every opportunity to destroy their foes.

Consider the events surrounding Uganda's "Anti-Homosexuality Bill" in 2009. As it became clear that prominent American activists, including Abiding Truth Ministry's Scott Lively and Exodus Global Alliance's Don Schmierer, had visited the country shortly before the bill's proposal, gay groups headlined the U.S. linkage to what they dubbed the "death to gays" bill. The New York-based Astraea Lesbian Foundation stated that its allies were in "a fight for their lives" – and indeed, in 2011, one Ugandan activist was killed. Other activists took the opportunity to tar more moderate opponents of gay rights. Political Research Associates insisted that one of America's most powerful evangelicals, Rev. Rick Warren of the Saddleback Church, sever his ties to a Ugandan church supportive of the bill. The strategic rationale for this demand? As PRA's Kapya Kaoma put it, these "challenges on conservatives' home territory provide vital support for LGBT Africans under attack."[28]

In the firestorm of criticism, the Holy See joined with rights groups to condemn the "death to gays" bill at a UN press conference. Rick Warren cut his links with the Ugandan preacher. Even the original American interlopers backpedaled. Schmierer, whose group helps homosexuals overcome "unwanted same-sex attraction," swore that he had been "duped" into appearing in Kampala and stated that "some of the nicest people I have ever met are gay people." Scott Lively told an interviewer he was

---

[28] Astraea spokesperson Mai Kang quoted in Jeffrey Gettleman, "Americans' Role Seen in Uganda Anti-Gay Push," *New York Times*, Jan. 3, 2010, http://www.nytimes.com/2010/01/04/world/africa/04uganda.html; Kaoma, "The U.S. Christian Right."

"very disappointed" that the bill included "such incredibly harsh punishments." On his "Defend the Family" blog, however, he showed less repentance: amend the bill to reduce punishment and emphasize rehabilitation, and "it would deserve support" from "advocates of marriage-based culture around the world." Unwilling to be shamed, Lively struck back: gay advocates were patronizing Africans by blaming Americans for the bill. In fact, Ugandan views stemmed from indigenous disgust at a nineteenth-century ruler, King Mwanga, who required men to have sex with him on penalty of death – and in 1886 gruesomely executed twenty-two converted Christians who refused his advances.[29]

To summarize, each side advances its goals by building its own network, using threats posed by the other to scare constituents into action. At the same time, each assaults the other, hoping to weaken and unbuild it. Both networks have been battered, but even the scars are used to fuel anger – and therefore their constituents' support.[30]

Institutions Picked, Packed, and Invented

Even as they build and unbuild, the rival networks make crucial decisions about the institutions in which to fight. As we have seen, gay groups have campaigned aggressively at the UN. Its centrality to international politics makes that imperative, even though many member states oppose the sexual-orientation concept. The perils of operating there, however, influence the specific

---

[29] Schmierer quoted in Gettleman, "Americans' Role Seen"; Exodus Global Alliance, "Missions," http://exodusglobalalliance.org/missionss6.php; Lively quoted in National Public Radio, "U.S. Evangelical Leaders Blamed For Uganda Anti-Gay Sentiment," interview transcript, Dec. 18, 2009, http://www.npr.org/templates/story/story.php?storyId=121605529; Scott Lively, "The Death Penalty in Uganda," Defend the Family International, Jan. 5, 2010, http://www.defendthefamily.com/pfrc/newsarchives.php?id=4480922. See generally Marc Epprecht, *Heterosexual Africa? The History of an Idea from the Age of Exploration to the Age of AIDS* (Athens, OH and Scottsville, South Africa: Ohio University Press and University of KwaZulu-Natal Press, 2008), 42–43.

[30] See, e.g., ILGA, "ILGA's Public Stance against Paedophilia and Commitment to the Protection of Children," July 13, 2006, http://ilga.org/ilga/en/article/861; Ruse, "Toward a Permanent United Nations Pro-Family Bloc."

UN venues activists choose. Early on, the NGO forums at international conferences offered easy accreditation and a chance to raise consciousness. Consensus decision making has proven an impediment, however. Gay activists have therefore targeted low-level UN institutions such as quasi-judicial commissions, treaty monitoring bodies, expert committees, and special rapporteurs, which sometimes do not rule by consensus. Many of these are staffed by international bureaucrats friendly to gay issues and accountable primarily to the UN. As well, these institutions operate for the most part out of the public eye.

For their part, religious traditionalists have been similarly ambivalent. After all, the UN launched outrages such as the Convention on the Elimination of All Forms of Discrimination Against Women (CEDAW), which "strips the family of all autonomy and authority," and the Convention on the Rights of the Child, which "subvert[s] the authority of parents over their children."[31] Nonetheless, religious conservatives have decided that the UN cannot be neglected. It is too important and offers avenues for their interests to be realized – or their opponents' to be foiled. Thus, they cultivate certain states and play the UN's arcane rules to block and harass. Of course, these NGOs, like their ideological enemies, have limited resources. Notwithstanding vows to fight for the family wherever it is threatened, members of the network must be selective. Like the opposition, they too focus on institutions whose outcomes they can influence – in their case, those in which consensus rules make it easier to sink foes' proposals. Least tractable are restricted venues in which appointed officials such as special rapporteurs are sympathetic to the opponent. In these cases, the primary response has been condemnation.

Given the volleys they face in regular UN venues, both sides hunger for alternatives – sites where they can promote their goals unimpeded. In some cases, they have fabricated such institutions, dolling them up with the trappings of authority, hoping thereby to influence policy.

---

[31] Carlson, "A History of 'the Family' in the United Nations."

Frustrated by a decade of UN failure to recognize gay rights, two supportive NGOs, International Service for Human Rights (ISHR) and the International Commission of Jurists (ICJ), hand-picked a "distinguished" group of like-minded "international human rights experts" in 2006. After several weeks in steamy central Java, they drafted and issued the Yogyakarta Principles. Accompanied by press release and Web site, these are described as "a universal guide to human rights which affirm binding international legal standards with which all States must comply." In essence, they proclaim that existing rules already mandate gay rights. In twenty-nine "principles" and hundreds of "directives," Yogyakarta holds that states must therefore "embody . . . equality and non-discrimination on the basis of sexual orientation and gender identity" in their constitutions and laws.[32]

Religious groups too have forged their own institutions, issuing authoritative-sounding proclamations supporting their views. One example is the 2004 Doha International Conference for the Family, marking the tenth anniversary of the International Year of the Family. Superficially, Doha resembled recent international conferences where homosexual activists have promoted their issues. It was endorsed by a UN resolution, advertised by a worldwide call for participation, preceded by regional preparatory meetings, and attended by hundreds of state and nongovernmental delegates. Its ideological polarity, however, was switched. The NGO Working Committee was made up of representatives from Brigham Young University's World Family Policy Center, the Family Research Council, and C-FAM. The Doha Declaration, quoting the Universal Declaration of Human Rights, reaffirmed the "right of men and women" (only) to marry and the family as the "natural and fundamental group unit of society." In the conference's wake, the government of Qatar established

[32] ISHR and ICJ, Yogyakarta Principles, 2006, http://www.yogyakartaprinciples .org/index.html; ibid, http://www.yogyakartaprinciples.org/principles_en. htm, prins. 2, 3. See also ICJ, "Sexual Orientation and Gender Identity in Human Rights Law," Geneva, Switzerland, Oct. 2006, 14, www.icj.org/ IMG/UN_References.pdf.

the Doha International Institute for Family Studies, headed by Brigham Young's Richard G. Wilkins. Finally, organizers memorialized the conference with a Web site and three-volume book. Its preface, penned by Her Highness Sheika Mozah Bint Nasser Al-Missned of Qatar, decreed: "all divine laws have blessed this sacred institution [the family], which forges a strong bond between males and females, a bond which conforms to human nature in bearing and raising new generations that, in turn, contribute to building civilization."[33]

Gay advocates gave Doha a miss, but beyond the fact that committed activists avoid hostile arenas, the analytic lesson is subtler. If an institution such as the UN plays a critical role in a policy area, activists will enter it notwithstanding disadvantages they may face, if only to hamstring their foes. Nor will they stop at that. Inventing friendly new arenas is another option.

Cascade Wars

Yogyakarta and Doha might seem reflexive and meaningless responses to international arenas riddled with adversaries. In fact, they are more: integral parts of broader strategies to institutionalize favored norms as international law. Taking a liberal view, the ICJ and ISHR argue that states' customary practices, international organizations' quasi-judicial rulings, and legal scholarship should all count. On that basis, these NGOs claim that UN

---

[33] UN, General Assembly Resolutions 58/15 (2003) and 59/111 (2004); A. Scott Loveless and Thomas B. Holman, eds. *The Family in the New Millennium: World Voices Supporting the "Natural" Clan* (Westport, CT: Praeger, 2007), 1: ix, xiii; Doha International Conference for the Family, http://www.yearofthefamily.org/Doha.htm; Doha Declaration, 2004, http://www.yearofthefamily.org/declaration.html; Doha International Conference for the Family, *The World Unites to Protect the Family* (Qatar and Provo, Utah: Supreme Council for Family Affairs and the World Family Policy Center, Brigham Young University, 2004), www.yearofthefamily.org/.../ The_World_Unites_to_Save_the_Family_Reports.pdf. See also Richard G. Wilkins, "International Law and the Family: Building on the Doha Declaration," in *The Family in the New Millennium*, ed. Loveless and Holman, 3: 365–84.

recognition of gay rights "would not create 'new rights'" but merely codify existing ideas and practices.[34]

Of course, this controverted process does not just happen. Custom and scholarship transform themselves into law only through activism: selecting favorable sources while ignoring or distinguishing inconvenient ones; calculating how to advance agendas while staving off ambushes; framing favorably while framejacking or smashing rival images; and finding policy makers already receptive to goals while avoiding those unwilling to listen. At best, change is contingent on the force of opposition. If it occurs, it is slow and incremental. Nonetheless, gay advocates have embraced the strategy, hoping that gradual gains will eventually unloose a cascade of advances. In the following sections, I show first how they used the strategy, then how opponents attacked it.

Setting the Gay Agenda

Two broad periods of the incremental strategy are discernible at the UN. From the mid-1970s until the early 2000s, advocates worked quietly in low-level venues using limited achievements at one site to bootstrap additional gains elsewhere. From about 2003 onward, the strategy has been conducted more publicly. The earlier approach stemmed from a lack of strong partners and the "venom of the opposition."[35] The later strategy hinged on the advent of powerful state allies willing to promote the issues openly even as they came under withering fire from the religious network.

In the first period, one small but important victory occurred in a 1994 decision of the Commission on Human Rights rejecting an Australian sodomy law. The basis for this ruling was privacy rights, not equality principles, but activists have nonetheless

---

[34] ICJ, "Sexual Orientation and Gender Identity in Human Rights Law," Geneva, Switzerland, Oct. 2006, 14, www.icj.org/IMG/UN_References.pdf. See generally Koh, "Bringing International Law Home."
[35] Wilson, "Lesbian Visibility," 217.

touted it in the broader battle.[36] More commonly in the 1990s, activists inched their agenda forward against harsh attack, under the guise of women's rights. At international conferences, they endorsed vanilla verbiage that arguably but not explicitly included homosexuals and their concerns. At the 1994 Cairo population conference, gay activists joined women's groups in lobbying for its Programme of Action. This affirmed "reproductive rights" and "reproductive health," including a "satisfying and safe sex life" free of coercion and discrimination. The broad language did not expressly cover homosexuals, and by some lights might be thought to exclude them. When it was adopted despite opposition, however, gay activists hailed this as an advance.[37]

In the lead-up to 1995's Beijing women's conference, advocates went further. At preparatory meetings, they succeeded in inserting the term "sexual orientation" as bracketed text, for debate at the main meeting. But what flew in regional conclaves where gays had political clout fell in the global meeting where they did not. It is true that the sexual orientation concept's international visibility increased. It was debated by state delegates for more than an hour. In the end, however, Beijing's Platform for Action declared only that women should "have control over ... their sexuality, including sexual and reproductive health" – omitting all proposed references to sexual orientation. Still, this too has been portrayed as progress and precedent.[38]

In the late 1990s, there were attempts to insert sexual orientation and gender identity language into other UN documents. The first official UN reference came in 2000 in a Commission on

---

[36] *Toonen v. Australia*, Communication No. 488/1992, U.N. Doc CCPR/ C/50/D/488/1992 (1994); Sarah Pritchard, "Gay Rights Victory at UN," *Human Rights Defender*, 1994, http://www.austlii.edu.au/au/journals/HRD/ 1994/2.html.

[37] UN, "Programme of Action of the United Nations International Conference on Population & Development," A/CONF.171/13, Oct. 18, 1994, Ch. VII, A7.2, http://www.un.org/popin/icpd/conference/offeng/poa.html.

[38] UN, "Platform for Action of the Fourth World Conference on Women," Sept. 1995, para. 96, http://www.un.org/womenwatch/daw/beijing/platform/plat1. htm; ARC International, "Building on the Past," 2.

Human Rights resolution on extrajudicial executions. Renewed in later years, this urged states to investigate killings motivated by any discriminatory reason, including sexual orientation. As discussed in the next section, however, Islamic and African states backed by religious NGOs made repeated attempts to rip the original reference from the underlying document. More generally, the sexual-orientation concept itself remained unaccepted at the UN and even in the Commission (or Human Rights Council, as it became in 2006).[39]

This slow, closeted approach changed in 2003. Brazil, acting on its own initiative and with significant domestic support for gay rights, proposed the binding resolution on "Human Rights and Sexual Orientation" noted in this chapter's introduction. The fierce opposition it engendered – from the UFI's Lynn Allred, her Egyptian superhero Amr Roshdy, and many others – killed it. The next year, Brazil resubmitted the resolution, this time in coordination with NGOs such as Human Rights Watch, which bootstrapped the foregoing "well grounded... human rights standards and United Nations precedents" in urging the Commission to adopt the resolution. The traditional families network blocked again, however, and Brazil withdrew the resolution in 2005. In reaction, the gay rights network led by New Zealand took a lesser step, submitting a similarly worded joint statement – nonbinding and requiring no vote for introduction – signed by thirty-two countries. Norway did the same in 2006, attracting fifty-four governments. In both cases, however, state and nonstate opposition remained strong, with Organisation of the Islamic Conference (OIC) countries submitting their own opposing joint statement.[40]

---

[39] UNCHR, "Extrajudicial, Summary or Arbitrary Execution," E/CN.4/RES/22000/31, para. 6 (2000); UNCHR, "Extrajudicial, Summary or Arbitrary Executions," E/CN.4/RES/2002/36 (2002); HRW, "Anatomy of a Backlash," 86; ARC International, "Building on the Past," 2.

[40] UN, "Human Rights and Sexual Orientation"; HRW, "Sexual Orientation and Gender Identity: Human Rights Concerns for the 61st Session of the U.N. Commission on Human Rights," Mar. 10, 2005, http://www.hrw.org/node/83524; ILGA, "UN: 32 Countries Support New Zealand," Apr. 20, 2005, http://ilga.org/ilga/en/article/533; ILGA, "Statement by Norway–UNHRC 2006," May 12, 2006, http://ilga.org/ilga/en/article/944.

A similar, if more prominent, attempt occurred in the UN General Assembly in 2008. A cross-regional grouping led by France and backed by numerous NGOs introduced a statement – again requiring no vote – urging a commitment to "promote and protect the human rights of all persons, regardless of sexual orientation or gender identity." Joined by sixty-six states, although not the United States until the Obama administration took office in 2009, the statement drew vehement opposition: a rival statement joined by fifty-seven states and publicized by NGO members of the traditional families network. Only in 2011 did the Human Rights Council pass a nonbinding resolution using the terms sexual orientation and gender identity. Applauded by the gay rights network, the 23-19 vote expressed "grave concern" over abuses on those bases, commissioning a study about the issue.[41]

Whether uncloseted as in these more recent cases or closeted as in the older ones, members of the gay rights network have long deployed the incremental strategy. They promote humble steps in one low-level arena to encourage advances in others, hoping that the groundswell will eventually change international law. As one further example of this strategy, the Yogyakarta Principles are now cited and recited by sympathetic scholars. Advocates brandish them to press their positions, and institutions disposed toward gay rights, such as the Council of Europe, refer to them as authoritative. This may in fact deepen the Yogyakarta Principle's authority – but only among the like-minded.[42]

---

[41] UN, "General Assembly Adopts 52 Resolutions, 6 Decisions Recommended by Third Committee on Wide Range of Human Rights, Social, Humanitarian Issues," Dec. 18, 2008, http://www.un.org/News/Press/docs/2008/ga10801 .doc.htm; OIC, "Response to SOGI Human Rights Statement"; UN Human Rights Council, A/HRC/17/L.9/Rev.1, June 15, 2011; ILGA, "ILGA Underlines Historic Significance of UN's First Ever LGBTI Rights Resolution," June 17, 2011, http://ilga.org/ilga/en/article/n266Zb11iS.

[42] Commissioner for Human Rights, "Human Rights and Gender Identity," Council of Europe, July 29, 2009, 6, http://www.transvestit.dk/Human%20rights%20and%20gender%20identity%20COE.pdf; Parliamentary Assembly of the Council of Europe (PACE), "Discrimination on the Basis of sexual Orientation and Gender Identity," Mar. 23, 2010, http://assembly.coe .int/Main.asp?link=/Documents/WorkingDocs/Doc10/EDOC12185.htm. See

Unsetting the Homosexual Agenda

For their part, opponents have condemned incrementalism as a stratagem for covertly creating controversial new rights. As Women for Faith & Family (WFF) complained in 1999, lobbying in obscure UN forums and grafting homosexual rights onto existing international treaties are nothing more than "maneuver[s]" to "by-pass ratification and avoid ... confrontations" with states having "contrary ... national culture[s] and religious values." In the related fight over abortion, C-FAM termed UN treaty bodies "opaque, complex, and largely unaccountable," usurping proper policy-making institutions and undermining citizens' ability to control their own societies.[43]

Even the recent, more open approach pioneered by the 2003 Brazilian resolution provoked censure. In this view, soft law has no legal value and threatens the integrity of international law. In challenging the 2008 UN General Assembly resolution on sexual orientation, OIC countries condemned "'new rights' or 'new standards' [created] by misinterpreting the Universal Declaration and international treaties to include ... notions ... never articulated nor agreed by the general membership." Not only did the resolution undermine the intent of the drafters and signatories, but also it "seriously jeopardize[d] the entire international human rights framework." C-FAM has similarly rejected the Yogyakarta Principles as "an attempt by activists to present an aspirational, radical social policy vision as a binding norm." Yogyakarta's lead author, Michael O'Flaherty, an Irish Catholic priest and

generally Kelly Kollman and Matthew Waites, "The Global Politics of Lesbian, Gay, Bisexual and Transgender Human Rights: An Introduction," *Contemporary Politics* 15, no. 1 (2009): 1–17, 5 (noting that the Yogyakarta Principles can be "criticized for the limited inclusiveness of processes leading to their articulation, and their content").

43 WFF, "UN Frontline Report: UN Declares Abortion a Universal Right; 'Enforced Pregnancy' an International Crime," *Voices Online Edition* XIV, no. 1, Spring 1999, http://wf-f.org/UN-AndersonSp99.html; Douglas Sylva and Susan Yoshihara, "Rights By Stealth: The Role of UN Human Rights Treaty Bodies in the Campaign for an International Right to Abortion," C-FAM International Organization (IORG) White Paper Series No. 8, n.d. (2007), vi, 4.

professor of politics, has come under harsh ad hominem attack. The gay groups' accomplishments have been deprecated too. In 2011, C-FAM minimized both the Human Rights Council vote – "nonbinding" and "feeble" – and the network's "baseless" trumpeting of it as a victory – "predictable for a movement that has been based on misleading terms and gross misstatements of international law."[44]

Opponents have learned, however, that puncturing soft law, denigrating international organizations, or even pillorying priests is not enough. The Doha Institute's Richard G. Wilkins warns that, "international norms are beginning to shape the content of domestic law ... [and] being used to deconstruct long-standing notions of family life." He therefore advises his own network "to avoid negative outcomes and promote positive ones."[45] The goal is to stuff the international system with soft law contradicting and counteracting that of the gay network. That done, it becomes hard to identify which of numerous contrary statements constitutes the norm. Just as important, it becomes difficult to shame reluctant states into joining a purported but nonexistent consensus.

In this, the Baptist-burqa network uses stealth and incrementalism itself. In November 2010, Islamic and African states quietly deleted the longstanding reference to sexual orientation in UN human rights resolutions on extrajudicial killings. The ambush was soon discovered and reversed, but the shift could only raise doubts about the sexual orientation concept's viability

---

[44] OIC, "Response to SOGI Human Rights Statement"; Piero A. Tozzi, "Six Problems with the 'Yogyakarta Principles,'" C-FAM IORG Briefing Paper No. 1, 2007, 1, 4; Terrence McKeegan, "Editorial: The 'Landmark Gay Rights Resolution' That Wasn't," C-FAM, Friday Fax, June 23, 2011, http://www.c-fam.org/fridayfax/volume-14/editorial-the-landmark-gay-rights-resolution-that-wasn%E2%80%99t.html. See also ARF, "A Legal and Policy Commentary on the Proposed PACE Draft Resolution 'Discrimination on the Basis of Sexual Orientation and Gender Identity' (Document12087)," letter memorandum, Apr. 7, 2010, 16, 28 (in author's files).

[45] Wilkins, "International Law and the Family," 370.

even in this rarefied venue.[46] As another example of rival standards floated not only to express heartfelt beliefs but also to blur soft law's already fuzzy meaning, consider the Doha conference. As Richard Wilkins boasted, "the outcomes of the Doha Conference, including the Doha Declaration, take their place in the canon of declarations, platforms, and agendas from which international legal norms are derived by political leaders, judges, and lawyers."[47] Similarly, the OIC statements issued in response to the Brazilian, New Zealand, and French resolutions are as much soft law as the originals. Selecting one or the other as the real soft law is a political act, satisfying only those who believe in the chosen principle beforehand.

Zombie Rights Policy

What in fact are the outcomes of this decades-long international contest? As we have seen, international law remains unsettled, reflecting the diversity of states' domestic policies. At a more abstract level, the battle continues. Consider the core concepts of sexual orientation, gender identity, and gay rights. Then consider how gay groups have fought back on the Baptist-burqa network's own sacred ground, religion.

Sexual Orientation – or Disorientation?
For proponents such as Human Rights Watch, sexual orientation is "the way in which a person's sexual and emotional desires are directed." Gender identity is a "person's deeply felt, internal

---

[46] UN, "Resolution on Extrajudicial, Summary, or Arbitrary Executions," A/C.3/65/L.29/Rev.1. See generally Tanya Domi, "UN General Assembly Votes To Allow Gays To Be Executed Without Cause," *New Civil Rights Movement*, Nov. 20, 2010, http://thenewcivilrightsmovement.com/un-general-assembly-votes-to-allow-gays-to-be-executed-without-cause/ politics/2010/11/20/15449; C-FAM, "US Forces Vote on 'Sexual Orientation' in General Assembly," Friday Fax, Dec. 23, 2010, http://www.c-fam .org/publications/id.1758/pub_detail.asp.

[47] Wilkins, "International Law and the Family," 370. Cf. San Jose Articles, 2011, http://www.sanjosearticles.org/.

sense of belonging to a gender." Both are innate but variable aspects of human nature. Supporting this view are scientific societies led by the American Psychological Association, although its shifting positions on the sources of homosexuality now seem to have settled into a vague compromise – that "nature and nurture both play complex roles." Promoting nature with consummate certainty are moral authorities in the gay rights network. South African Archbishop and Nobel Peace laureate Desmond Tutu states that just as black people were made to suffer "for something we could do nothing about – our very skins. It is the same with sexual orientation. It is a given."[48]

Opponents, however, have disputed and defamed the very concepts of sexual orientation and gender identity. For the ex-gay ministry Exodus Global Alliance, homosexuality is a "multicausal, developmental disorder that can be overcome with the help of professional counselors and . . . the healing power of Jesus Christ." Others such as UFI do not seek to "cure" gay people but bandy their own "wealth of peer reviewed social science data" claiming that homosexuality is nothing more than a lifestyle choice, passing social trend, or a fad. Using those same authorities, they go on to warn of the "dangers of homosexual behavior to individuals, families, and societies." To further disparage the concept, the OIC highlights its vagueness and warns of slippery slopes: the "notion of orientation spans a wide range of personal choices that expand way beyond the individual's sexual interest in copulatory behavior with normal consenting adult human beings, thereby ushering in the social normalization

[48] HRW, "Sexual Orientation and Gender Identity: Human Rights Concerns for the 61st Session of the U.N. Commission on Human Rights," press release, Mar. 10, 2005, http://www.hrw.org/en/news/2005/03/10/sexual-orientation-and-gender-identity-human-rights-concerns-61st-session-un-commiss; APA, "Answers to Your Questions: For a Better Understanding of Sexual Orientation and Homosexuality," APA, 2008, 2, www.apa.org/topics/sorientation.pdf; Desmond Tutu, "Homophobia Is as Unjust as That Crime against Humanity, Apartheid." *Times Online*, July 1, 2004, http://www.timesonline.co.uk/tol/comment/columnists/guest_contributors/article451901.ece.

and possibly the legitimization of many deplorable acts including pedophilia." Less theatrically, the Catholic hierarchy argues that the "natural structure of the family," "inscribed in human nature itself," involves the union of man and woman in marriage. As such, homosexuality is incoherent and violates human dignity. Moreover, the concepts of sexual orientation and gender identity have "no recognition or clear and agreed definition in international law."[49]

Gay advocates dismiss these views. Human Rights Watch lambasted attacks on the Brazilian resolution as "misinformation" involving "the distortion of language and medical fact." Instead, it has urged that sexual orientation should be defined "as understood in ordinary speech as well as in repeated references in official U.N. documents" – as referring only to heterosexual or homosexual desires.[50]

Regarding gender, the traditional families network has not kept every mention of this less sensitive term out of UN documents. It has succeeded in keeping the term traditionally defined, however. A skirmish over the Rome Statute of the International Criminal Court in the late 1990s is instructive. Rights activists sought to insert the term gender into the Statute, as one type of "identifiable group or collectivity" whose persecution would constitute a "crime against humanity." The religious network, however, saw this as recognizing homosexuality. Conflict flared, the result being an emphatically delimited definition of gender:

[49] Exodus International, "Policy Statements," 2010, http://exodus.to/content/view/34/118/; Allred, "Thwarting the Anti-Family Agenda"; OIC, "Response to SOGI Human Rights Statement"; Pope Benedict XVI, "Address to Members of the European People's Party on the Occasion of the Study Days on Europe," Mar. 30, 2006, http://www.vatican.va/holy_father/benedict_xvi/speeches/2006/march/documents/hf_ben-xvi_spe_20060330_eu-parliamentarians_en.html; Holy See, "Statement at the 63rd Session of the General Assembly of the United Nations on the Declaration on Human Rights, Sexual Orientation and Gender Identity," Dec. 18, 2008, http://www.vatican.va/roman_curia/secretariat_state/2008/documents/rc_seg-st_20081218_statement-sexual-orientation_en.html.

[50] HRW, "Anatomy of a Backlash," 86. For similar definitions, see, e.g., Amnesty International, "Crimes of Hate, Conspiracy of Silence: Torture and Ill-Treatment Based on Sexual Identity," 2001.

"the two sexes, male and female, within the context of society. The term 'gender' does not indicate any meaning different from the above." As C-FAM's Austin Ruse stated in an interview, "we have been content to believe we have won.... Additionally, language in other nonbinding documents has to be understood as traditionally understood."[51]

Rights: Equal or Special?

Beyond recognition of sexual orientation and gender identity, a central goal of gay groups is equal rights in all spheres. A matter of simple justice, explicit rights protection would create legal tools helping millions. In this view, sexual orientation and gender identity should never form the basis for discrimination, and laws that differentiate on these bases require revision. For advocates such as ILGA, this has meant domestic and international campaigns aimed at repealing sodomy statutes, equalizing age-of-consent laws for homosexuals and heterosexuals, passing hate crimes and hate speech prohibitions, and recognizing same-sex unions.

For strategic and moral reasons, many activists in the traditional families network oppose punishment for homosexual activity among consenting adults, although penal sanctions are still popular in African and Caribbean societies. The idea that same-sex relations should be a right, however, is anathema. Rather, as UFI puts it, homosexual rights constitute "*special* human rights (rather than *equal* human rights)." They aim to protect a behavior rather than a status. They open the door to other perversions. In the guise of same-sex marriage, they threaten "our very civilization." NGOs such as Human Rights Watch, fight back, decrying the "conflation of human rights principles with 'protecting bestiality.'" There is no question, however, that repulsing the attacks costs them scarce time and resources.[52]

---

[51] Rome Statute Art. 7, secs. 1, 3; Austin Ruse, telephone interview with author, June 29, 1010 (audiotape).
[52] Allred, "Thwarting the Anti-Family Agenda" (emphasis in original); HRW, "Anatomy of a Backlash," 86.

Culture: Established or Evolving?

So even while defending bedrock empirical and normative propositions, gay advocates work to undermine their foes' own fundamental beliefs. Most importantly, they have questioned "traditional" understandings of religion. The targets are statements such as Pakistan's opposing gay rights because they "contradict[] the tenets of Islam and other religions."[53]

As one sally, rights proponents feature religious liberals at international forums. There they challenge orthodox views, their presence and proclamations embodying more open, faith-based values. The rationale for this strategy was best articulated by activist Jennifer Butler in the context of women's rights: "[T]he Religious Right demonizes feminists in part by painting the feminist movement as a movement of 'Godless radicals.' A feminist religious stance shakes up this simplistic dichotomy and makes demonizing feminists more difficult." Following a similar approach, the British based Lesbian and Gay Christian Movement (LGCM), formed in 1976, "constantly challenge[s] homophobic and transphobic comments made by faith leaders."[54] As another strategy, activists forge deauthenticating groups in civil society. One example we have already met: Catholics for Choice (CFC), its raison d'etre to provide a Catholic alternative to the Holy See and C-FAM. CFC may be representative of its liberal members. Conservatives, however, reject it as "vigorously anti-Catholic," a "'playboy's dream'" that has collaborated with Planned Parenthood and been funded by "'philanthropists'" such as the Rockefeller Foundation, Turner Foundation, and *Playboy* magazine.[55]

[53] Pakistani statement quoted in WorldNetDaily.com, "Global 'Gay' Rights Measure before U.N.: Opponents Fear Resolution Will Advance Homosexual Agenda Worldwide," Apr., 25, 2003, http://www.wnd.com/?pageId=18458.

[54] Jennifer Butler, "300 Religious Right Participants Attend Beijing PrepCom," Global Policy Forum, June 1, 2000, http://www.globalpolicy.org/component/content/article/177/31727.html; Lesbian and Gay Christians, "About Us," http://www.lgcm.org.uk/about-us/.

[55] WFF, "UN Frontline Report." See also C-FAM, "War on the Faith: How Catholics for a Free Choice Seeks to Undermine the Catholic Church," IORG Research Paper No. 1, n.d.

In a further attempt to undercut their foes' philosophical foundations, gay groups enlist moral authorities whose ethical eminence rivals the Pope's. In 2006, the Dalai Lama issued a statement at activists' request. It opposed "violence and discrimination based on sexual orientation and gender identity and urge[d] respect, tolerance, and the full recognition of human rights for all." More vocal still, South Africa's Tutu champions gay partnerships and attacks fellow churchmen for "being almost obsessed with questions of human sexuality." In this battle, Tutu has transcended his faith, going so far as to declare, "If God, as they say, is homophobic, I wouldn't worship that God."[56]

Confronting retrograde religions, Human Rights Watch has savaged the "false ideologies of cultural uniformity that exploit sexuality with no other real goal than to reject, exclude, and destroy." In this view, "traditions" are invented and cultures undergo "*bricolage*[,] . . . constant change and interchange." The Arcus Foundation of New York City and Kalamazoo, one of the gay movement's primary funders with more than $155 million in assets and twenty-five employees, has put these ideas into practice. Arcus, which promotes equal rights for the world's LGBT communities as one of its two core goals (the other being conservation of the world's great apes), has started a Program on Religion and Values. Targeting "faith traditions" such as Anglican, Episcopal, Jewish, Methodist, and Lutheran, the Program has ambitious aims: to "refute beliefs that portray gay . . . people as sinful and immoral"; to "achiev[e] long-term change in cultural attitudes and religious institutions"; and to "creat[e] a positive shift in cultural attitudes and values toward sexuality in general and GLBT . . . issues in particular." Other activists go further, chipping away at core religious texts including the Bible. Rightly interpreted, properly updated, the Good Book supports homosexuality, even same-sex marriage! Or, as *Newsweek*'s 2008

---

[56] "Dalai Lama Urges Respect and Tolerance for LGBTs," *Fridae*, Apr. 3, 2006, http://www.fridae.com/newsfeatures/2006/04/03/1605.dalai-lama-urges-respect-and-tolerance-for-lgbts; "Tutu Chides Church for Gay Stance," *BBC News*, Nov. 18, 2007, news.bbc.co.uk/2/hi/7100295.stm.

cover story, "Our Mutual Joy," claimed, "Opponents of gay marriage often cite Scripture. But what the Bible teaches about love argues for the other side."[57]

Far from loosing joy on the world, however, the article's framejacking unleashed a fury that swept well beyond the United States. Many religious leaders remain unmoved by calls for change and toleration, no matter how authoritative the source. Well-financed, persistent strategies such as Arcus's may influence religious moderates already receptive to homosexuals. Even an irresistible ethical force like Desmond Tutu, however, cannot budge the immovable moral objects of the traditional families network. For the Catholic Church, "recognition and promotion of the natural structure of the family – as a union between a man and a woman based on marriage" with an "irreplaceable social role" is "not negotiable."[58]

Of course, Pope Benedict XVI does not speak for other religions. Still, his words reflect the uncompromising views of traditionalists, whatever their faith. In India in 2009, B. P. Singhal, a member of the Hindu nationalist Bharatiya Janata Party (BJP), decried a court decision overturning an Indian statute, originally imposed by the British colonial government, criminalizing "carnal intercourse against the order of nature." The case had been promoted by international advocates including Human Rights Watch and Naz Foundation International (NFI), an "international MSM [men who have sex with men] development agency" based in Britain. Rejecting cultural *bricolage* in

---

[57] HRW, "Anatomy of a Backlash," 89, 74; Arcus Foundation "Arcus Foundation Appoints Tom Kam to Lead Program on Religion and Values," press release, Feb. 26, 2007, http://www.arcusfoundation.org/pages_2/news_arch_template.cfm?ID=20; ARCUS Foundation, "Arcus Foundation Ends Year with New Awards Totaling over $9.6 Million; Brings 2007 Grant Making Total Over $16.8 Million," press release, Mar. 18, 2007, http://www.arcusfoundation.org/pages_2/news_arch_template.cfm?ID=44; Lisa Miller, "Gay Marriage: Our Mutual Joy," *Newsweek*. Dec. 6, 2008, http://www.newsweek.com/id/172653. See also Lesbian and Gay Christian Movement, "Faith and Sexuality Education Resource," http://www.lgcm.org.uk/2010/08/the-faith-and-sexuality-education-resource/

[58] Pope Benedict XVI, "Address to European People's Party."

this instance, gay activists claimed that the *Naz Foundation v. Delhi* verdict returned India to its precolonial tolerance of varied gender identities. For his part, the BJP man was untroubled by the sodomy law's foreign origins – despite the party's usual partiality toward indigenous Hindu culture. Singhal, like religious conservatives worldwide, disparaged the "trap of homosexual addiction," terming it "inherently immoral, grossly unnatural and...the very antithesis of the lofty ideals, lofty values and lofty objectives" sustaining Indian civilization.[59]

Conclusion

Gay advocates have achieved some of their initial goals at the UN, in particular raising visibility of homosexuality. More importantly, sodomy laws have gone by the wayside and equality provisions have increased in Western Europe, the Americas, and elsewhere, as reflected in the stance of these countries at the UN. Discrimination too has declined in these states, although the role of the UN in these important achievements appears limited.

On activists' core problem, however – the UN's failure to recognize gay rights and sexual orientation – nonpolicy is the rule, although an occasional zombie policy staggers off UN plaza. As should be clear, this is not because the gay network lacks density, resources, or persuasion. Rather, it is because of fervent opposition that has exploited UN rules to mount potent dissuasive strategies. They have deconstructed the sexual orientation concept and unbuilt the gay rights network. They have delegitimated institutions and invented new ones. They have bashed activists' frames, slashed their grafts, and trashed their authorities. Of course, rights advocates have not taken any of this lying down. They have fought back, unleashing their own battery of negative

---

[59] *Naz Foundation v. Govt. of NCT of Delhi*, 160 Delhi Law Times 277 (2009); NFI, "What Is Naz Foundation International?" http://www.nfi.net/about .htm; Singhal quoted in Amy Kazmin, "Gay Indians Seek Sexual Equality." *Financial Times*, June 30, 2009, http://www.ft.com/cms/s/0/5f059856-650d-11de-a13f-00144feabdco.html.

tactics against their foes. The resulting conflict influences every aspect of the issue, not least the contending forces themselves. Their behavior, not only their interactions with one another but also their internal politics, is strongly affected.

To have focused only on the gay network's affirmative efforts would have missed all this, and might even have suggested that a new norm was emerging. That is a fine hope, but the reality is bleaker. As human rights scholar Jack Donnelly, has observed, "[i]n the short and medium run, there is no chance of anything even close to an international consensus on even a working text for a draft declaration on the rights of homosexuals."[60]

[60] Jack Donnelly, *Universal Human Rights In Theory and Practice* (Ithaca, NY: Cornell University Press, 2003), 237.

4

Litigating for the Lord

American Attorneys and European Sexualities

A quiet Sunday in the sleepy Swedish town of Borgholm; a few dozen worshippers filing into the local Pentecostal church; at the pulpit, sixty-two-year-old Åke Green, bald, bespectacled, avuncular: then the unassuming minister began spouting fire and brimstone. "Is homosexuality genetic or an evil force that plays mind games with people?" Invoking scripture and science, he found an answer. "Humans are slipping into clearly unbiblical and clearly inhuman relations. It is not a private matter or a right to live in a sexual manner other than what the Bible dictates. . . . [It is] a deep cancerous tumor in the entire society." Its effects: everything from bestiality to pedophilia. Yet Sweden did nothing to excise the malignancy! On the contrary: politicians and press promoted homosexuality, even public displays of gay love. And, gallingly, the government ignored Christians who "cannot bear to see such things," thereby risking "violence."[1] This time, however, prosecutors caught Green's words. Days after his July 2003 tirade, they indicted him for violating a new law criminalizing "disrespect" for groups defined by sexual orientation. Later he was convicted and sentenced to thirty days in jail.

---

[1] Åke Green, "Is Homosexuality Genetic or an Evil Force that Plays Mind Games with People?" June 20, 2003, Anders Falk and Debra Sandstrom, trans., http://www.eaec.org/bibleanswers/ake_green_sermon.htm.

But Green never served time. To his rescue flew an unlikely angel: out of Fairfax, Virginia, a powerful Christian lawyers' group, Advocates International. Dispatching top attorneys, it and other overseas NGOs prepped Green's local counsel, submitted amicus curiae briefs in Swedish courts, and mustered religious groups in Europe, North America, and elsewhere. Under this legal and political barrage, an appellate court overturned Green's conviction in February 2005.

Swedish and European gay groups demanded more jail time, however. In an unusual move, the prosecutor appealed to the Högsta Domstolen (Supreme Court), calling for Green's sentence to be upped to six months. Nor did the Americans go home, instead redoubling their efforts. Months later, as protesters faced off on Stockholm's streets, the top court reluctantly found in Green's favor. Meanwhile, Advocates International and others had made Green a cause célèbre among conservative Christians worldwide – a victim of homosexual rights and bellwether of coming intolerance against traditional religions. For their part, gay advocates at home and abroad portrayed Green as a bigot, epitomizing the larger threat of homophobia. He became a powerful symbol, invoked by both sides in many countries, even making a cameo appearance in the 2008 fight over California's Proposition 8, ending same-sex marriage in the state.

Advocates International's intervention in Green's case might seem surprising. However members of the Baptist-burqa network have established similar ties around the world, paralleling linkages the gay rights network has forged with local activists. This chapter expands on the prior one by examining contention within countries, both those whose citizens receive and send international support. In fact, that terminology, although convenient, is misleading. The relationships are two-way. "Receivers" gain from support, but "senders" reap reciprocal benefits. They use overseas clashes to bolster their own side in analogous domestic dustups or in international disputes. This chapter adds to the prior one and the scholarly literature by highlighting legal activism – clashes among lawyers of diverse political views. Today, transnational advocacy means not just general political activism, but also advocacy strictly defined: filing briefs, strategizing trials, and interrogating witnesses.

The chapter begins with brief discussion of the impulse driving attorneys, especially conservative Americans, to overseas "cause lawyering" – much like progressive attorneys have long done. Next, I analyze how rival networks organized around the *Green* case, the tactics they deployed in contending with one another, and the ways they redeployed the case overseas. In the final sections, I turn to a very different European country, Romania, the continent's most religious nation and one of the least friendly to gay rights. After years of internationalized controversy over its harsh sodomy laws, Romania in the late 2000s became the scene of a related battle over same-sex marriage – or, more precisely, over importation of an American-derived defense of marriage law. I examine the ways in which foreign antagonists entered Romania, linked with rival activists, and contended with one another in a fight that has implications well beyond that country.

Why Sweden? Why Romania? These countries are not the only ones in which religious groups have engaged in transnational advocacy, as earlier mention of German, Nicaraguan, Indian, and Ugandan clashes shows. Nor can I claim that conflict in these two countries is necessarily representative of events elsewhere. Sweden and Romania, however, illustrate the scope of right-wing advocacy and highlight the need for alternative approaches to analyzing transnational activism.

Foreign Law in American Courts

Overseas work by cause lawyers has a long history. Attorneys founded important human rights groups such as Amnesty International, Human Rights Watch, the International Commission of Jurists, and Human Rights First. These groups aimed to use international law and legalistic methods to advance their visions of justice worldwide, occasionally entering foreign or international courtrooms to make their cases. More recently, environmental, women's rights, and social justice groups based in the

United States and Europe have adopted similar approaches, using lawyerly techniques of investigation, argumentation, and litigation. Just as in the United States, however, where cause lawyering began on the left but soon faced powerful opposition, conservative legal activists have internationalized in recent years.[2]

Part of this is a strategic response to ideological foes. In addition, among powerful groups based in the United States, changes in American jurisprudence explain this expansion. U.S. courts have long rejected foreign law as precedent. Until the 2000s, it was unusual for them even to cite such law as supportive of a decision. Since then, however, the Supreme Court has referred to overseas practice as "instructive for its interpretation" of American law, as it stated in a 2005 case about juvenile executions. Many on the left welcomed this and other decisions for their use of foreign law. The American Civil Liberties Union (ACLU), backed by the Ford Foundation, began new programs to "bring human rights home" to the United States, where judicial and even political incorporation of international human rights, as opposed to domestic civil rights, has been meager.[3]

The decisions enraged conservatives, starting with Justice Antonin Scalia in a series of fiery dissenting opinions. Liberal judges would import law, especially from Europe, to justify desired outcomes in American jurisprudence. To fight the threat, those seeking to "strengthen American independence and

---

[2] Austin Sarat and Stuart Scheingold, *Cause Lawyering and the State in a Global Era* (Oxford: Oxford University Press, 2001); Hans J. Hacker, *The Culture of Conservative Christian Litigation* (Lanham, MD: Rowman & Littlefield, 2005); Steven M. Teles, *The Rise of the Conservative Legal Movement: The Battle for Control of the Law* (Princeton, NJ: Princeton University Press, 2010).

[3] *Roper v. Simmons*, 543 U.S. 551, 575 (2005); Alan Jenkins and Larry Cox, "Bringing Human Rights Home," *The Nation*, June 27, 2005, 27; Columbia Law School, Bringing Human Rights Home Lawyers' Network, http://www.law.columbia.edu/center_program/human_rights/HRinUS/ BHRH_Law_Net. For other cases referring to foreign law, see *Lawrence v. Texas*, 539 U.S. 558 (2003) (Constitution protects consensual adult homosexual activity); *Goodridge v. Department of Public Health*, 798 N.E.2d 941 (*Mass.* 2003) (Massachusetts state constitution provides right to same-sex marriage). See also Cynthia Soohoo, Catherine Albisa, and Martha F. Davis, *Bringing Human Rights Home* (Westport, CT: Praeger, 2007).

self-government" took to the media and the courtroom, "opposing global governance and transnational progressivism."[4] At the same time, however, key activists strategically pirouetted, entering foreign jurisdictions to blunt or preempt the menace at its source. Powerful groups such as Advocates International, the Alliance Defense Fund, and the American Center for Law and Justice now work overseas to change "bad" laws or implant "good" ones, as this chapter makes clear. In this, they resemble the Doha Institute's Roger Wilkins, who we met in Chapter 3, promoting alternative norms in international forums. As a result, those hoping to use foreign laws or cases in U.S. courts must fight not only over their admissibility, but also, in foreign jurisdictions, over what the law will be.

Swedish Hate Speech Globalized

The *Green* case illustrates how local battles become part of larger transnational wars. Its roots run deeper than the pastor's fiery 2003 sermon. It began with the growing political power of groups such as the Swedish Federation for Gay, Lesbian, Bisexual, and Transgender Rights (RFSL), founded in 1950. Sweden was one of the first countries to legalize homosexual activity, to pass antidiscrimination laws, and in 2006 to permit same-sex marriage. RFSL was an important member of ILGA-Europe, working with the international network to promote Europe-wide initiatives. After years of lobbying, they achieved notable successes in the late 1990s, capped by the European Union's passage of the Treaty of Amsterdam in 1999. Among other things, it urged governments to fight discrimination and violence directed against people because of their sexual orientation. In the treaty's wake,

---

[4] Solidarity Center for Law and Justice (SCLJ) and Sovereignty Network, Amicus Brief in *Graham v. Florida*, 130 S. Ct. 2011 (2010), www.lexis-nexis.com. The brief was filed on behalf of Americans United for Life, Catholic Family and Human Rights Institute, Center for Security Policy, Concerned Women for America, Family Advocacy International, Family Watch International, Freedom Alliance, Hudson Institute, The Cato Institute, The Competitive Enterprise Institute, and United Families International.

ILGA-Europe together with the European Union (EU) and Council of Europe strengthened programs to end one of the perceived sources of the problem, fear and hatred of homosexuals: homophobia. These included proposals to prohibit and punish hate crimes and hate speech.[5]

As part of this larger drive, in 2002, RFSL and other Swedish gay groups urged amendment of the country's Act on Persecution of Minority Groups, passed after World War II to protect religious and ethnic minorities. Grafting their cause to those cases, they argued that hate speech threatened the rights of gays. The amendment criminalized "agitation" against groups defined by their sexual orientation, including threats or "expressions of contempt." In the debate over the proposal, Sweden's justice minister, suggested that certain church sermons declaring homosexuality sinful might be criminal. Gay groups went further: there would be no pass for pastors. We will "report hate speech irrespective of where it occurs," stated RFSL president Sören Andersson.[6]

If the bill pleased gay advocates at home and abroad, it antagonized Sweden's small number of religious traditionalists. International networks came to their aid too, concerned about the broader menace posed by European initiatives on homophobia. Turning the homosexuals' framing on its head, the World Evangelical Alliance (WEA), which claims to serve 600 million evangelicals worldwide, criticized the amendment for violating the

[5] See ILGA-Europe, "After Amsterdam: Sexual Orientation and the European Union," Sept. 1999, http://www.ilga-europe.org/home/publications/reports_and_other_materials/after_amsterdam_sexual_orientation_and_the_european_union_1999; Amnesty International, *Crimes of Hate, Conspiracy of Silence: Torture and Ill-Treatment Based on Sexual Identity* (London: Amnesty International, 2001).

[6] Justice minister quoted in Tomas Dixon, "'Hate Speech' Law Could Chill Sermons," *Christianity Today*, Aug. 5, 2002, http://www.christianitytoday.com/ct/2002/august5/15.22.html?start=1#related; Andersson quoted in ibid. For the debate surrounding amendment of Swedish Penal Code BrB16: 8, see *Prosecutor General v. Åke Ingemar Teodor Green*, Supreme Court of Sweden, Case No. B 1050–05, Nov. 29, 2005, 4-7, http://www.domstol.se/Domstolar/hogstadomstolen/Avgoranden/2005/Dom_pa_engelska_B_1050–05.pdf (official English translation).

Universal Declaration of Human Rights. Severing the graft to minority rights, WEA argued that the amendment would place Sweden "on level with China, with the state defining which theology is permissible." The threat was broader: "Europe, still a stronghold of religious freedom, seems about to change directions in an alarming fashion" and "churches must awaken to the danger."[7] In 2003, however, the Swedish parliament passed the amendment. Its solution to homophobia was jail sentences up to two years – or four years for especially threatening, extremely disrespectful, or widely disseminated verbiage.

For clergy such as Åke Green, the new law was an affront. God's word condemning homosexuality could no longer be spoken, even in His own church. "Deeply grieved" by how "sodomy [had] started to invade our country," Green began studding his services with Biblical warnings on homosexuality. But preaching to the converted, especially his small rural flock, did little to save Sweden. He would have to make himself a sacrificial lamb in the lion's den of Swedish public opinion. So Green exhorted journalists to heed his weekly homilies, hoping for publication and prosecution – a test case that might undermine the new law.[8]

The media ignored the provocative parson, however, including his July 2003 blast delivered to about fifty parishioners. Frustrated, Green sent a summary to a local newspaper, which finally covered the sermon. With that, an RFSL representative made good on the group's earlier threat to hound haters even in the sanctuary. Pressured, the prosecutor indicted Green, leading to

7 WEA official Johan Candelin quoted in Dixon, "Hate Speech." See also RFSL, "Stanley Sjoberg Continues to Condemn the Homosexual Lifestyle," press release, May 3, 2002, http://www.rfsl.se/?aid=7480&p=3815. For a brief government description of the statute and punishments, see Government Offices of Sweden, Ministry of Integration and Gender Equality, "Equal Rights and Opportunities Regardless of Sexual Orientation or Transgender Identity or Expression," fact sheet, Oct. 2009.

8 Green quoted in Katherine Britton, "A Swedish Perspective on California's Gay Marriage Debate," *Crosswalk.com*, Oct. 31, 2008, http://www.crosswalk .com/11584257/. See also Dale Hurd, "Swedish Pastor Sentenced for 'Hate Speech,'" *CW News*, Sept. 10, 2004, http://www.akegreen.org/Links/L14/L14 .html.

the first but not only trial for violating the law. The case attracted one of Sweden's top lawyers, Percy Bratt of the Swedish Helsinki Committee for Human Rights, who defended Green by raising free expression rights under Swedish, European, and international law.[9] A year after the sermon, however, the court sided with the prosecutor and sentenced Green to jail.

Deterring Hate

With Green on the brink of imprisonment, both sides internationalized the case. How and why did this occur? With resources scarce and contention sharp, only a small number of local conflicts draw the attention of international networks. Yet Green's did – and for similar reasons on both sides. This was a case of great import not only to the Swedish combatants, but also to their overseas backers.

Hours after Green's sentencing on June 29, 2004, RFSL president Andersson welcomed his conviction: "freedom of religion should never imply agitation against persons." Internationally, ILGA took only a day to place an English translation of RFSL's exultant press release on its Homophobia Web page. The network then tracked the case as it wended its way through Sweden's appellate system. After all, its import went beyond the minimal direct damage done by Green's words or even the sermon's publication in a local newspaper. With Sweden's passage of the hate speech amendment and with Green's prosecution, the country was an international trendsetter. His jailing would authenticate the homophobia fight, demonstrate the gay network's power, and deter haters elsewhere. As Andersson stated, "It is [Green's] type of agitation that foments hate crimes against homosexual, bisexual and transgender persons." To accept this outrage would have handed a default victory to the religious network. Some gay activists at home and abroad condemned the prosecution, predicting it would backfire. RFSL, however, supported by ILGA and other European gay activists, applauded the law's execution.

[9] Percy Bratt, Chairman, Civil Rights Defenders, personal interview, Stockholm, April 14, 2011.

As opposition to the case grew at home and abroad, the network promoted a campaign defending prosecution, gay rights, and the fight against homophobia.[10]

Defending Truth

For religious conservatives, overseas attention to the case was equally decisive. A few days after Green's conviction, Slovakia's interior minister attacked Sweden for "a left-wing liberal ideology [that] was trying to introduce tyranny." (In turn, a Slovak opposition figure upbraided him for making Slovaks "look like total idiots.") Weeks later, America's Republican Party alluded to Green in fundraising letters for the 2004 presidential race. In late August, Canada's *National Post* editorialized against Sweden's "censoring the Bible." In the fall, American conservatives invited Green's Swedish allies for a Washington visit. By early 2005, a host of foreign attorneys had flown to Green's aid. Over ensuing years in many countries, Green would be anointed a "religious dissident," even a "martyr," albeit living and unjailed.[11]

---

[10] RFSL president Sören Andersson quoted in ILGA, "Sweden: 1 Month Imprisonment for Anti-Gay Sermon," June 30, 2004, http://www.ilga .org/news_results.asp?LanguageID=1&FileCategory=9&ZoneID=4&FileID= 236. For similar statements, see Hurd, "Swedish Pastor Sentenced." For the gay community's debate over the prosecution, see Jim D'Entremont, "Gay Sweden," *The Guide*, Dec. 2005, http://www.guidemag.com/magcontent/ invokemagcontent.cfm?ID=F1C88B05-935D-4609-9C496059FE13EB9B; Joe Perez, "A Rant against Misguided, Extreme Queer Activism" and response from RFSL information head, Robert Karlsson Svärd, MyOutSpirit.com, July 16, 2004, http://gayspirituality.typepad.com/blog/2004/07/this_makes_me_s .html.

[11] Slovakian officials quoted in WorldNetDaily.com, "Pastor's Imprisonment for Sermon Protested," July 30, 2004, http://www.worldnetdaily.com/news/ article.asp?ARTICLE_ID=39687; David D. Kirkpatrick, "Republicans Admit Mailing Campaign Literature Saying Liberals Will Ban the Bible," *New York Times*, Sept. 24, 2004, 22; *National Post* (Canada), "Censoring the Bible," Aug. 23, 2004, A11; World Magazine, *Prop 8 and Åke*, Nov. 1, 2008 http:// www.worldmag.com/articles/14572; Nicholas George, "Swedish Pastor – Bigot or Christian Martyr?" *Financial Times*. Jan. 22, 2005, http://www.ft .com/cms/s/928484ca-6c1b-11d9-94dc-00000e2511c8,Authorised=false .html?_i_location=http%3A%2F%2Fwww.ft.com%2Fcms%2Fs%2Fo% 2F928484ca-6c1b-11d9-94dc-00000e2511c8.html%3Fnclick_check%3D1 &_i_referer=&nclick_check=1.

How did Green become an overseas cause célèbre? Most important was mobilization by local activists, who alerted their own and mainstream journalists. A primary player was Advocates International's Swedish affiliate. Founded in 1991 by Samuel Ericsson, a Swedish-born American and Harvard Law School graduate, Advocates International was one of the first Christian legal groups to work abroad. Its chosen method is the "L-O-R-D" strategy, "putting legs to Jesus' final words" through local meetings (L), national organizations (O), regional networks (R), and global disciples and mentoring (D). Linking more than 30,000 "followers of Christ within the legal profession" in 158 nations, Advocates International encourages and funds them to be "proactive locally, nationally, regionally and globally."[12] In Sweden, Advocates International's representative Mats Tunehag grasped the *Green* case's broader import in fighting perceived homosexual threats to religion. He then acted like "the Paul Revere of the Internet," as one admirer put it, alerting the global conservative media to the horror story of a pastor sentenced to jail for a sermon. In the fall of 2004, Tunehag attended Advocates International's global convocation in McLean, Virginia, where he lobbied Ericsson and convinced him to champion Green.[13]

Apprised of the case, the Washington-based Religious Freedom Coalition (RFC), a nonprofit group promoting family based legislation, unleashed its formidable firepower. The RFC's head, William J. Murray (also director of the Government Is Not God political action committee), brought several of Green's Swedish supporters to Washington in October 2004. Days after this visit, Murray penned an account in his print and Internet newsletter

---

[12] Advocates International, Newsletter, Feb. 2008, http://www.advocatesinternational.org/newsletters/feb08; Advocates International, "Miracle in Slow Motion," 2009 (author's files); Advocates International, "Who Needs an Advocate?" 2009 (author's files).

[13] Mats Tunehag, Global Council of Advocates International, personal interview, Stockholm, April 14, 2011 (audiotape); Benjamin Bull, Chief Counsel, Alliance Defense Fund, telephone interview, July 22, 2009 (notes). See also Samuel E. Ericsson, "Sex, Politics and Religion," Advocates International Newsletter, Feb. 2005 (author's files).

under the electrifying but inaccurate title, "Pastor Jailed for 'Hate Crime.'" Innocently or not, other reports transmitted the error. To move the story beyond the Beltway, the RFC arranged for the Swedes to appear on a nationally syndicated Family Research Council radio program, visit the Heritage Foundation, strategize at Paul Weyrich's Coalitions for America luncheon, and speak at a National Clergy Council (NCC) dinner.[14]

All this generated an angry buzz across right-wing circuits. Republican congresswoman Jo Ann Davis, liaison to the European Union, promised to pressure the Swedish government not to "arrest...pastors because of what they say." More concretely, the attention galvanized legal aid from the Alliance Defense Fund, a powerful advocate for America's "first liberty," religious freedom. Founded in 1994 and based in Scottsdale, Arizona, and Bratislava, Slovakia, ADF "defend[s] the right to hear and speak the Truth" – "the Bible [as] the inspired, infallible, authoritative Word of God." Homosexuality has increasingly taken center stage in this fight. ADF promotes defense of marriage acts in American states. It publishes a book titled *The Homosexual Agenda: Exposing the Principal Threat to Religious Freedom Today*. Most importantly, it litigates high-profile cases such as *Perry v. Schwarzenegger*, the federal court challenge to California's 2008 Proposition 8 referendum barring same-sex marriage. In all this, as chief counsel Benjamin Bull told me in an interview, ADF refuses even to use the term "gay," referring instead to "homosexual behavior."[15]

Regarding the *Green* case, although ADF has opposed the U.S. Supreme Court's use of foreign law, it had pragmatically

---

[14] RFC, "Pastor Jailed for 'Hate Crime,'" Chairman's Action Report, Oct. 10, 2004, http://www.rfcnet.org/pdfs/04F16.pdf. See also, e.g., Bob Unruh, "Congress Debates 'Jail Grandma' Hate Speech: Warnings Issued over 'Most Dangerous Bill in America,'" WorldNetDaily.com, Apr. 18, 2007.

[15] Davis summarized in RFC, "Pastor Jailed"; ADF, "What We Believe," http://www.alliancedefensefund.org/about/Purpose/whatwebelieve.aspx; Bull interview. See also ADF, "The Truth about International Law," leaflet, n.d., http://www.alliancedefensefund.org/issues/ReligiousFreedom/International Law.aspx; Rachel Morris, "Crusaders in Wingtips," *Legal Affairs*. Mar./Apr. 2006, http://www.legalaffairs.org/printerfriendly.msp?id=1005.

crossed the international threshold in 2004. As a response to the ACLU's "Bringing Human Rights Home" program, ADF trained an "army of allied attorneys to defend America's sovereignty" and fight against "importation of foreign case law." ADF also did a transnational turnabout. As its Website states, it opted to "strategically litigat[e] key religious liberty cases abroad" to "prevent the creation of harmful foreign case law that might otherwise be imported by the ACLU into American courts." Explaining the contradiction, Bull told a reporter, "We're forced to do it, because if we don't, we're going to lose according to the rules of a game we never created." Preemptively forging overseas law into something less dangerous, more ambiguous, or outright helpful, ADF does not wait for distant dissidents to walk into its offices. Its staff members scour the Internet. Its foreign scouts raise obscure cases to Scottsdale's attention. All of this allows ADF to be involved "without appearing to be interlopers from America."[16]

In the *Green* case, the latter mechanism was central. Tunehag and Ericsson pressed ADF chief counsel Bull: "you must get involved" to fight the "homosexual agenda" worldwide. Bull was at first skeptical because ADF's limited resources require it to be selective. "It is always a triage; there are more cases than we can get involved in. We have to learn to say 'No,'" even to those whose ideals mesh with ADF's. In addition, Bull was uncertain about the client: was Åke Green a "crank, a flame-thrower – or a serious-minded humble man who was not looking for publicity?" In April 2005, Bull met Green at a UN meeting in Geneva where the pastor was declaiming on religious liberty. After talking with him, Bull decided to take the case. "I said, 'What can we do for you? We can work with other lawyers, we can pound the table in the Christian and secular media.'" In this, ADF was

---

[16] ADF, "International Law," http://www.alliancedefensefund.org/Home/ADF Content?cid=3169; Bull quoted in Morris, "Crusaders in Wingtips." See also ADF, "Defending Religious Freedom at Home and around the World," http://www.alliancedefensefund.org/Global ("Confining our fight to defending America from foreign law carries the significant risk of winning a domestic battle while potentially – in time – losing the world").

acting as American cause lawyers, both left and right, have long done at home, going back at least to the *Scopes* monkey trial of the 1920s. As Bull states, we "fund or finance the action, even if the defendant or plaintiff has no funds, we are very proactive and not afraid to pick up the phone. Where we see an opening, we try to seize it."[17]

Why did ADF come to Green's aid? Green had able Swedish counsel. Sweden is a functioning democracy with a history of adherence to the rule of law, if not always the world's broadest views of free speech. In no sense was Green blocked from defending himself using domestic resources. Nor was ADF moved simply by sympathy for an aging churchman facing thirty days in a Swedish slammer.

ADF and other foreign groups rallied to Green's aid because they saw the appeal as a test of principles "significant in our areas of interest." As Bull told me, ADF selects cases using several criteria: "Does the case have potential to adversely impact American jurisprudence? Does the case have potential to positively influence events in the States? Is the case of significance locally: has it made the media; is it precedent setting?" The *Green* case met these criteria. According to an ADF press release, it authenticated the view that "'tolerance' of the homosexual agenda means silencing and punishment of those who disagree." Taking the appeal was therefore "critical for freedom of religious expression in America, too. If the ACLU and its radical activist allies have their way, the laws of Europe will soon be the laws of America."[18] Whether or not one believes that – and America's First Amendment makes any similar hate speech provision unlikely – ADF saw Green's prosecution as overreaching by a government egged on by radical activists. Fighting the case

---

[17] All quotations from Bull interview. See also Edward J. Larson, *Summer for the Gods: The Scopes Trial and America's Continuing Debate over Science and Religion* (New York: Basic Books, 2006), 87–89.

[18] Bull interview; ADF, "ADF Protecting Religious Liberty Internationally, Assisting Defense of Pastor in Sweden," press release, Nov. 9, 2005, http://www.alliancedefensefund.org/news/pressrelease.aspx?cid=3587.

therefore sent a signal of resolve against key goals of its gay foes in the United States and elsewhere.

As an additional reason for foreign intervention, this horror story – a pastor dragged from pulpit to prison by radical homosexuals – was already shocking religious believers worldwide. The benefits of taking the case were therefore high. As Advocates International crowed to its members afterward, the "result of all this publicity" was phenomenal: "over 250,000 hits [on Advocates International's website] in recent months!"[19] Win or lose, the case would create a powerful global symbol helpful to the cause and its proponents.

In sum, activists on both sides formed their networks not so much because of the gravity of Green's words, the severity of his sentence, or the want of Swedish justice. More important was the case's value in larger transnational wars over gay rights. Both sides used the case not only to galvanize their constituents, but also to authenticate their contrary views of reality: for gay groups, that homophobic hate speech is a serious global problem requiring a punitive solution; for religious groups, that the "homosexual agenda" threatens religion. Nor did elevation to the international arena happen automatically. Each side carefully executed the maneuver, placing its foe's perfidy at the center of its move.

Swedish Litigation, American-Style

Backing Green

The American attorneys supported Green in both the courts and the press, working closely with his Swedish lawyer. Most importantly, they framejacked the gay groups' most potent images: vulnerability and rights. Gays were not the vulnerable minority; Christian believers were. Nor should Sweden's gay rights govern the case; international protections for religious liberty and free

---

[19] Advocates International, Letter, n.d. 2005, http://www.advocatesinternational.org/resources/AGbrief.htm; Bull interview.

speech should. As ADF and others argued, Green's views may have been "unpopular" or "'offensive'" in the secular country, but European law vindicated Green's right to express his views. To bolster these arguments, the Americans translated documents, wrote legal memoranda for Green's attorney, and prepared him for court sessions.[20]

Advocates International and ADF also stretched the rules of Swedish jurisprudence, introducing a new litigation tactic, amicus curiae briefs. Common in American cases, particularly in cause lawyering by left-wing and, more recently, right-wing activists, amicus briefs were previously unknown in Sweden. The courts had no rules for them, but none against, so the Americans seized the opening. At both appellate and Supreme Court levels, they filed briefs and mustered filings by other intervenors, including America's Becket Fund, Family Research Council, and Focus on the Family, Canada's Christian Legal Fellowship, and Britain's Jubilee Campaign. As Advocates International's brief stated, "Law now operates in a global village," and Green's prosecution "creates dangerous ripples around the globe." More concretely, Advocates International, ADF and others raised legal principles under the International Covenant on Civil and Political Rights, the European Convention on Human Rights, and associated case law.[21]

At home and abroad, the religious groups mounted political and journalistic campaigns, attacking homosexual extremism. Advocates International's Mats Tunehag coordinated a Swedish public relations blitz, distributing letters of concern written by affiliates in the United Kingdom, Portugal, Bulgaria, Canada, and

---

[20] Advocates International, Newsletter, Feb. 2005; ADF, "Swedish Pastor Beats 'Hate Crime' Conviction," press release, Nov. 29, 2005, http://www.alliancedefensefund.org/news/story.aspx?cid=3606. See also ADF, "ADF Protecting Religious Liberty."

[21] Advocates International, "Legal Opinion Submitted by Advocates International in the Court of Appeals for Göta Hovrätt, Case # B 1987–04, Re: Åke Green," Jan. 19, 2005, http://www.advocatesinternational.org/resources/AGAIOp.htm. See also Becket Fund, "Brief of the Becket Fund for Religious Liberty," n.d., available at http://www.becketfund.org/index.php/article/388.html; ADF, "ADF Protecting Religious Liberty."

the United States (including two Congressmen). Samuel Ericsson was interviewed by the media, including the national Channel 2 network and the *Financial Times*. Knowing his moment in the midnight sun would be brief, he concocted two sound bites: Green was the first pastor ever sentenced to prison for preaching about sexual morality; and his jailing would undercut Sweden's standing to criticize countries for religious persecution.[22] A Becket Fund attorney authored an opinion article opposing the prosecution on religious freedom grounds. Meanwhile, in the United States, Christian groups orchestrated a deluge of calls to the Swedish embassy, protesting Green's prosecution. All of this, according to Green's Swedish lawyer, was critical in showing politicians and jurists that the world's eyes were on the case.[23]

Blackening Green

Gay groups and their allies fought back, with the American intervenors and their arguments condemned in the Swedish press. For instance, the Becket Fund opinion piece faced a "very hostile response" from Swedish journalists who cried, "you don't understand our culture. This man should go to jail for two years – not six months!"[24] More damningly, gay activists tarred Green with an unwanted and extreme trans-Atlantic meddler: Fred Phelps, the rabidly antihomosexual founder of Topeka, Kansas's tiny but obstreperous Westboro Baptist Church. After Green's conviction, Phelps erected a "monument" on Westboro's Web site – the first time Phelps had so honored someone, other than an

---

[22] Bratt interview; Tunehag interview. Later, in Advocacy International's internal newsletter, Ericsson confessed that the first sound bite was inaccurate. At least one other holy man, none other than John the Baptist, was sentenced – and beheaded – for a sex sermon. Ericsson absolved himself, however, declaring that he "didn't want to confuse things." Advocates International, Newsletter, Feb. 2005.

[23] Becket Fund, "The Becket Fund on Åke Green in *Varlden Idag*," Dec. 17, 2004, http://www.becketfund.org/index.php/article/387.html.

[24] Lee Duignon, "Swedish Pastor Faces Jail For Preaching Against Homosexuality," *Chalcedon Report*, n.d. 2005, http://chalcedon.edu/Research/Articles/Swedish-Pastor-Faces-Jail-For-Preaching-Against-Homosexuality/; Bratt Interview; Tunehag Interview.

enemy whose death he was applauding. Later the monument linked to Westboro's "God Hates Sweden" campaign. It heartlessly asserts that Swedish victims of the 2004 Asian tsunami suffered God's wrath because of the country's liberal homosexuality laws.

For Swedish gay groups, Phelps's intervention in the *Green* case was a godsend. After all, as journalist Lars Lindstrom noted, "With friends like Fred Phelps, Åke Green doesn't need a single enemy." Forging a toxic tie between the two was easy. As RFSL pointedly warned, "Phelps' and Green's agitation against homosexuals leads to persecution and legitimization of violence against LGBT people...[and] is a threat to what we have achieved." For Green, this tarring was a catastrophe. With the outrage echoing in the media – and Phelps himself threatening to visit Sweden in the weeks before the Supreme Court hearing – Green denounced Phelps's support as "appalling," "extremely unpleasant," and "harm[ing] Christianity." Green even contacted U.S. newspapers to wonder, without irony, why American authorities had not silenced Westboro.[25]

Notably in this incident, Green had not sought Phelps's help. Nor, apparently, had Phelps contacted Green beforehand. Yet Green's foes seized on this tenuous transnational link, forcing Green to scramble to repudiate it. (For his part, Phelps dismantled his monument to the newfound Swedish traitor.) On the other hand, this smearing with the Phelps fringe did not change Green's views, as he made clear at the supreme court hearing. In his sermon, Green had sounded much like Phelps, even if he conceded that God loves all people: As the land "vomit[ed] out [Sweden's] inhabitants," there could be "earthquake[s]...or monsoon rains that drown thousands of people."[26] The broader

---

[25] Lindstrom quoted in "Minister of Hate to 'Hunt Down' Swedish King," *The Local*, Aug. 25, 2005, http://www.thelocal.se/discuss/index.php?showtopic= 7157; RFSL, "Hate Pastor Fred Phelps Is Not Alone," press release, Sept. 2, 2005, http://www.rfsl.se/?p=324&aid=2458; Green quoted in James Savage, "Swedish Pastor Disowns US Hate Site," *The Local*, Jan. 7, 2005, http://www.thelocal.se/article.php?ID=818&date=20050107.

[26] Green, "Is Homosexuality Genetic?"

analytic point remains, however: tarring is a powerful negative tactic in activist arsenals, used to create guilt by association, even when the target does not collude with the pariah.

Judgment and Afterlife

At the supreme court hearing on November 9, 2005, international observers and advocates sat inside. Outside, protesters on both sides marched, prominently including a congregation of Ethiopian evangelical immigrants living in Stockholm. Because of the controversy, the court approved an unprecedented live national radio broadcast of the session. As LifeSiteNews reported, Green "capitalized on the occasion to evangelize the nation." His original sermon was replayed, and Green defended his views. Asked by the prosecutor whether he believed that his sermon might be offensive to homosexuals, he agreed but insisted, "When you tell the truth to a person, it can hurt."[27]

On November 29, the Supreme Court affirmed the appellate decision, dismissing Green's conviction. In doing so, the court upheld the hate speech law's constitutionality, finding Green in violation for "express[ing] contempt for homosexuals as a group." Green's case had not rested solely on Swedish law, however, as his local and foreign lawyers had insisted. Praising the overseas amicus briefs for raising these points, the court held that the European Court of Human Rights would likely overturn Green's conviction on free-speech grounds, requiring his exoneration.[28]

The decision was hardly the last word, however. Both sides took the opportunity to promote or demote. Angry gay activists

---

[27] John-Henry Westen and Terry Vanderheyden, "Homosexual Hate Crime Trial of Swedish Pastor Used as an Opportunity for Evangelization," LifeSiteNews.com, Nov. 15, 2005, http://www.lifesitenews.com/ldn/2005/nov/05111504.html; Green quoted in Mattias Karen, "Swedish Pastor Defends Anti-Gay Sermon," Associated Press Online, Nov. 9, 2005. See also WorldNetDaily.com, "Swedish Minister Acquitted of Hate Speech Charges," Nov. 29, 2005, http://www.worldnetdaily.com/news/article.asp?ARTICLE_ID=47633.

[28] *Prosecutor General v. Åke Ingemar Teodor Green*, 8.

highlighted the court's holding the hate law constitutional but denounced the final ruling as a rights violation and license to bash. In foreboding phrases internationalized on the ILGA Web site, RFSL chairman Soren Andersson predicted "growing religious agitation from right-wing extremist Christian groups who use the church as a forum to spread their message of hate." To shock their supporters into action, RFSL launched a postcard campaign yoking Åke Green to moral monsters. This featured photographs of a Green look-alike depicted as a Nazi preacher. One of Sweden's largest newspapers, *Aftonbladet*, editorialized that, "If you can say that homosexuals are a cancerous tumor, then what can you not say?"[29]

For his part, a relieved Green sang the praises of his international backers on the ADF Web site: "Because of ADF, I am a free man." ADF in turn universalized the decision as a "major victory for the religious freedom of pastors and Christians worldwide." Advocates International's Ericsson went them one better, crediting "our Client above all other clients" for "connect[ing] all the loose threads in the Green case to show a beautiful tapestry of freedom and justice."[30]

Globalizing Green

Whether beautiful or not, the tapestry did more than influence Swedish law and politics. Far from Scandinavia, rival activists deployed the *Green* case, albeit in contrasting terms. Analyzing these uses and their effects is important in understanding how local battles are incorporated into broader transnational wars.

---

[29] Andersson and *Aftonbladet* quoted in Mattias Karen, "Swedish Pastor to Stop Criticizing Gays," Associated Press Online. Nov. 29, 2005; RFSL, "RFSL Launches Postcard Debate Campaign with Photographer Elisabeth Ohlson Wallin to Focus on Implications of the Supreme Court's Acquittal of Åke Green," press release, Dec. 20, 2005, http://www.rfsl.se/?p=324&aid=2664. See Elisabeth Ohlson Wallin, "In Hate We Trust," http://www.ohlson.se/utstallningar_inhatewetrust.htm.

[30] Green and Bull quoted in ADF, "Defending Religious Freedom at Home and around the World"; Ericsson quoted in Advocates International, Newsletter, Feb. 2005.

ADF has brandished Green's victory worldwide to "deter other attempts to censor Christian ministers from delivering Bible-based messages against harmful homosexual conduct." More important than the outcome's deterrent effect, the pastor's earlier conviction made him a potent mobilizing tool against proposed hate statutes. Many countries and international organizations debated these in the 2000s. In the United Kingdom, there was the Racial and Religious Hatred Bill, opposed by the Lawyers' Christian Fellowship (LCF) which transported Green to its 2006 annual meeting where he railed against the bill. At the UN and elsewhere, the Becket Fund used Green's prosecution to argue that hate speech statutes foster censorship and "intolerance towards disfavored minorities."[31]

In the United States in 2004, Green's conviction influenced Congressional debate on the Matthew Shepard hate crimes bill, named after the young gay man murdered in 1998. Foes fought this evocative framing with their own: the "thought crimes," "pedophile protection," or "send your grandma, your pastor, or you to jail" law. For the National Clergy Council's leader Robert Schenck, Green's jail sentence for a "traditional moral expression of the church . . . in a very modern, sophisticated, Western state" excited "a fear we are heading in a similar direction." A political cartoon distributed in Christian media made a similar point, linking Green's prosecution to cases in the United States and Canada. In October 2004, the Religious Freedom Coalition invited two

---

[31] ADF, "Swedish Pastor Beats 'Hate Crime' Conviction"; LCF, "A Personal Stand – Pastor Åke Green," Annual Conference, 2006, http://www.lawcf.org/index.asp?page=Annual%20Conference%202006; Becket Fund, "UNCHR Speech on Åke Green, April 14, 2005," press release, n.d., http://www.becketfund.org/index.php/article/386.html. See also Becket Fund, "Sweden's Conviction of Pastor for Preaching from the Pulpit Violates International Law," press release, Jan. 11, 2005, http://www.becketfund.org/index.php/article/333.html; Becket Fund, "Pennsylvania's Amended Hate Crimes Law and the Chilling of Religious Speech," letter to 9,000 houses of worship, June 18, 2004 (author's files); ARF, "Letter of Protest re: Council of Europe's Attempts to Impose Same-Sex Marriage on Member States," June 28, 2008, www.telladf.org/UserDocs/ARFletter.pdf, 4.

of Green's allies to meet with Congressional leaders and "warn
Christians" about the Shepard bill's dangers.[32]

More broadly, Christian activists used the case to rally believers and stymie homosexuals. Consider the million-member Coral
Ridge Ministries. It featured Green in its "10 Truths about Hate
Crime Laws" booklet, Web site, and DVD. These allow church-
goers "to intelligently share *why* you believe, *what* you believe"
at any time because "the battle wages at the water cooler," as
well as "at the mall, on the golf course, [and] at the beauty
salon," and "it is so very important to always be ready." "Truth
8" – hate crime laws "jeopardize free speech" – reviewed the
Green parable. It surveyed other "horrors beyond our borders,"
in Australia, Britain, and Canada, where Christians faced prosecution for Biblically based expression. Among other "truths":
hate crime laws are a "solution in search of a problem," are
"about recognition, not fighting crime," are a "vehicle for identity politics," "advance the homosexual agenda," and "violate
equal justice under the law."[33]

For their part, gay groups had long hailed Sweden for forging the path to full equality. When Green turned Sweden from
positive to negative model, incensed advocates first denounced
the ruling, much like RFSL did in Sweden. Soon, however, they
sought to turn the loss to their advantage. At the European Parliament, they warned of "religious leaders" using "inflammatory or

---

[32] Unruh, "Congress Debates 'Jail Grandma' Hate Speech"; Schenck quoted in
Keith B. Richburg and Alan Cooperman, "Swede's Sermon on Gays: Bigotry
or Free Speech?" *Washington Post*, Jan. 29, 2005, A1; RFC, "Pastor Jailed
for 'Hate Crime,'" 1. See also Faith2Action, "Bill to Expand Federal Hate
Crime Laws," http://www.f2a.org/index.php?option=com_content&view=
article&id=746:hate-crimes-expansion-house-vote-wednesday&catid=42:
homosexuality&Itemid=141.

[33] Coral Ridge Ministries, "10 Truths Series: The Battle Wages at the Water
Cooler," http://www.coralridge.org/equip/10TruthsSeries/default.aspx (em-
phasis in original); Coral Ridge Ministries, "Truth # 8: Hate Crime
Laws Jeopardize Freedom of Speech," http://www.coralridge.org/equip/10
TruthsSeries/10%20TRUTHS%20ABOUT%20HATE%20CRIMES/Hate%
20Crimes%20-%20Truth%208.aspx; Coral Ridge Ministries, "10 Truths
About Hate Crime Laws," http://www.coralridge.org/equip/10TruthsSeries/
10%20TRUTHS%20ABOUT%20HATE%20CRIMES/Default.aspx.

threatening language," often "hidden behind justifications based on . . . religious freedom." Weeks later, the Parliament passed the first of many annual resolutions demanding an end to homophobic hate speech. In 2009 too, the European Union Agency for Fundamental Rights cited "intolerant statements by religious leaders" to bolster calls for national and EU actions against homophobia. In addition, consider the Yogyakarta Principles, propounded months after the Swedish supreme court's decision as a guideline to legal requirements concerning gay rights worldwide. Principle 19E calls on states to "ensure" that "freedom of opinion . . . does not violate the rights . . . of persons of diverse sexual orientations." Portraying this point as settled law, the document did not mention the Swedish hate speech statute or Green's victory. Rather its "jurisprudential annotations" cited a UN committee report noting "with satisfaction" a Maltese statute on "freedom of public expression, which criminalizes insults . . . based on real or supposed sexual orientation."[34]

In the United States, gay activists narrowed, distinguished, or reinvented the *Green* case in the battle over the proposed hate speech law. In 2005, Lambda Legal's Kevin Cathcart responded to those "trying to twist" the case, differentiating it as "not relevant" to gay rights or religious freedom because of America's First Amendment. Later, advocate Jim Burroway argued that, far from demonstrating any risk to faith, Green's absolution in fact proved the opposite: even in Sweden, "strong exceptions have been made," with religious leaders "perfectly free to hate as long as they wrap their hatred around religious themes." Despite these efforts, a U.S. hate crimes provision repeatedly failed, with Green's horror story probably playing some role. Only in 2009

---

[34] European Parliament, "Homophobia in Europe," Resolution, Jan. 18, 2006, P6_TA-PROV(2006)0018; European Parliament, "Homophobia in Europe," Resolution, Apr. 26, 2007, P6_TA(2007)0167; European Union Agency for Fundamental Rights, "Homophobia and Discrimination on Grounds of Sexual Orientation and Gender Identity in the EU Member States, Part II – The Social Situation," 2009, 3; Yogyakarta Principles, prin. 19E; Jurisprudential Annotations to the Yogyakarta Principles, prin. 19E, p. 47, n. 127, http://www.yogyakartaprinciples.org/principles_en.htm.

did it pass – with special protections for religious speech. Even then Congressman Tom Price and Focus on the Families' James C. Dobson, derided the bill as "thought crimes" legislation "to muzzle people of faith who dare to express their moral and biblical concerns about homosexuality."[35]

Greening California

Beyond conflicts over hate speech, Green became an international symbol in related issues. In 2008, Ethiopian Lutherans invited him to their country. Swedish Lutherans had proselytized there decades earlier. Rifts had grown, however, as the home church integrated homosexuals, whereas the Africans recoiled at doing so. Green, despite his Pentecostalism, was therefore a welcome spiritual and strategic advisor on how "to protect [the Ethiopian church] against the gay movement."[36]

In addition, Green became part of the international fight over same-sex marriage. Invoked from Chicago to Bucharest, his influence was most striking in California's fight over Proposition 8, one of several 2008 voter questions that America's Christian Right considered more important than the year's presidential election. As born-again Christian leader Charles Colson stated, "This vote on whether we stop the gay-marriage juggernaut in California is Armageddon [for] freedom of religion."[37] In May 2008, the state's Supreme Court had struck down California's

[35] Cathcart quoted in Richburg and Cooperman, "Swede's Sermon"; Burroway, "'Jailed' Swedish Preacher Campaigning For Prop 8," Oct. 29, 2008, www.boxturtlebulletin.com/2008/10/29/5506; Price and Dobson quoted in Jim Adams, "House Votes to Expand Hate Crimes," *Milwaukee Journal Sentinel*, May 4, 2007, 6A.

[36] Jonas Adolfsson, "Åke Green Speaks at Seminary in Lutheran Mekane Yesus Church in Ethiopia; Last Summer [Lutheran] Archbishop Anders Wejryd Was Refused When He Sought to Visit the Same Church," *Varlden Idag*, Nov. 25, 2008, http://www.varldenidag.se/index.php?option=com_content&task=view&id=3308&Itemid=98.

[37] IFI, "Homosexual Protesters Blast Moody Church as 'House of Hate,' then Picket Cardinal George's Residence," press release, Feb. 13, 2005, http://www.illinoisfamily.org/informed/contentview.asp?c=22904; Charles Colson quoted in Laurie Goodstein, "A Line in the Sand for Same-Sex Marriage Foes," *New York Times*, Oct. 27, 2008, http://www.nytimes.com/2008/10/27/us/27right.html?pagewanted=print. See also Illinois Family

defense of marriage act (DOMA), so permitting gay marriage.[37a] Within weeks, the ProtectMarriage.com coalition collected enough signatures for a voter initiative to overturn the ruling. Proposition 8 proposed that the state's constitution be amended to affirm, "Only marriage between a man and a woman is valid and recognized in California."

In the months before the vote, the Family Research Council (FRC) held a high-profile Washington conference on "religious liberty in the crosshairs." With ADF and the Becket Fund featured, Green's prosecution drew attention as a demonstration of the threat same-sex marriage could pose to religious expression. Similar arguments soon reverberated across California. According to Rev. Jim Garlow of San Diego's Skyline megachurch, Green's ordeal was "a symbol of what is ahead. When you have . . . homosexual marriage[,] . . . the government . . . must declare anything in opposition to that hate speech." In the campaign's tempestuous final weeks, the "Yes on 8" committee even transported Green to California, where he embodied both the menace of the "homosexual agenda" and the power of resistance. Portrayed by the Christian *World* magazine as a "religious dissident," Green toured the Golden State, recounting his ordeal. On Sunday, October 19, he was a featured guest on "The ABCs of Protecting Marriage," a ninety-minute satellite simulcast to about 200 churches packed with thousands of ProtectMarriage.com pastors. Speaking through an interpreter, Green exhorted them to be "bold and courageous," a "political power" that would "stand up in the defense of our children . . . both the present ones and those still not born, [who] have nobody to defend what's in their interest if we remain silent."[38]

Insitute, "Homosexual Protesters Blast Moody Church as 'House of Hate,' then Picket Cardinal George's Residence," press release, Feb. 13, 2005, http://www.illinoisfamily.org/informed/contentview.asp?c=22904.

[37a] The state legislature had passed the DOMA in 1977 to eliminate inadvertent ambiguities in prior law. In 2000, a California voter initiative had limited recognition of out-of-state marriages to those between man and woman.

[38] FRC, "Religious Liberty in the Crosshairs," July 10, 2008, http://www.frcaction.org/get.cfm?i=WA08G15; Garlow quoted in Goodstein, "A Line

Of course, Green was only a small part of the Proposition 8 fight. Gay groups could not let him go unchallenged, however, deriding references to Green's conviction as incomplete and to his "jailing" as untrue. As one put it, "Anti-gay extremists who warn that advancement of equality... mean [sic] that their freedoms will be curtailed... are either woefully ignorant of the Constitution... or they are lying."[39] Nonetheless, with Green helping rally activists, Proposition 8 passed by a 52 percent to 48 percent margin among California's electorate.

It is impossible to determine how much Green influenced this and other outcomes. His case, however, is wielded to stoke fear and drum up activism among believers. Nor have gay activists been able to ignore it. Rather they use it – and especially its occasionally false deployment – to fire up their own supporters and prove their foes' deceit. More generally, the Green controversy illustrates key aspects of contemporary policy wars. Advocates undertake overseas forays, using the results of one battle, whether positive or negative, on the other fronts they contest.

Romanian Marriage Globalized

It is not only gay rights proponents who take the initiative, either. Sometimes their foes turn the tables, working to implant "good" laws overseas and pushing gay groups to the defensive. Romania's 2009 enactment of an American-style defense of marriage law exemplifies this in a country very different from Sweden.

in the Sand"; *World*, "Prop 8 and Åke," Nov. 1, 2008, http://www.worldmag. com/articles/14572; News Kitchen, "Californians Rally to Defend Marriage: Churches across State Host Simulcast Event to Arm Congregants with 'ABCs of Protecting Marriage' to Share with CA Voters," press release, Oct. 22, 2008; Green quoted in Adrienne S. Gaines and Felicia Mann, "Pastors Ramp Up Marriage Fight," *New Man eMagazine*, Nov. 5, 2008, http://www. newmanmag.com/e-magazine/110508/story8.php; Green quoted in Britton, "A Swedish Perspective." See also Åke Green, "Freedom to Proclaim the Gospel," interview with Åke Green, SkylineChurch.org archives, mp3 recording http://www.skylinechurch.org/resources/audio/5p10182008.mp3.
39 Burroway, "'Jailed' Swedish Preacher."

Background

About 87 percent of the nation's highly religious population is Romanian Orthodox, with conservative evangelical churches important too. Under communism, Romania had an active policy criminalizing homosexual behavior – Article 200 of the penal code. As late as 2008, a Eurobarometer poll found that the country's 22 million citizens were some of the least likely of all Europeans to feel comfortable with a gay neighbor (Swedes were most likely).[40]

In this oppressive context, a Romanian gay movement formed late. In 1994, a group of "mainly foreign citizens residing in Romania" organized the Bucharest Acceptance Group (BAG, later ACCEPT), its main goal the repeal of Article 200. Among its leaders was American Scott Long, a Fulbright lecturer at a Romanian university, who, by 1995, worked for the International Gay and Lesbian Human Rights Commission (IGHLRC) and later directed Human Rights Watch's LGBT division. From its early years, ACCEPT's "main supporter" was the Dutch government agency MATRA, and its "main partner organization" was the Dutch gay group Centre for Culture and Leisure (COC).[41] In 1995, the Dutch embassy and UNESCO sponsored a symposium, "Homosexuality: A Human Right?" which urged "a more gay Romania," taught that "modern democrac[ies] separate law from religious morality," and warned that the world would monitor Romania's policies. At the conference, however, government and

---

[40] European Commission, "Discrimination in the European Union: Perceptions, Experiences and Attitudes," Special Eurobarometer 296, Table QA 6.3, July 2008. For historical background, see Ingrid Baciu, Vera Cîmpeanu, and Mona Nicoara, "Romania," in *Unspoken Rules – Sexual Orientation and Women's Human Rights*, ed. Rachel Rosenbloom (IGLHRC, 1995); Lavinia Stan and Lucian Turcescu, *Religion and Politics in Post-Communist Romania* (Oxford: Oxford University Press, 2007), 171–80.

[41] ACCEPT, "Brief History of ACCEPT," http://accept.ong.ro/englishscu. html; HRW, "Scott Long: Director, Lesbian, Gay, Bisexual & Transgender Rights Division," http://www.hrw.org/en/bios/scott-long; ACCEPT, "ACCEPT Today," http://accept.ong.ro/englishpro.html; COC Netherlands, International Newsletter, http://www.coc.nl/dopage.pl?thema=any&pagina= algemeen&algemeen_id=274.

Orthodox officials defended criminalization, denounced homosexuality as "sin" and "plague," and commended "the beauty of the Romanian woman" as an inspiration to procreate.[42]

If the symposium did not change minds, foreign intervention eventually lifted Romania's harsh sodomy law. In 1998, Long "enthusiastically and skillfully, drew the initial version" of a legislative amendment repealing Article 200. When the campaign kindled a blistering nationalist backlash, the Council of Europe, European Union, European Court of Human Rights, and United Nations all applied pressure. Romanian accession to the EU soon became a critical leverage point, and in 2001, the legislature removed the old statute.[43]

Romania's Marriage Problem

Several years later, a new battle broke out. The country's constitution and family law, formulated decades earlier, innocently defined marriage as the relationship between two "spouses" without mentioning their gender. As such, these provisions were inadvertently ahead of their time. According to gay activists, they permitted same-sex marriage in line with evolving EU practice.[44]

For traditional believers, however, the country's laws were a menace, made sharper as Romania's small gay community held its first annual pride march in 2004. When Spain, a Roman

---

[42] ACCEPT, "For a More Gay Romania," n.d. 2000, http://accept.ong.ro/foramoregayromania.html; BAG under the Patronage of UNESCO, "Report on the Symposium Homosexuality: A Human Right?," May 31, 1995, http://www.france.qrd.org/assocs/ilga/euroletter/35-Romania.html.

[43] ACCEPT, "Draft Bill to Amend Penal Code Provisions Related to Sex Life," http://accept.ong.ro/macoveien.html#proiectsus. See generally ILGA-Europe and ACCEPT, "ILGA-Europe Calls on Romanian Senate to Repeal Laws Criminalising Same-Sex Relations," press release at "ACCEPTing Diversity: 22nd European Conference of ILGA," Oct. 8, 2000, http://accept.ong.ro/Conference2000.html#conferinta2000; Human Rights Watch, *Public Scandals: Criminal Law and Sexual Orientation in Romania* (New York: Human Rights Watch, 1998).

[44] Human Rights Watch, "Letter to the Romanian Government Urging Protection of All Families without Discrimination," Feb. 6, 2008, http://www.hrw.org/en/news/2008/02/06/letter-romanian-government-urging-protection-all-families-without-discrimination.

Catholic "defector" from the traditional families network, approved same-sex marriages in 2005, a group of Romanian evangelical pastors felt particularly threatened. For help, they turned to Peter Costea, son of a Romanian preacher and at the time a lawyer practicing in Houston, Texas. According to Costea, his group believed that the "homosexual agenda ... promotes ... radical changes that would permeate every aspect of society – affecting freedom of expression, association, religion, education, media, culture, pulpit, and the legal system."[45]

Initially, Costea and the Romanian clerics opted for an unprecedented campaign to amend the country's constitution by popular initiative. Costea wrote the amendment, which defined marriage as between a man and a woman, with support from Britain's Lawyers Christian Fellowship and America's Rutherford Institute. The pastors worked with the Catholic Church and much larger Orthodox Church to collect the 650,000 signatures needed for the referendum. The group orchestrated online petitions from overseas Romanian citizens, endorsements from major Romanian-American newspapers, and letters from Baptist and Pentecostal churches in the United States.[46]

In reaction, the gay community, backed by its own international supporters, worked to unset the religious groups' agenda. In the spring of 2006, it launched what ACCEPT spokesman Florin Buhuceanu called "the most focused drive yet to change opinions on gay marriage in Romania." This began at Bucharest's May 2006 Gay Fest, only the country's third after major controversy and violent protests against the previous year's pride march. Provocatively themed "Same-Sex Marriage and Civil Unions in Romania," the multiday event attracted foreign participants and

---

[45] Information and quotations in this paragraph from Peter Costea, president, Association of Romanian Families, telephone interview, Mar. 11, 2010 (audiotape).

[46] Costea interview; "Normal Romania: Homosexual Marriage Excluded from Family Code by Romanian Senate," interview with Peter Costea, *Romanian Tribune* (Niles, IL), Feb. 22, 2008, http://www.romaniantribune.net/a941_Rom226nia_normala_Casatoria_intre_homosexuali_exclusa_din_Codul_Familiei_de_catre_Senatul_Romaniei.aspx.

sponsors, including the EU, Open Society Institute, Astraea Lesbian Foundation for Justice, and British Council. In a symbolic gesture, ACCEPT's Buhuceanu married his same-sex Spanish partner. This was a public, although not legally binding, ceremony blessed by the small Romanian outpost of the Abilene, Texas-based Metropolitan Community Church (MCC). With churches in twenty-three countries – the Romanian one headed by Buhuceanu himself – MCC is a Protestant denomination with a special mission of promoting same-sex marriage. All of this, according to ACCEPT's president, would "show the government where public opinion stands on the issue."[47]

In fact, however, this was not so clear. Hours before the Gay Fest, political parties, NGOs, and the Orthodox Church sponsored a rival march. Gay activists were assaulted by extremists. Nor did ACCEPT's campaign slow the petition drive for the ballot initiative. Organizers such as Costea rejected violence, punishment, and workplace discrimination against homosexuals – but they nonetheless opposed same-sex marriage as a threat to traditional Romanian values and the rights of the community. By December 2006, the Romanian religious groups had gathered the necessary signatures for validation by the Romanian Constitutional Court.[48]

Bolstering the court submission, Costea engineered the filing of amicus curiae briefs, a tactic unprecedented in Romanian jurisprudence. In addition to its own, his pastor's group solicited a brief from a "prestigious" international authority. After consulting fellow Houston lawyers, Costea contacted the

---

[47] ACCEPT spokesman and president statements in Associated Press, "Romanian Gay Activists Begin New Drive to Legalize Gay Marriage," May 30, 2006. See also GayFest 2006, http://www.gay-fest.ro/gayfesto6RO.htm; Marina Dohi, "Gay Chief's Religious Marriage Yesterday," *Libertate* (Romania), June 5, 2006, http://www.libertatea.ro/stire/seful-homosexualilor-s-a-insurat-religios-ieri-154747.html.

[48] See generally "Clashes Mark Romanian Gay Pride," *BBC News*, June 4, 2006, http://news.bbc.co.uk/2/hi/europe/5045352.stm; "Normal Romania: Homosexual Marriage Excluded from Family Code by Romanian Senate," interview with Peter Costea, *Romanian Tribune* (Niles, IL), Feb. 22, 2008, http://www.romaniantribune.net/a941_Rom226nia_normala_Casatoria_intre_homo sexuali_exclusa_din_Codul_Familiei_de_catre_Senatul_Romaniei.aspx.

Alliance Defense Fund, which for years had championed American defense of marriage acts. ADF leaders, unfamiliar with Costea, investigated him – "I expected that; if it had not happened, I would have been suspicious." Satisfied, ADF then reviewed Costea's brief and filed its own. This claimed that the proposed amendment was constitutional under Romanian and European Union law and argued for Romania's "traditional rights" and culture, not gay rights.[49]

Faced with the petition and accompanying briefs, ACCEPT countered with its own amicus brief. This too cited domestic and foreign laws – but to contrary effect. It argued that the proposed amendment would contravene the Romanian constitution and international standards. Even if the Romanian people approved the amendment, the "so-called consensus of the majority" would be void if it violated gay peoples' fundamental rights to equality and marriage. In addition, ACCEPT tarred the initiative committee as bigots: the proposed amendment did not express authentic Romanian culture but instead was an "affirmation and perpetuation of discrimination based on sexual orientation."[50]

In July 2007, the Constitutional Court upset plans for the referendum – not on ACCEPT's grounds, but on a technicality. The petition failed to meet the Constitution's geographic distribution requirement for citizen initiatives. Touted by ACCEPT, this decision was only a temporary setback for Costea's group. Within months, the Romanian pastors had created a formal organization, the Alliance of Romania's Families (ARF).

Costea, its president, describes ARF as "absolutely... model[ed] on the Family Research Council, Focus on the Family, ADF." Providing "inspiration" at the ARF's launch was ADF senior counsel Glen Lavy who, according to Costea, urged, "You need to get involved – [or] you will begin to lose your freedom of religion and values, like in the US and Western Europe." Summarizing ADF's influence, Benjamin Bull stated, "There was

---

[49] Costea interview; Bull interview.
[50] ACCEPT, "Amicus Curiae on Proposal to Conduct a Referendum to Amend Article 48 of the Constitution of Romania," Mar. 7, 2007, 2, 8 (author's files).

clearly a need and desire there. We simply helped shape and
define the organization." One way it did so was by hosting
Costea at one of its multiday, all-expenses-paid National Litigation Academies (NLA), discussing everything from American to
international law. As an "ADF-allied attorney," Costea's ties to
the group are strong; when I interviewed him, Costea volunteered
that ADF chief counsel Benjamin Bull had earlier confirmed me
as "a balanced person" who didn't "look at us as a bunch of
wackos."[51]

Romanian Lawmaking, American-Style

ARF has borrowed many tactics from America's Christian Right:
litigating, lobbying, electioneering – and linking to transnational
networks. This potent mix was on display in ARF's first campaign, to rid Romanian law of its accidental openness to same-
sex marriage. The plan this time: amend the marriage statute
with a defense of marriage provision similar to those in the
United States. The effort began early in 2008 when legislators
introduced an amendment to the country's family code. The Senate's judiciary committee quickly passed it. Within days, ADF
sent a congratulatory letter offering "to assist any government in
defending its marriage laws." Focus on the Family, the American
Family Association, and the Family Research Council joined in
the praise.[52]

As in the initiative campaign, however, ACCEPT and its overseas allies opposed these efforts. Human Rights Watch urged
Romania to reject an amendment "motivated by prejudice and
predicated on exclusion," which would "trap" Romania in

---

[51] Costea interview; Bull Interview. See also ADF, "National Litigation
Academy: Attorney Network," https://nla.alliancedefensefund.org/Login
.aspx?ReturnUrl=%2fDefault.aspx.

[52] Costea interview; ARF, "Despre Advocacy," http://www.protejarea-familiei
.com/advocacy.html; ADF, "Letter to Mr. Peter Eckstein Kovacs, President,
Senate Judiciary Commission of Romania," Feb. 11, 2008, www.alliance
defensefund.org/UserDocs/RomaniaLetters.pdf.

"preemptive and discriminatory prohibition." In a letter resembling a legal brief, HRW argued that the provision would violate Romanian, European, and international standards including the Yogyakarta Principles that "draw together these international protections for family and for non-discrimination." At the UN, ACCEPT, IGLHRC, and ILGA-Europe joined in the outcry. They cited the proposed amendment as violating "existing legal provisions and the constitutional principles of human rights equality and the universality of rights."[53]

Days later, however, ADF shot back with its own hard-hitting legal arguments. It defended the amendment as "sound social and public policy" that "merely codifies the existing tradition, custom, and law of Romania." It attacked HRW for its "error," "improper assertions," and "attempt at confusion." A special target was the Yogyakarta Principles – "nothing more than a one-sided effort to influence international leaders . . . not, in any way, law or binding authority upon any government." A few weeks later, another long-range salvo: the World Congress of Families sent a "Petition in Support of Romania's Defense of Marriage," signed by more than 100 pro-family leaders from 20 countries. This praised Romania as "a socially conservative country whose citizens are overwhelmingly religious." It exalted traditional marriage as a "divinely ordained institution which predates governments and on whose health the future of society depends." Finally, it warned that EU bureaucrats might attempt to "intimidate" the Romanians, as they had other member-states "defending traditional marriage and the natural family." In early April, ARF delivered the petition to the Romanian parliament at its annual prayer breakfast.[54]

[53] HRW, "Letter to the Romanian Government Urging Protection of All Families without Discrimination," Feb. 6, 2008, http://www.hrw.org/en/news/2008/02/06/letter-romanian-government-urging-protection-all-families-without-discrimination; ACCEPT, IGLHRC, and ILGA-Europe, "Romania: The Status of Lesbian, Gay, Bisexual and Transgender Rights," Feb. 8, 2008, www.iglhrc.org/binary-data/ATTACHMENT/file/000/000/74-1.pdf.
[54] ADF, "Memorandum," Feb. 19, 2008, www.alliancedefensefund.org/UserDocs/RomaniaLetters.pdf; WCF, "Petition in Support of Romania's

The WCF petition proved prophetic, even if its language was overwrought. In 2008, the Parliamentary Assembly of the Council of Europe (PACE) debated same-sex marriage as a means of fighting inequality and discrimination against homosexuals. PACE policies do not bind the Council of Europe's forty-seven member-states, and it is unlikely that the debate was aimed only at Romania. Nonetheless, this European elevation of the Romanian conflict hit a nerve.

ARF sent PACE a stinging letter of protest. This was signed by other Romanian, American, and Canadian NGOs, posted on ADF's Web site, and publicized in Christian media worldwide. It demanded that PACE "immediately desist" from "impos[ing]" same-sex marriage on Romania and other countries. Denying the underlying problem, ARF denounced such marriages as a "mere fad." Framejacking, ARF claimed the unions would violate freedom of religion and the rights of children. Problematizing the purported solution to marital "inequality," ARF cited huge "social costs" for a continent threatened by low birthrates. Attacking PACE's "radical" intervention, ARF disparaged the international organization for threatening sovereignty and democracy.[55] Despite all this, PACE remained unmoved. Taking another step toward European recognition of same-sex marriage, it initiated a report on "various forms of marital and non-marital partnerships."[56] In turn, the Romanian parliament ignored PACE, listening instead to ARF and its allies. Overwhelmingly, it amended the old marriage statute with a new defense of marriage provision.

Still the battle raged, next in Romania's fall 2008 parliamentary elections. Following methods pioneered by its American

Defense of Marriage," 2008, http://www.worldcongress.org/WCF/wcf
.leadership.romania.0804.htm.

[55] ARF, "Letter of Protest re: Council of Europe's Attempts to Impose Same-Sex Marriage on Member States," June 28, 2008, http://www.telladf.org/UserDocs/ARFletter.pdf.

[56] PACE, "Equal Rights for Homosexual Partnerships, Doc. 11956," June 20, 2009, http://assembly.coe.int/main.asp?Link=/documents/workingdocs/doc09/edoc11956.htm#P43_3809.

mentors, ARF surveyed the candidates, asking about their stands on "morality issues." As Costea recalled, "Just like in the U.S. where the Christian Coalition puts out voter guides in Texas, we did the same except in electronic form... blasting out thousands and thousands of emails to ordinary voters." ARF made all candidates "aware, just like in the US, that if you want to get elected, take the time to talk to us."[57] Although the effects of ARF's efforts are unclear, many of its candidate picks were elected.

The new parliament's conservatism became clear in early 2009, when the government announced plans to revise the country's civil code. Seizing the opportunity, ARF worked with ADF and Romanian legislators to draft defense of marriage language even broader than the recent amendment. The resulting bill prohibited adoptions by same-sex couples and rejected recognition of such marriages performed elsewhere. (In addition, ARF drafted civil code amendments on issues such as divorce, cohabitation, organ transplants, euthanasia, and adoptions.)[58]

ACCEPT objected to the sweeping new provisions. With few friends in the Romanian parliament, however, it relied on international supporters. In a joint letter with IGLHRC, it again sought to lift the battle to European and international turf. At the Bucharest Gay Pride march, it urged Romania to adopt a 2009 European Parliament resolution calling for mutual recognition of same-sex partnerships. European parliamentarians lobbied the Romanian president and parliament. To no avail: Romania approved the new civil code, including all of ARF's suggested provisions on same-sex marriage. For good measure, when the new code came into operation in December 2009, Parliament held a three-day conference, "The Family in Crisis," at which ARF was invited to make presentations. ACCEPT, IGLHRC, and ILGA-Europe could do no more than remonstrate at

---

[57] All quotations from Costea interview.

[58] ADF, "Romania Adopts Strong Civil Codes Protecting Marriage: ADF, ADF-Allied Attorney Provided Instrumental Legal Counsel to Romanian Parliament," n.d. 2009, http://www.alliancedefensefund.org/news/pressrelease.aspx?cid=5013; Costea interview.

Romania's violating international protections for people not following the "traditional heterosexual model."[59]

For the time being, the victory was the ARF's – and that of its international supporters. As the ARF Web site acknowledges, ADF, WCF and other pro-family NGOs played "a major role in protecting marriage and the family in Romania," providing "legal guidance and international solidarity." WCF president Allan Carlson returned the compliment: "While some countries are choosing 'diversity' over natural law and common sense, Romania is standing firm for marriage and the natural family. . . . This shows the value of forging an international pro-family movement."[60]

For ADF, the victory was more strategic: "Americans told by same-sex 'marriage' advocates that the rest of the world considers the U.S. out of step when it comes to affirming marriage as the union of one man and one woman need only point to examples like Romania to demonstrate that such an assumption is false: 'Romania is one country where American judicial activists will find no support.'"[61] Thus if American gay activists bolster their case with European law, groups such as ADF will have a ready rebuttal: a spanking-new, if American-influenced, marriage law in a European democracy similar to the United States in the crucial area of religious observance and belief.

Conclusion

These Romanian and Swedish contests demonstrate the frequency with which both sides in the gay rights fight jump borders

---

[59] ACCEPT, IGLHRC, and ILGA-Europe, "Letter to Traian Basescu, President of Romania, July 30, 2009," http://www.iglhrc.org/binary-data/ATTACHMENT/file/ooo/ooo/298-1.pdf; Mediafax, "Bucharest Gay Pride Parade Ended without Incident," May 23, 2009, http://www.mediafax.ro/english/bucharest-gay-pride-parade-ended-without-incidents-4443267; ADF, "Romania Adopts."

[60] ARF, press release, June 10, 2009 (author's files); Carlson quoted in WCF, "Alliance of Romania's Families Achieves Victory for Marriage and the Family," http://www.worldcongress.org/wcfnl/htm/2009/wcfnl.0906.htm.

[61] ADF, "Romania Adopts" (quoting ADF legal counsel Roger Kiska).

and cross institutions. Similar battles in places as diverse as Belize, Malawi, and Singapore involve transnationally linked domestic groups as well. In this as in other issues, litigation and lawmaking join boycotts and sanctions as potent arrows in activist quivers. To quote a Human Rights Watch official touting India's 2009 *Naz Foundation* case striking down the country's sodomy laws: "It's a very shrunk world for gay-rights activists.... [This] will set a precedent for other activists."[62]

For religious groups, however, the world is equally shrunken. They too are strategizing and litigating across borders. They too use cases such as Green's or statutes such as Romania's as precedents and symbols in other places. The result is transnational and even global warfare over any number of prominent policies. As WCF leader Allan Carlson put it in praising the pro-family network's global "solidarity" in the Romanian conflict: "[A] threat to the natural family anywhere is a threat to the natural family everywhere." Overseas activists such as the Alliance Defense Fund and Advocates International are fighting round after round with their local partners against rival networks. In turn, those foes take a similarly expansive view of the struggle. In challenging African homophobia, for instance, Political Research Associates urges gay groups to continue "taking the fight to conservatives and putting them on the defensive at home," in churches in the network's American strongholds.[63]

---

[62] HRW official quoted in Kazmin, "Gay Indians Seek Sexual Equality." For the Belize conflict, see. C-FAM, "Christian Churches File Court Papers Today in Fight over Sodomy in Belize," May 13, 2011, http://www.c-fam.org/publications/id.1853/pub_detail.asp; News5, "Caleb Orozco and UNIBAM take Gay Rights to the Courts," Feb 4, 2011, http://edition.channel5belize.com/archives/48258. For Malawi, see International Commission of Jurists, "Sex Between Women Now a Crime in Malawi: New Law Violates Human Rights Obligations of Malawi," press release, Feb. 8, 2011, http://www.icj.org/default.asp?nodeID=349&sessID=&langage=1&myPage=Legal_Documentation&id=23698. For Singapore, IGLHRC, "Singapore: Update – Law Against Homosexuals To Remain," Oct. 24, 2007, http://www.iglhrc.org/cgi-bin/iowa/article/takeaction/resourcecenter/483.html. See generally Human Dignity Trust, "What We Do," http://www.humandignitytrust.org/how_we_do_it.html.

[63] Carlson quoted in "Pro-Family Leaders Rally to Romania's Defense of Marriage," *World Congress of Families Newsletter* 2: 4 (Apr. 2008),

This chapter and the broader perspective developed in this book show how these wars are waged at ground level, not only in national legislatures and popular referendums, but also in courtrooms and the press. Most importantly, the chapter illustrates the necessity of analyzing rival sides, not just those promoting change, to explain outcomes. In both the Swedish and Romanian cases, dueling networks, each transnationally linked, grappled over the identity of the policy problem. Their contradictory solutions created crises for their opponents. To set agendas and persuade decision makers, the sides unleashed an array of positive and negative tactics. Along with advancing themselves through lobbying and litigating, they assailed their foes. Frames were hijacked, leaders tarred, and institutions smeared. Examining only one side to these conflicts could not have revealed these critical dynamics or explained the outcomes that, for the moment, prevail.

www.worldcongress.org/wcf/wcf.nl/wcf.nl.0804.0204.pdf; Kaoma, "U.S. Christian Right."

5

Shootout at United Nations Plaza

Warring over Global Gun Control

It was a warm evening in June 2006, and delegates to the Small Arms Review Conference crowded the narrow atrium at United Nations headquarters. An official had just dedicated the Five Year Report on the UN's Programme of Action to control the illicit trade in small arms and light weapons (SALW), a policy activists and diplomats had worked years to develop. Celebrating the fight against the global "gun crisis," the throng of dark suits and knee-high dresses sipped drinks at the open bar and munched shrimp, cheeses, and petits fours.

But just below the surface, things were amiss. The event's organizers had forgotten to check the recorded music track. As the delegates gobbled and gabbed, Bob Marley's "I Shot the Sheriff" blared – its refrain, "but I swear it was in self-defense," sounding a consistent theme of the Programme's sworn enemies, the National Rifle Association (NRA) and the World Forum on the Future of Sport Shooting Activities (WFSA). For them, gun deaths were not one of the world's most pressing human rights problems. On the contrary: the real threat came from firearms control, undermining the most basic of human rights – preserving life, if necessary at the barrel of a gun. Thanks to the NRA and WFSA, the UN festivities were bittersweet. Despite high hopes, the Programme of Action had become, in the words of one early proponent, Human Rights Watch (HRW), little more than a "program of inaction," its bland principles nonbinding. Much of the responsibility for this gutting could be laid at the feet of the gun groups, whose representatives sat in their own dark suits on the U.S. delegation.[1]

This chapter analyzes international efforts at small arms control both before and after the 2006 UN conference, seeking to explain this zombie policy. In the early 1990s, NGOs, UN agencies, and states began targeting these weapons as causes and multipliers of violence. Immediately, however, their nemesis took the field: national gun organizations preemptively organized their own global network, encompassing civil society and governments. As the chapter shows, the bitter, if budding, rivals affected one another, the problem's definition, and the outcomes of the UN process.

What are "small arms and light weapons?" They include pistols, revolvers, ordinary rifles, semiautomatics, and other weapons carried by individuals (small arms), and automatic rifles, machine guns, mortars, and missile or rocket launchers (light weapons). For my purposes, these distinctions are of secondary import; I use the terms "small arms," "firearms," or "guns," avoiding the deadly UN acronym, SALW. There is disagreement about their number in the world today, but one widely cited estimate from the Small Arms Survey was 875 million in 2007. Deployed in warfare, such weapons are also involved in crime, accidents, and suicide. In these and other contexts, about 740,000 people per year are killed worldwide by small arms, according to the UN. This firearms statistic, however, like most others, has been challenged not only for its accuracy, but also for its failing to account for lives *saved* by guns in the hands of police, soldiers, or citizens.[2]

---

[1] HRW, "U.N.: 'Program of Inaction' on Small Arms," press release, July 18, 2001, http://hrw.org/english/docs/2001/07/19/global308.htm.

[2] Small Arms Survey (SAS), *Small Arms Survey 2007: Guns and the City* (Cambridge: Cambridge University Press, 2007), 39; Geneva Declaration on Armed Violence and Development Secretariat, *Global Burden of Armed Violence*, 2008, http://www.genevadeclaration.org/measurability/global-burden-of-armed-violence.html; David B. Kopel, Paul Gallant, & Joanne D.

Dueling Networks

Guns have been weapons of choice in conflicts around the world for centuries. For centuries, too, journalists, artists, and humanitarians have deplored the carnage. But a sustained international movement to control small arms began only after the Cold War ended. Initially, efforts were led by two distinct networks, each with its own members, goals, and strategies. The first network viewed weak gun laws as a crime problem, seeking broad international limits on civilian ownership and usage. A second, more prominent approach conceived of small arms narrowly, as a disarmament matter affecting countries torn by violent internal conflicts. Only in 1998 did these two control networks merge, driven in part by the pro-gun activism their initial organizing had fueled.

Crime Prevention Network
The crime control effort began earlier, with a tragic event that propelled the Japanese government to the frontlines of international gun politics. In October 1992, Yoshihiro Hattori, a Japanese exchange student living in Baton Rouge, Louisiana, donned a Halloween outfit and headed to a party. He made one fatal error: approaching the wrong house, whose trigger-happy resident gunned him down. The killing – and the shooter's acquittal under a law allowing homeowners to use deadly force to defend their dwellings – outraged Japan. There, restrictive policies prevent most citizens from owning firearms. More than 1.6 million signed a petition urging stronger U.S. laws. In Louisiana, Hattori's parents won a $650,000 civil judgment, using the money to establish a foundation pressing American gun control.[3]

As for the Japanese government, it devoted itself to the UN (but did nothing to curb its large, export-oriented firearms

Eisen, "How Many Global Deaths from Arms? Reasons to Question the 740,000 Factoid Being Used to Promote the Arms Trade Treaty," 2010, http://works.bepress.com/cgi/viewcontent.cgi?article=1034&context=david_kopel.

[3] Isabel Reynolds, "Shot in the Dark: Exchange Student's Parents Keep the Memory Alive," *Daily Yomiuri* (Tokyo), Apr. 15, 2000, 7.

industry or its booming business in Hawaiian gun tours).[4] Hoping to convince the world to adopt stricter control measures, in 1993 the Japanese pushed for the Economic and Social Council's (ECOSOC) Commission on Crime Prevention and Criminal Justice to begin a multiyear study on gaps in national, regional, and international laws covering civilian firearms. Later in the decade, Japan spearheaded the Commission's negotiations on new gun controls.

Disarmament Network

Parallel to the UN's crime prevention process, a separate disarmament campaign began. As the Cold War waned, the world paid greater attention to appalling death tolls in countries such as Angola, Liberia, and Colombia. Wars also erupted in Yugoslavia, and genocide ripped Rwanda. In this context, the UN undertook humanitarian missions and peacekeepers died. Fueling the apparent spikes in internal warfare were AK-47s, Uzis, and M-16s, sold legally or illegally. In response, pundits and blue-ribbon international commissions decried a "new world disorder" and a "coming anarchy," with "immediate, powerful ramifications for all of humanity."[5] It is less certain whether any of the underlying developments were in fact threatening – or merely "myths or misunderstandings" that "originated in the media [or] were propagated ... by, international organisations and NGOs," as one

---

4 Maria Haug, Martin Langvandslien, Lora Lumpe, and Nicholas Marsh, "Shining a Light on Small Arms Exports: The Record of State Transparency," Occasional Paper No. 4, Small Arms Survey and Norwegian Initiative on Small Arms Transfers, Jan. 2002, 24, n. 67; Luke Burbank, "Japanese 'Gun Tourists' Flock to Hawaiian Ranges," *National Public Radio*, Dec. 21, 2005, http://www.npr.org/templates/story/story.php?storyId=5064621.

5 Ted Galen Carpenter, "The New World Disorder," *Foreign Policy*, Fall 1991, 24; Robert D. Kaplan, "The Coming Anarchy," *Atlantic Monthly*, Feb. 1994, http://www.theatlantic.com/magazine/archive/1994/02/the-coming-anarchy/4670/; Carnegie Commission on Preventing Deadly Conflict (CCPDC), *Preventing Deadly Conflict: Final Report* (New York: Carnegie Corporation, 1997), xiv.

authoritative analysis later concluded. Nonetheless, the calamitous view held sway at the time.[6]

Of equal import to these perceptions – or misperceptions – in the early 1990s, arms control experts began looking for new issues as the Cold War ended. As analyst William Hartung described the view among those who had specialized in heavy weapons control, "conventional arms sales other than small arms [are] history, they don't matter. We're . . . dinosaurs; we have to re-tool to be relevant." At the UN, the Department of Disarmament Affairs (DDA) was "fighting for its existence and wanted to be seen as relevant," according to a former staff person.[7]

Moved by these moral and material factors, a group of activists based in North America and Western Europe convened in February 1994 at the American Academy of Arts and Sciences (AAAS). Those attending included several who would become key small arms control advocates: Aaron Karp (Old Dominion University), Edward Laurance (Monterey Institute), and Natalie J. Goldring (British American Security Information Council [BASIC]). Under AAAS auspices, the group prepared the first major study of small arms as a global problem, *Lethal Commerce: The Global Trade in Small Arms and Light Weapons*. The book examined what its authors already took to be "the *growing* international proliferation of small arms and light weapons [and] the impact of such weapons on ethnic and nationalist conflicts." Also in 1994,

---

[6] Human Security Center, "Overview," *Human Security Report 2005: War and Peace in the 21st Century* (Oxford: Oxford University Press, 2005), 2. See also John Mueller, *Overblown: How Politicians and the Terrorism Industry Inflate National Security Threats, and Why We Believe Them* (New York: Free Press, 2006), 117–38.

[7] William Hartung, director, Arms Trade Resource Center, World Policy Institute, personal interview, Oct. 11, 2007, Pittsburgh, PA (audiotape); Chantal De Jonge Oudraat, United States Institute of Peace; former Senior Research Associate, UN Institute for Disarmament Research, telephone interview, Apr. 12, 2007 (notes). See also Aaron Karp, "Small Arms – The New Major Weapons," in *Lethal Commerce: The Global Trade in Small Arms and Light Weapons*, ed. Jeffrey Boutwell, Michael T. Klare, and Laura W. Reed (Cambridge, MA: AAAS, 1995), 17.

the Ford Foundation made a critical $224,000 grant to support a small arms network. According to its program officer at the time, the Foundation had felt "no real demand" for the network from people in conflict zones, so the grant went to BASIC. Led by Goldring, BASIC's task was to define and measure the small arms problem, propose policies to solve it, and develop implementation strategies.[8]

Spurred by its own disarmament mission, DDA also became active at this time, hiring Laurance. More prominently, UN Secretary General Boutros-Boutros Ghali targeted small arms in January 1995: "The world is awash with them," requiring "micro-disarmament" of the weapons "that are actually killing people in the hundreds of thousands." Later that year, the UN General Assembly established the Panel of Governmental Experts on Small Arms, chaired by Japanese Ambassador Mitsuro Donowaki, to report on the problem, with Laurance again tapped as a consultant.[9]

Gun Network

As the crime prevention and disarmament networks took shape, however, domestic gun organizations fought back. At the network's core was America's National Rifle Association (NRA), one of the nation's most powerful lobbying groups. Like the control forces, a mix of moral and material factors motivated it and other groups.

Most important was a perceived peril to rights – gun rights and the right to self-defense. In the early 1990s, this menace came

---

[8] Boutwell, Klare, and Reed, *Lethal Commerce*, 5 (emphasis added); Geoffrey Wiseman, University of Southern California, Los Angeles; former program officer, Ford Foundation, telephone interview, Aug. 1, 2007 (notes).

[9] UN, "Supplement to an Agenda for Peace: Position Paper of the Secretary-General on the Occasion of the Fiftieth Anniversary of the United Nations," A/50/60S/1995/1, Jan. 1995, paras. 63, 60; UN, "Report of the Panel of Governmental Experts on Small Arms," A/52/298, Aug., 1997. See generally Natalie J. Goldring, "Domestic Laws and International Controls," in *Light Weapons and Civil Conflict: Controlling the Tools of Violence, Carnegie Commission on Preventing Deadly Conflict Series*, ed. Jeffrey Boutwell and Michael Klare (Lanham, MD: Rowman & Littlefield, 1999), 108.

partly from domestic lawmaking in various countries. In 1992, a leader of the Sporting Shooters' Association of Australia (SSAA) addressed the NRA's annual meeting. Under attack at home, the Australians urged a global network to "protect... the rights of firearms owners wherever they are threatened." The NRA agreed, helping found the International Conference on Firearms Legislation (ICFL) in 1993, long before a formal control network formed. As top NRA official Tanya Metaksa later stated, "When guns are being confiscated in Australia and Britain... N.R.A. members must stand shoulder to shoulder to defend the Second Amendment."[10]

Gun forces also viewed early international control efforts as threats. As NRA official Thomas Mason stated, "any U.N. action is bound to affect national firearms legislation in this country.... Our position is that gun-control is an internal matter – and an extremely complex subject." International standards endangered not only civil rights but also unique cultures, with "non-hunting societies... seek[ing] to impose their values on hunting societies." As the Canadian Institute for Legislative Action's Tony Bernardo later put it, global controls would hogtie a "land which was founded with a rifle in one hand and a beaver pelt in another." To further authenticate these concerns, Bernardo referred to Canada's indigenous populations who "in the harsh regions of the country's north, depend on firearms for their protection." Gun groups have also expressed more cosmopolitan motivations. In the words of NRA Executive Director Wayne LaPierre, the "innocent have a right to own firearms to defend themselves anywhere and everywhere."[11]

[10] SSAA official quoted in Goldring, "Domestic Laws," 111, n. 53; Metaksa quoted in Katharine Q. Seelye, "National Rifle Association Is Turning to World Stage to Fight Gun Control," *New York Times*, Apr. 2, 1997, http://query.nytimes.com/gst/fullpage.html?res=9901E6DE163DF931A35757C0A961958260&sec=&spon=&pagewanted=all.

[11] Mason quoted in Thalif Deen, "NRA Fighting U.N. over Weapons Curb," InterPress Service, Aug. 4, 1997, http://www.monitor.net/monitor/9708a/nra-un.html; Bernardo quoted in UN, "Civil Society Groups Highlight Impact of Firearms Injuries, Gun Ownership Rights in Small Arms Conference Debate," press release, DC/2792, July 16, 2001; LaPierre, *The Global War*

Beyond such moral motives lay material factors. For arms manufacturers, it is good business to minimize regulations. Gun rights groups, who take a more public role, also used foreign bogeymen to shock their constituencies into opening their wallets. As the NRA's Metaksa stated in 1997: "We put it in some of our mail – that the U.N. has this ongoing effort, funded by the Japanese and managed by the Canadians, to regulate guns worldwide." Nine years later, Wayne LaPierre reviled the UN as "the most lethal threat ever to our Second Amendment rights," as "complicit in genocide," and as "pro-terroris[t]" – the hyperbole suggesting that the NRA uses a global bugbear to shake its national money tree.[12]

In 1997, ICFL was superseded by the World Forum on the Future of Sport Shooting Activities (WFSA), spanning gun rights groups, sport shooting associations, and gun manufacturers. Linked to the NRA, WFSA's early members included five other U.S. firearms groups, as well as gun sports and manufacturers organizations from Belgium, France, Germany, Italy, Netherlands, and the United Kingdom. WFSA saw its main challenges as UN efforts to "promote international gun control schemes" as well as "proposed gun bans" that could "end . . . shooting sports in several nations." Among its first activities, the fledgling WFSA would "establish a presence" at UN forums to "insure that correct and unbiased information is available."[13]

In short, by the mid-1990s, two rival blocs confronted one another, both motivated by moral and material considerations and both spanning NGOs, states, and, in the control case, the

on Your Guns: Inside the U.N. Plan to Destroy the Bill of Rights (Nashville: Nelson Current, 2006), 185.

[12] Metaksa quoted in Seelye, "National Rifle Association"; LaPierre, *Global War*, 59, 149, 185.

[13] NRA-ILA, "World Forum on the Future of Sportshooting Activities Established," Fax Alert 4, no. 28, July 11, 1997, quoted in Goldring, "Domestic Laws," 112, n. 62; "World Forum Seeks to Save Sport Shooting," *Gun News Digest*, Fall 1997, 20, quoted in ibid, 112, n. 61. See also WFSA, "About WFSA," http://www.wfsa.net/about.html.

UN bureaucracy. Locked in combat, each shaped how the other defined the issues, organized itself, and struggled for its goals.

Conflicting Crises

Gun Crisis

To take the control side first, both the nascent crime prevention and disarmament networks faced the same strategic dilemma: how to construct the problem. On one hand, leading activists affirmed that it was major: gun "proliferation" is "one of the most important and least studied international security problems of the post–Cold War era."[14] On the other hand, apart from such stock claims, the problem's other aspects were ambiguous. In formulating these, the two distinct control networks took different tacks, influenced by their own internal politics and by potential foes' anticipated reactions.

This dynamic is clearest for disarmament advocates. With many based in countries having strong domestic gun lobbies, they were well aware that making small arms control a global issue would further inflame resistance. As Natalie Goldring told me, "We always assumed that there would be opposition, . . . that any talk of controlling small arms and light weapons was going to bring us into the domestic debate here" in the United States. Indeed, she wrote as much in 1997, reviewing ICFL activities and urging strategies to "overcome domestic obstacles," including those of "'pro-gun' groups such as the National Rifle Association." Even at the AAAS's original 1994 meeting, participants flagged the "difficulties of enacting and enforcing strong international controls . . . when domestic gun control legislation is so contentious."[15]

---

[14] Boutwell, Klare, and Reed, *Lethal Commerce*, 9, 13.
[15] Natalie J. Goldring, Georgetown University; former staff member, British American Security Institute (BASIC), Washington, personal interview, May 11, 2006, Washington, DC (audiotape); Natalie J. Goldring, "Links between Domestic Laws and International Light Weapons Control," AAAS and CCPDC conference on Controlling the Global Trade in Light Weapons, Washington, DC, Dec. 11–12, 1997, http://www.basicint.org/WT/plw/97-links_

At first, therefore, the nascent network opted for a constrained description of the problem. This was contentious, with some activists such as Goldring doubting that it would limit resistance. In 1994-98, however, the dominant approach to dealing with opponents was avoidance. As Edward Laurance stated, "We did not want to legitimize the NRA internationally. We didn't think the [NRA] had anything to do with anything. . . . It detracts from these very real problems we have [in conflict zones] where there is no structure, no capacity. . . . It's a tremendous amount of energy wasted." The budding disarmament network therefore narrowed the issue, as exemplified in the 1997 report of the UN's panel of governmental experts. First, the panel limited it geographically, to the "most protracted armed conflicts," with "a recurring cycle of violence, an erosion of political legitimacy and a loss of economic viability." Second, aware that responsible parties use guns to quell violence, the panel restricted the problem to "excessive and destabilizing accumulations." These "exacerbat[ed] conflicts by increasing the lethality and duration of violence." Finally, the panel constricted the definition of small arms: weapons manufactured to "military specification for use as lethal instruments of war."[16]

The disarmament network also tailored its solutions to avoid antagonizing gun groups. Activists such as Laurance realized that a "blanket ban" in an "age of increasingly brutal ethnic conflicts" would be a "nonstarter." Rather, "proliferation" should be fought by "disposal and destruction" of "excess" arms in "post-conflict" sites. More fundamentally, the international community should curb the weapons' trade with war-torn countries.

between.htm; Boutwell, Klare, and Reed, *Lethal Commerce*, 11. See also R. T. Naylor, "The Structure and Operation of the Modern Arms Black Market," in Boutwell, Klare, and Reed, *Lethal Commerce*, 44.
[16] Edward Laurance, Dean, Graduate School of International Policy Studies, Monterey Institute of International Studies, Monterey; former consultant, UN Department of Disarmament Affairs, telephone interview, June 8, 2007 (audiotape); UN, "Report of the Panel of Governmental Experts," Foreword by Secretary General, paras. 1, 17, 20, 24, 28. See also Boutwell, Klare, and Reed, *Lethal Commerce*, 11. For a contrary view, see Goldring, "Domestic Laws," 118.

Some activists called for restrictions on both legal and illegal commerce, but most, including the UN panel, proposed only policies covering "illicit" manufacturing and trafficking. Some of these measures potentially had broader applications, but the target was illegal trade in conflict zones.[17]

By contrast, ECOSOC's early crime prevention efforts defined the gun crisis expansively: excessive civilian gun possession and permissive gun laws worldwide. ECOSOC also mooted sweeping solutions: limits of one firearm per person; upper as well as lower age restrictions on ownership; and a ban on private gun collections.[18] Why did ECOSOC at first define the problem so broadly, whereas the disarmament activists had opted for narrower constructions? For years, the crime control process was dominated by the Japanese, with their strict domestic controls, weak arms lobby, and lingering outrage over the Hattori killing. In addition, the United States took a hands-off approach to the ECOSOC process early on, and the NRA had little ability to influence the Clinton administration prior to formal negotiations in the late 1990s. In short, whereas the disarmament network at first sought to defuse conflict, leaders of the ECOSOC process, less worried about foes, did not calibrate their approach.

Gun Ban Crisis

In reaction, the NRA and other firearms proponents denounced ECOSOC's crime prevention efforts as "absurd" and "radical." In addition, they attacked the disarmament network. Far from being assured by the splitting of crime and disarmament processes, advocates lumped them together as a single threat to "your guns."[19] They denied almost every aspect of the small arms problem. Most important, they portrayed the solutions

[17] Edward J. Laurance, "Addressing the Negative Consequences of Light Weapons Trafficking: Opportunities for Transparency and Restraint," in Boutwell, Klare, and Reed, *Lethal Commerce*, 149; UN, "Report of the Panel of Governmental Experts," para. 79, 80.

[18] UN ECOSOC, "Criminal Justice Reform and Strengthening of Legal Institutions: Measures to Regulate Firearms," E/CN.15/1998/4, 1998, 5.

[19] LaPierre, *Global War*, 33, 34.

proposed by the control network as a competing crisis – a global gun ban.

The assault began with definitions. Controls must not cover civilian weaponry, which should be construed broadly, including firearms used in all manner of legal pursuits whatever their percussiveness. As for the limitation to those "designed for military purposes," advocates such as Dave Kopel scoffed that "almost all guns are derivative of military designs" and warned that the language was "a wedge for near-total gun prohibition." "Excessive and destabilizing accumulation" of weapons? The terms were ambiguous and begged whether there could ever be too many guns. Nor did prohibiting sales to conflict zones bring comfort. Freedom fighters need arms! More generally, as we shall see, gun advocates impugned the control side's studies on everything from factual issues such as casualty figures to causal matters such as the relationship between guns and crime.[20]

Just as vehemently, the gun groups stigmatized the control network's solutions. This happened at every level, starting with their effectiveness, epitomized by contemptuous critiques that "gun destruction" days drew only unusable or archaic weapons. The most impassioned broadsides concerned repercussions. Banning guns would produce human rights and security disasters. It would leave innocents around the world vulnerable to crime, repression, and genocide—arguments I detail in the section on clashing frames.

To summarize, disarmament activists failed in their strategic attempt to minimize hostility. The gun network mobilized anyway. Only on the blandest points was there agreement. Gun advocates such as Dave Kopel concurred that the illicit trade was wrong; they had no truck with criminals. They also agreed "at the

---

[20] Dave Kopel, "Score One for Bush: A U.N. Conference Concludes without Too Much Permanent Damage," *National Review Online*, July 30, 2001, http://old.nationalreview.com/kopel/kopel073001.shtml. See also Mason quoted in Deen, "NRA Fighting U.N." Notably, even staunch supporters of control, such as the Small Arms Survey, have admitted that some of the "first efforts to articulate estimates" for such issues as "global firearm totals" used "nothing more than a sense of feel" to reach their conclusions. SAS, *Survey 2007*, 41.

highest level of generality" that prohibiting arms sales to human rights violators is a "very good idea." In the same breath, however, they railed that authoritarian governments "have extreme laws against citizen gun ownership" and claimed that control forces sought to push the world in that despotic direction.[21]

Gun Crisis Reinvented

In this contentious context, leaders of the informal disarmament network opted to institutionalize, just as the gun groups had done earlier with ICFL and WFSA. In 1998, they established the International Action Network on Small Arms (IANSA), merging the distinct disarmament and crime prevention networks – a lumping that the gun groups had already made. Critically, this merger broadened the disarmament network's goals and openly challenged firearms advocates. For that reason, some disarmament activists opposed the expanded mission. The young IANSA, however, came to include powerful domestic gun control organizations. Their leaders, long at odds with national gun groups, opted for confrontation, rather than avoidance, as the preferred strategy for IANSA.

This shift in the disarmament network's identity began inadvertently. When Edward Laurance attended the signing ceremony for the Landmines Treaty in December 1997, he asked one of its sponsors, Canadian Foreign Minister Lloyd Axworthy, to support a small arms campaign. Axworthy encouraged Laurance: "'Get a critical mass of NGOs [to] sign up...and I'll fund a meeting [to] start the campaign.'" Laurance soon established the online Preparatory Committee for a Global Campaign on the Spread and Unlawful Use of Small Arms and Light Weapons (Project PrepCom). As Laurance put it, "When I started the website, I'm looking for *anybody*...to get Axworthy to sign on." By 1999, he had attracted 129 NGOs. Many came from the developing world and some from conflict zones. (For Brazil,

---

[21] Dave Kopel, "UN to World: You Have No Human Right to Self Defense," *America's 1st Freedom*, Nov. 2006, 26, http://www.davekopel.org/2A/Foreign/UN-To-World.htm.

see Chapter 6.) These groups were useful in authenticating the issues and legitimating the network, which previously had been dominated by Northerners from countries at peace. But some new members had little knowledge of disarmament, joining for other reasons. As Laurance put it, "NGOs started coming to us – they're always begging. . . . They needed money, and they were looking at a budding international organization." In some cases, they joined without believing in PrepCom's goals. A leader of a Nicaraguan group asked Laurance incredulously: "'You want to . . . take all the guns out of Nicaragua so only the police are left with them? . . . Come down and spend a week with the police and try to imagine what it will be like.'" Nonetheless, the Nicaraguan signed onto PrepCom.[22]

In addition to attracting new and needy NGOs, PrepCom accepted large and established gun control groups from the United States, Canada, and Australia. With their entry, however, conflict developed over the network's mission – a debate conducted with strategic concerns about WFSA and the NRA very much in mind. Laurance and other disarmament hands argued against confusing ruthless insurgencies and government death squads with criminals, accident victims, and suicides. Lumping the two would stir more opposition, internationalize unproductive domestic gun debates, and blur the network's core humanitarian aims. But national groups, led by Canada's powerful Coalition for Gun Control, pushed a more aggressive approach. They allied with a minority of disarmament activists who had long questioned the feasibility of avoiding confrontation. Little familiar with international disarmament, the national groups portrayed the two issues as one: *The Global Gun Epidemic: From Saturday Night Specials to AK-47s*, as a later book by domestic

---

[22] Information and quotations from Laurance interview (emphasis original). See also Project PrepCom, http://web.archive.org/web/19990429182831/www .prepcom.org/text/index.html; Aaron Karp, "Laudable Failure," *SAIS Review* 22, no. 1 (2002): 177–93, 185–86; Denise Garcia, *Small Arms and Security: New Emerging International Norms* (New York: Routledge, 2006), 50–51.

activists is titled. Nor did these organizations quail at provoking the gun lobby, who they had long combated at home.[23]

Indeed, participants at IANSA's founding conference went out of their way to goad. The new network should "reduc[e] the availability of weapons to civilians"; "discourage gun possession and use"; "delegitimiz[e] the possession of weapons"; "eliminat[e] the reliance and use of private arms for self-defence"; and "'stigmatiz[e]' actions of state and non-state actors seen to be contributing to the problem of small arms."[24] Stoking the fire, IANSA's facilitation committee chose Rebecca Peters, an official at George Soros' Open Society Institute and a former chairperson of Australia's National Coalition for Gun Control, as the network's first head. With Peters's recent success at bringing stringent controls to Australia, few figures would have been more likely to enrage gun groups.

In the end, IANSA veered far from the original vision. Disarmament advocates had inaugurated it in the name of international humanitarianism, with a strategy of avoiding unrelated squabbles over gun control in peaceful countries. With the addition of powerful new members already engaged in those conflicts, however, the old approach fell by the wayside. In all this, the threat and reality of opposition shaped the very nature of the control network and its definitions of the problem.

Competing Mobilization

IANSA quickly became the lynchpin of the transnational control movement. Central to its activism is the view that "gun proliferation is a global problem" and therefore requires a "global

---

[23] Laurance interview; Wendy Cukier and Victor W. Sidel, *The Global Gun Epidemic: From Saturday Night Specials to AK-47s* (New York: Praeger, 2005).

[24] International NGO Consultation, "Report on an International NGO Consultation on Small Arms Action," Lake Couchiching, Canada, Aug. 17–19, 1998, http://www.ploughshares.ca/libraries/Control/Couchiching.html#Participants.

solution." Based in London, it enjoys funding from major foundations and governments, especially in Europe. In 2008, it had more than 800 member organizations in more than 100 countries. On this basis, IANSA claims to "represent the voices of civil society on the international stage."[25]

To marshal them, IANSA trumpets the perils of proliferation and the virtues of control. Slaughter will continue unless we "stop the global gun crisis." More pointedly, IANSA uses the threat posed by the pro-gun network to energize and enlarge its own. IANSA portrays itself as a valiant David fighting a sinister, gun-slinging Goliath: the "overpowering" NRA whose "immense clout" is a "greater force than all the 180 [control] NGOs [at the UN] combined," as Aaron Karp put it. To call attention to the menace, IANSA has even faced off against the NRA in person. Consider the "Great Gun Debate," a live, internationally televised wrangle between NRA Executive Director Wayne LaPierre and IANSA leader Rebecca Peters in October 2004. There was strong disagreement about the debate's wisdom within IANSA. Peters, however, decided that the NRA was enough of a bogeyman in Europe that a high-profile exchange would advance the cause. In the aftermath, IANSA has made an edited transcript available on its Web site.[26]

Simultaneously, IANSA seized opportunities to embarrass and unbuild the enemy network – and mobilize its own. In this, it highlighted what it considered to be outrageous and extreme statements made by the gun groups. In early 2007, the draft of an NRA fundraising pamphlet, "Freedom in Peril," leaked

---

[25] IANSA, "UN Arms Talks Meltdown: Conference Allows Global Gun Crisis to Continue," press release, July 7, 2006, http://www.iansa.org/un/review2006/ documents/IANSA%20press%20release%20-7%20July%202006_.pdf (quoting Rebecca Peters); IANSA, "What Is IANSA," http://www.iansa.org/ about.htm.

[26] Aaron Karp, "Small Arms: Back to the Future," *Brown Journal of World Affairs* IX, no. 1 (2002): 179–91, 186; Rebecca Peters, Director, IANSA, personal interview, July 7, 2006, New York, NY (audiotape); Starcast Productions Ltd., "The Great UN Gun Debate," DVD, 2004; IANSA, "IANSA Director in Gun Debate with the NRA," http://www.iansa.org/action/nra_debate .htm.

to the press. Replete with inflammatory rhetoric and unflattering caricatures, "Freedom in Peril" opened by describing the UN and IANSA as "part of a marching axis of adversaries far darker and more dangerous than gun owners have ever known." Days later, IANSA topped its Web site with a link to the online version of this "scathing attack on gun control advocates, NGOs, the United Nations, feminists and the media."[27] It is unlikely that these statements gave pause to the gun network, but they raised questions among wider audiences and roused control advocates to stronger efforts.

On the other hand, with IANSA's formation, control forces drew intense fire. WFSA expanded, by 2007 including thirty-eight national organizations and forging ties to others, such as those in Brazil, who could not afford its dues. America's NRA remained WFSA's most outspoken member, but other country's gun groups supported its views even if they did not voice them as boldly. In some cases, these domestic organizations owed their membership in WFSA to the NRA. As Tony Bernardo, Executive Director of the Canadian Institute for Legislative Action (CILA), reported to his members in 2001:

We have worked hand in hand with the NRA regarding international issues for the past three and a half years. In fact, the NRA was instrumental in the formation of CILA and was one of our sponsors into the World Forum.... The NRA provides CILA with tremendous amounts of logistic support.... The NRA Constitution prevents them from providing money. They freely give us anything else.[28]

Domestic organizations used the threat of IANSA to stoke support. Reversing the control groups' David-and-Goliath imagery, the NRA portrayed itself as a callow "newcomer" to an international process driven by a "frightening network of activists"

---

[27] NRA, "Freedom in Peril: Guarding the 2nd Amendment in the 21st Century," 2007, 1, http://www.boingboing.net/images/NR-F8_PERILFINAL.pdf; IANSA, "Additions to the site: 05.01.07, http://www.iansa.org/whats-new/new1-7jan2007.htm.

[28] CILA, "Defending Canada's Heritage," Cdn-Firearms Digest 3, no. 897, July 11, 2001, http://www.canfirearms.ca/archives/text/v03n800-899/v03n897.txt.

and "career bureaucrats...whose jobs depend on negotiating agreements, not making principled stands." Worse, firearms proponents were "vastly underfunded compared to the billions of dollars received by NGOs in 'international aid and development' grants." Underwriting the nefarious plots were IANSA's "sugar daddy" George Soros, various "left-wing foundations," and "socialist" European governments.[29]

Just like control forces, gun groups use unbuilding tactics to malign their enemy and draw support to themselves. They have spotlighted such statements as Rebecca Peters's – if shooters "miss your sport" after firearms are restricted, they should "take up another" – to build belief that IANSA and the UN seek a "global gun ban." They specialize in name-calling and unflattering photographs aimed at making the diminutive Rebecca Peters look sinister. More generally, the NRA derides global gun control as, among other things, an "old socialist fantas[y]." Singled out to tar IANSA is one of its financers, the Samuel Rubin Foundation, because its namesake, "not coincidentally, was a member of the Communist Party U.S.A."[30] Whether these attacks deter potential IANSA members is unclear, but their intentions are broader – galvanizing their own constituents and sowing doubts about the enemy among outside audiences.

Manipulating Institutions

Biasing the United Nations

From 1999 onward, the two networks would tussle repeatedly. Battles broke out in many democracies, with Brazil, discussed in the next chapter, a major theater. In organizations such as the Organization of American States, fights raged over regional control conventions. Most importantly, debate roiled the UN, where both crime prevention and disarmament bureaucracies continued their work separately even after IANSA came to encompass the two civil society networks.

---

[29] LaPierre, *Global War*, xxiv, 13, 8, 11, xxii.
[30] LaPierre, *Global War*, xxi, xxii, 1–4, 11, 35.

For IANSA, the UN was a logical institutional choice, given its global reach and symbolic value. The UN's centrality also reflected the extent to which it was part of the control network itself. Like the civil society activists with whom it worked, the UN promoted the small arms problem and international controls. It was by no means neutral.

For firearms organizations, therefore, the UN was hostile territory. To see this, according to NRA leader Wayne LaPierre, one need look no further than the "infamous" knotted gun sculpture squatting balefully outside UN headquarters. Indeed, groups such as Gun Owners of America refused to legitimate the UN by their presence. They worked to defund or otherwise cripple the organization. In the mid-1990s, however, first the NRA and then other gun organizations began monitoring the UN. By November 1996, the NRA had received NGO consultative status at ECOSOC. Given the NRA's derision of the UN, this application was strategic, a case of plugging one's nose to "get into the dialogue at an earlier point in time and have a voice in the process rather than just reacting to proposals," as Tanya Metaksa stated. WFSA received ECOSOC roster status in 2002.[31]

Notably, control advocates, aware of the NRA's ECOSOC application in the 1990s, considered contesting it. It was not just that the gun group disparaged UN diplomacy. By some lights, it undercut the UN's mission. After lengthy debate, however, the activists decided not to mount a challenge. It would have consumed scarce resources and stood little chance of success. Worse, it might have backfired, handing gun groups a potent argument: that control forces craved to skew participation and squelch debate.[32]

These concerns did not stop the UN itself from limiting or excluding civil society, however. Superficially applying to all

---

[31] LaPierre, *Global War*, 27; Larry Pratt, Executive Director, Gun Owners of America, personal interview, Apr. 23, 2009, Pittsburgh, PA (audiotape); Metaksa quoted in Seelye, "National Rifle Association." The country of Luxembourg donated the knotted gun sculpture to the UN to commemorate the 1980 shooting of John Lennon.

[32] Goldring interview.

NGOs, these efforts hit gun groups hardest, given the UN's close ties to the control network. The effects were greatest in the crime prevention process, with ECOSOC voting in 1995 to limit NGO participation to four closely managed workshops. The NRA disputed this "systematic exclusion" of NGOs, ridiculing the UN's claim that "sensitive 'law enforcement matters' were being discussed."[33] To little avail: the workshops became the primary forum for civil society input. At the negotiations themselves, NGOs were excluded, although both pro-gun and pro-control groups used governmental ties to watch the UN and influence home state positions.

In 1997 in the UN's disarmament process, the Panel of Governmental Experts also planned to restrict NGO participation, but the NRA prevented it from doing so. Days before the Panel's first meeting, it flooded the Japanese mission, whose Ambassador Donowaki led the Panel, with written harangues from hundreds of NRA members. These reviled the UN as antidemocratic and upbraided top diplomats as high-handed. Shocked by this outpouring, Donowaki revised the rules and unsealed the process. As one disarmament advocate admitted, the NRA was "way ahead of all the other NGOs that were in favor of control."[34] Of course, in opening the issues, the NRA primarily helped its own, because control forces were close to the UN bureaucracy.

More aggressively, gun groups have sought to bully the UN into inaction. In 1997, NRA official Thomas Mason intimated that the group might stir up Congress, where "the topic of U.S. participation in the United Nations has undergone considerable debate." As Gun Owners of America noted in 2006 prior to a major UN meeting, Louisiana Republican Senator David Vitter had introduced the Second Amendment Protection Act to "withhold funding" from the UN if it "abridges" the U.S. Constitution. Vitter's bill never became law, but these and other threats put the UN on the defensive.[35]

---

[33] LaPierre, *Global War*, 33.
[34] Laurance interview. See generally LaPierre, *Global War*, 22.
[35] Mason quoted in Deen, "NRA Fighting UN"; Gun Owners of America, "UN 4th of July Gun Control Threat & Agenda," press release, June 7, 2006, http://gunowners.org/a060706.htm.

Skewing States

Although the UN bureaucracy had some autonomy on the small arms issue, binding international measures hinged on consensus decision making by states. Knowing this, both sides built close ties to key governments, primarily through domestic politics. For control forces, this meant linkages to political parties and bureaucrats in countries such as the United Kingdom, Canada, Netherlands, Sweden, Colombia, and South Africa. At times, IANSA members won seats on national delegations; at other times, sympathetic delegates kept IANSA apprised of negotiations among states. These contacts in turn have helped the control network set agendas and advance issues. Of course, the gun groups portray this in a different light, claiming that "the largest and most influential NGOs serve as puppet-masters for delegates who support their extremist agendas."[36]

Gun groups, too, seek influence on national delegations, especially the United States, but also others such as New Zealand and Switzerland. On an ongoing basis, WFSA members educate generalist diplomats about firearms minutiae and warn them of threatening UN developments. At international conferences, the George W. Bush administration invited top NRA members, such as Congressman Bob Barr, as "public" members on the American delegation. Meanwhile, they denied applications from American control advocates, such as the Center for Defense Information's Rachel Stohl. Whether the NRA should be considered the United States' puppet-master on international gun issues is unclear. But the U.S. government, especially under Republican administrations, listens to the NRA and often acts as the group wishes.[37]

Clashing Frames

Epidemic and Abuse

Notwithstanding these efforts to sway states beforehand, each side deploys an arsenal of arguments – scientific, historical, legal,

---

[36] La Pierre, *Global War*, x.
[37] Rachel Stohl, Senior Analyst, Center for Defense Information, telephone interview, May 10, 2006 (audiotape). See also LaPierre, *Global War*, xiii, 32.

and moral – as it seeks to advance its goals and destroy its foes. From early on, control activists sought scientific certification of their political goals, preparing studies on everything from the quantity of guns, to the value of the arms trade, to the number of shooting victims. By the 2000s, leading studies came from an epistemic community led by the UN Disarmament Commission and the Small Arms Survey (SAS). The latter, funded by European states supporting controls, bills itself as the "principal international source of impartial and public information" on small arms. The network also tapped moral authorities such as Archbishop Desmond Tutu and Hollywood celebrities such as UN Messenger of Peace Michael Douglas to deplore the illicit trade as "an issue that affects us all . . . fuel[ing] conflict, crime and violence."[38]

IANSA depicted small arms as a public health emergency: "1000 Killed Every Day," as one advocacy poster declared. The cure for this "epidemic" of injury and death? Slash gun ownership, and restrict the firearms trade. In addition, the network grafted small arms onto popular human rights concerns. Amnesty International and Human Rights Watch leant their authority, certifying the casualty toll as a major rights problem. Control proponents also transformed insurgents and terrorists into pernicious poster children for their proposal that only governments should be able to purchase small arms. As Canadian Foreign Affairs Minister Lloyd Axworthy argued, "non-state actors," should not be "armed and equipped as though they were armies themselves." For Axworthy, this held true even for movements "opposing repressive regimes [that] could legally arm themselves against their people." Stringent controls would assure that the "defining image of the 21st century is not that of ragged children aiming AK-47s at one another across a village street."[39]

---

[38] SAS, "About the Small Arms Survey," http://www.smallarmssurvey.org/about-us/mission.html; UN, "UN Messenger of Peace Michael Douglas Features in Public Service Announcement to Draw Attention to Illicit Trade in Small Arms, Light Weapons," press release, DC/3025, May 26, 2006.

[39] IANSA, "Gun Violence: A Global Epidemic," 2006, www.iansa.org/documents/2006/Gun-violence-a-global-epidemic.pdf; Axworthy, "Notes

For IANSA members, such controls must be international. Guns "do not respect borders," as the Million Mom March's Mary Leigh Blek told the UN. Those sold in indulgent jurisdictions such as the United States easily find their way to more regulated shores. As such, America's Second Amendment was an eighteenth-century anachronism – and a twenty-first-century aberration, if not abomination. Sharp restrictions on civilian possession, such as those in Japan, Britain, and Australia and in the prototype national laws put forth by activists, should be the model for forward-thinking societies. Only global solutions could solve the global problem.[40]

Genocide and Rights

The firearms network rejected all this. Most broadly, its members denied the existence of a "global gun crisis," instead warning that the control network's proposed solutions would constitute a "global gun ban." Regarding science, the NRA's LaPierre acknowledged the Small Arms Survey as a "dangerous [and] formidable foe" because of its "resources, credibility, and relationship to the UN." The shooting groups, however, developed their own epistemic community. This included WFSA's "project on myths" and encompassed scholars unaffiliated with SAS or

for an Address...to the International NGO Consultations on Small Arms Action," Aug. 19, 1998, http://wo1.international.gc.ca/Minpub/ PublicationContentOnly.asp?publication_id=375752&Language= E&MODE=CONTENTONLY&Local=False. Cf. the 1890 Brussels Convention, prohibiting arms exports to colonial Africa, ostensibly to control the slave trade but also to keep guns from nationalists (H.C. Engelbrecht and F.C. Hanighen, *Merchants of Death* (New York: Dodd, Mead: 1934), 267). For a critique of Axworthy's view from a control proponent, see Karp, "Laudable Failure," 179.

40 Blek quoted in UN, "Civil Society Groups Highlight Impact of Firearms Injuries, Gun Ownership Rights in Small Arms Conference Debate," press release, DC/2792. July 16, 2001. See generally Rebecca Peters, "The Great Gun Debate," Oct. 12, 2004, edited transcript at http://www.iansa.org/action/ nra_debate.htm; Parliamentary Forum on Small Arms and Light Weapons and CLAVE (Latin American Coalition for the Prevention of Armed Violence), "Model Law on Firearms, Ammunition and Related Materials," http://www.parliamentaryforum.org/.

the UN. Holding conferences and publishing in peer-reviewed outlets, they hacked away at the control network's authorities, dismantling their methods, disputing their findings, and dismissing their prescriptions. At the UN, Germany's Forum Waffenrecht and other gun groups used statistical evidence to reject any asserted relationship "between the number of firearms and the misuse of firearms, legal or illegal." Others challenged such basic "facts" as the number of firearms deaths worldwide.[41]

To counter the control network's celebrity endorsements, WFSA's image committee promoted "a true and accurate portrayal of the... heritage of the shooting sports." Annually, it honors a shooter who has made the greatest "social contribution" – luminaries such as the 2007 winner, Justice Antonin Scalia, who one year later wrote a landmark U.S. Supreme Court decision holding that Americans have an individual Constitutional right to own firearms.[42]

To fight the control groups' human rights appeal, the gun network framejacked, retorting that lack of arms is the real violation. As the NRA's LaPierre argued in dozens of footnote-studded pages, Rwanda's Tutsis, Indonesia's East Timorese, and Papua-New Guinea's Bougainvilleans suffered butchery in the 1990s because they did not have guns to protect themselves. Nor had a "morally bankrupt" international arms embargo on Yugoslavia stopped the fighting; instead, it had hastened the slaughter of defenseless people. The best preventive? Arm vulnerable populations! LaPierre put it baldly: "If every family on this planet owned a good-quality rifle, genocide would be on the path to extinction." Seizing on a major human rights cause of

---

[41] LaPierre, *Global War*, 12; WFSA, "Statistics: Program on Myths," http://www.wfsa.net/statistics.html; Forum Waffenrecht statement quoted in UN, "Civil Society Groups"; Kopel, Gallant, & Eisen, "How Many Global Deaths from Arms?" See also John R. Lott, Jr., *More Guns, Less Crime: Understanding Crime and Gun Control Laws* (Chicago: University of Chicago Press, 1998); Joseph P. Tartaro, "US Election Didn't Put an End To Global Gun Control Threat," *GunWeek.com*, Jan. 20, 2005, http://www.gunweek.com/2005/hso12005.html.

[42] WFSA, "Image Committee," http://www.wfsa.net/image.html; "Global Sport Shooting Group Honors Scalia," *New Gun Week*, Apr. 10, 2007, 1.

the 2000s, he advocated outfitting Darfur's refugees to "drive off the Janjaweed who come to . . . plunder, murder, and rape." That the UN did not do so demonstrated that the "international gun prohibition movement" is "morally blinded by its obsessive hatred of guns and gun owners."[43]

More generally, the gun network charged that the control side twisted the entire concept of human rights. Witness "the UN Plan to Destroy the Bill of Rights," NRA shorthand for the UN small arms process. Nor was this simply a matter of individual rights under attack. The UN also threatened the "cherished heritage" of vulnerable "hunting cultures," as WFSA warned. Those cultures should have the right to determine gun regulations grounded in their own histories and democratic processes. Viewed this way, the Second Amendment is not an anachronism, a blot, or a blip. It is "America's first freedom" – and the "birthright of all humankind."[44]

Seizing the offensive at UN conferences in 2001 and 2006, firearms groups also sought to shame the gun control forces into accepting another human right – to self-defense. One of the "inalienable natural rights of peaceful, law-abiding people," it has been recognized for millennia, according to Brazilian activist Jairo Paes de Lira. For the NRA's Wayne LaPierre, only the "U.N. and its proxies such as IANSA" could stand against this "vision of civilization" that "God inscribes on every human heart." Only the UN could float the "barbaric principle" that "self-defense is a privilege that the government can and should take away."[45]

---

[43] LaPierre, *Global War*, 98–104; 125–49, 136, 158, 148–49.

[44] LaPierre, *Global War*, 226; WFSA, "About." See generally Mason quoted in Deen, "NRA Fighting UN"; David B. Kopel, "U.N. to World: You Have No Human Right to Self-Defense," *America's 1st Freedom*, Nov. 2006, 26–29, 62–63, http://www.davekopel.com/2a/Foreign/UN-To-World .htm.

[45] Jairo Paes de Lira, Brazilian Coalition for Self Defense (Coalizão Brasileira Pela Legítima Defesa [PLD]), "A Mandate from Brazil," statement to UN Small Arms Review Conference, June 30, 2006, http://www.un.org/ events/smallarms2006/ngos.html; LaPierre, *Global War*, 185. See also Kopel,

But the barbarians begged to differ, refusing to be shamed and ridiculing the idea that more guns would mean less crime, let alone less genocide. As one Argentine activist told the UN, "Where I come from, firearms lead to violence and inequality . . . to [a] silent genocide." Stung by the gun groups' hijacking the human rights frame and trumpeting the right to self-defense, the UN counterattacked. In 2001, its Subcommission on the Promotion and Protection of Human Rights appointed a special rapporteur, law professor Barbara Frey, to report on "prevention of human rights violations committed with small arms and light weapons" and to authoritatively ascertain whether international law supported a human right to self-defense. After years of research, study, and consultation, Frey rejected such a right, holding too that international law did not require states to permit individuals to possess firearms for self-defense.[46]

In turn, the gun groups repudiated her work. They scorned the report as one-sided – its UN remit, only to study how firearms contribute to violations, not how they might avert them. They condemned its findings as "Orwellian" – insinuating that "America's first freedom amounts to a human rights violation." And they maligned Frey as biased – systematically ignoring NRA and WFSA ideas and an IANSA member before her appointment.[47] In short, the special rapporteur's study, meant to be authoritative and thereby settle – or, in WFSA's view, squelch – debate, only impressed those who already believed in control.

Watching the Watchers
To step back from the Frey fray, it is notable that this and other incidents were only possible because both sides scrutinize one

---

"U.N. to World." For uses of the right to self-defense argument in Brazil's conflict over gun control, see chapter 6.

[46] Martin Appiolaza, Fundación espacios para el progreso social (Argentina), in UN, "Civil Society Groups"; UN, "Prevention of Human Rights Violations Committed with Small Arms and Light Weapons," A/HRC/Sub.1/58/27/, paras. 19–25 (2006). The UN study did find that international law recognizes self-defense as a defense to criminal responsibility.

[47] La Pierre, *Global War*, 11, 59, 141, 185. See also Kopel, "U.N. to World."

another's every move. The result is intimate knowledge of the enemy, gleaned from its publications, Web sites, and conferences. In 2002, long-time activist Aaron Karp wrote two searching articles on the control network. He observed that it had "triggered a response from gun advocates" and must now "contend with organized opposition." Noting the opposition's repeated accusations of "an international conspiracy to get rid of their guns," he sardonically suggested that control activists "become more as they are described."[48]

As Karp eyed the gun movement, so it watched him. A *Guns & Ammo* article analyzed not the UN process – but Karp's articles. Lauding him for an "insightful assessment" of the "anti-gun community," the authors claimed that those points revealed its malevolent goals: disarming civilians worldwide. Citing Karp's conspiracy quip as his "let[ting] the cat out of the bag," the article concluded with a ringing warning: "The price of liberty is eternal vigilance."[49]

Opposing Agendas

If the UN was the institution of choice for the control network, its centerpiece was the 2001 UN Conference on the Illicit Trade in Small Arms and Light Weapons in All its Aspects. Its planning, preparation, and follow-up, the 2006 Conference to Review the Implementation of the Programme of Action on the Illicit Trade in Small Arms and Light Weapons (RevCon), occupied the network – and its opponents – for years. The plan: enact a binding agreement that would curb the scourge of gun deaths worldwide. Even as the control network set its agenda, however, gun groups worked to unset it. In discussing these conflicting processes, I primarily take a thematic rather than chronological approach,

---

[48] Karp, "Small Arms: Back to the Future," 186, 190. See also Karp, "Laudable Failure."
[49] Paul Gallant and Joanne Eisen, "Global Gun Ban A Bust," *Guns & Ammo*, Oct. 2003, http://www.gunsandammomag.com/second_amendment/global_1028/.

analyzing events that occurred both at the 2001 conference and the 2006 RevCon, which I attended as an observer.

Sparring started early, with contention over the 2001 conference's scope, as denoted by its title. Aware of resistance, the UN limited it to the "Illicit Trade." There was solace for the control network, however: the "in All its Aspects" verbiage, tacked to the conference's name. Potentially this opened the conference to discussion of relationships between legal and illegal trade and to issues as diverse as women's rights, child soldiers, and development. As the date of the conference approached, its location – Geneva or New York – also drew debate. UN officials and IANSA members worried about the "potential effects of the presence . . . of the US National Rifle Association" at a conference held in America.[50] In the end, however, the Swiss withdrew their bid, and New York became the venue for both the conference and RevCon.

Overt agenda-setting began at three regional PrepComs held in the months prior to the 2001 conference. To promote its goals, IANSA provided its members with position papers for lobbying at the conclaves and, more importantly, in national institutions beforehand. The gun groups took similar actions, although they held much of their fire for the conferences themselves. As a result, the draft Programme of Action (PoA) for the 2001 conference looked promising for control groups – and "objectionable" to gun groups such as the NRA. Although no treaty was proposed, the draft urged that states bind themselves to reduce small arms stocks, restrict manufacture and trade, record transfers, bar sales to nonstate actors, and promote a "culture of peace."[51]

[50] Jenni Rissanen and Rebecca Johnson, "Low-Key First Committee Seeks to Maximise Common Ground," *Disarmament Diplomacy* 52, Nov. 2000, http://www.acronym.org.uk/52lowkey.htm.

[51] IANSA, "How to Use These Documents," n.d., 2006, http://www.iansa.org/un/review2006/documents-english.htm; NRA News, "Internal IANSA Talking Points Memo for UN Conference on Small Arms Control," n.d. 2006, http://www.nranews.com/article.aspx?article=16; LaPierre, *Global War*, 25; UN, Draft Programme of Action to Prevent, Combat and Eradicate the Illicit Trade in Small Arms and Light Weapons in All Its Aspects (Revised Working paper by the Chairman of the Preparatory Committee, February 9, 2001), A/Conf.192/PC/L.4.Rev.1, sec. II, para. 39.

At the two-week-long conference and RevCon, both sides deployed a host of parallel strategies and contrary arguments. In addition to infiltrating national delegations, they mobilized their broader support bases. Prior to the 2006 RevCon, the NRA set up a special Web site, the "Fire a Shot Heard 'Round the World on the 4th of July!" complete with grave Wayne LaPierre webcast decrying UN perfidy and urging members to contact their legislators and the UN. The NRA and Gun Owners of America (GOA) provided prewritten messages to their constituents. For its part, the British Shooting Sports Council (BSSC) met with diplomats at the Foreign and Commonwealth Office to "discuss issues in advance . . . which provided assurance that there would be no surprises on our side."[52]

At the conferences themselves, both sides publicized the issues, hoping to attract media attention and pressure delegates to support their goals. UN Secretary-General Kofi Annan opened the conferences, stressing, "[t]hese weapons may be small, but they cause mass destruction." One conference day, July 9, 2001, was declared "Small Arms and Light Weapons Destruction Day," with IANSA affiliates organizing gun crushings and burnings around the world. Gun groups fought back, however, declaring July 9 National Firearms Purchase Day. In *National Review Online*, activist Dave Kopel denounced gun destruction as tantamount to Nazi book burnings that eventuated in the "burning of Jews and other un-German people." Going further, he warned that the UN might soon condone state-sponsored executions of gun law violators, as it already allegedly had for drug law violators.[53]

Both sides rallied their contingents for the conferences. The UN provided a hallway for NGOs to mount displays and

[52] NRA, "Fire a Shot Heard 'Round the World on the 4th of July!" 2006, http://www.stopungunban.html (author's files); GOA, "Are Members of Congress Lying to You about the UN Threat on July 4th?," email alert, June 7, 2006, reprinted in http://spofga.org/2nd/2006/june/un_gun_control.php; BSSC, Annual Report, 2006, 16, http://www.bssc.org.uk/dox/BSSC%20Annual%20Report%202006.pdf.

[53] UN, "Secretary-General's Address to the UN Small Arms Review Conference," press release, June 26, 2006, http://www.un.org/apps/sg/sgstats.asp?nid=2106; Kopel, "Score One for Bush."

distribute pamphlets, buttons, decals, and CDs. There, inches from one another for days on end, activists glared. On occasion, they heaped scorn across the ideological divide. Rarely, they sought to educate or shame approachable-seeming opposite numbers. To little result: far from convincing anyone, the usual aftermath of these fruitless exercises was best described by Natalie Goldring at the 2006 RevCon: "I just want to leave, go home, and take a shower."[54]

Under pressure from both networks, the UN allowed civil society groups to make statements at the conferences. On the appointed days, a UN hall resounded to the statistics, pleas, and attacks of forty NGOs. Germany's Forum Waffenrecht argued that "to eradicate firearms from societies means to disarm law-abiding citizens and encourage criminals." America's Single Action Shooting Society made the case for indigenous customs: "cowboy action shooting is part of our country's culture." Million Mom March leader Mary Leigh Blek gritted her teeth through these orations, then had this to say: "The gun lobby has been talking for 40 minutes. During that time, 40 people around the world have been shot dead with the weapons they promote and sell. That figure...is further proof that this country is at war."[55]

More publicly, both sides mobilized their constituents, raising pseudo-democratic claims. For the 2006 conference, the Control Arms campaign, led by IANSA, Oxfam International, and Amnesty International, tendered the "Million Faces" petition demanding effective action against the arms trade: head shots of one million people, uploaded to the Internet. Adding star power, actor Nicholas Cage, fresh off his role as an unscrupulous gunrunner in the film *Lord of War*, slammed the arms trade by videotape at a conference side event. For their part, the gun groups loosed a fusillade of member letters and e-mail messages insisting the UN keep its corrupt hands off citizens' guns. Nor should

54 Goldring interview.
55 Forum Waffenrecht, Single Action Shooting Society, and Million Mom March quoted in UN, "Civil Society Groups."

the UN schedule such a conference over July 4, "America's most revered national holiday," as it did in 2006.[56]

At both conferences, the sheer number of these angry if canned missives prompted the UN to issue special "Setting the Record Straight" press releases. These rebutted "myths" with paragraphs of "facts." The conference was not negotiating a treaty and was not a power grab by global diplomats. To the charge that the conference would not be "democratic, transparent or open," the UN noted that all sides would have equal chance to air views. The UN even felt the need to refute the July 4th charges: its offices would shutter on the day, while its grounds would welcome 10,000 (unarmed) patriots for the East River fireworks. Demonstrating the UN's enduring worry about the power of the original "myths," the first page of the RevCon's permanent UN Web site begins not with grand pronouncements about control but with the following excerpt from Kofi Annan's opening statement: "[T]his Review Conference is not negotiating a 'global gun ban,' nor do we wish to deny law-abiding citizens their right to bear arms." All of this indicated to gun groups such as the BSSC that their carefully orchestrated letter-writing campaign had "long-term value for the pro-shooting interest."[57]

Zombie Gun Policy

Programme of Action

Indeed, at the conferences themselves, the gun network demolished much of IANSA's careful preparatory work. On the 2001 conference's opening day, U.S. Undersecretary of State John

---

[56] ControlArms, "Join the Million Faces," http://www.controlarms.com/million_faces/en/index.php/register; NRA, "Shot Heard 'Round the World"; LaPierre, *Global War*, 225–26.

[57] UN, "Setting the Record Straight," July 2001, http://www.un.org/Depts/dda/CAB/smallarms/facts.htm; UN, Secretary-General's Statement, http://www.un.org/events/smallarms2006/; BSSC, Annual Report, 16. See also UN, "Press Briefing on Small Arms," July 5, 2001, http://www.un.org/News/briefings/docs/2001/SmallArmsConfBrf.doc.htm; UN, "Setting the Record Straight: The UN and Small Arms," 2006, http://www.un.org/events/smallarms2006/pdf/SettingRecordStraight.pdf.

Bolton unset months of UN agenda-setting in a harangue that delicate delegates found "undiplomatic" and even "un-UN-like."[58] Bolton lay down a series of "redlines," points the United States would not accept: a legally binding agreement; restrictions on legal trade and manufacture; restrictions on sales to nonstate actors; and promotion of international advocacy. These were also planks basic to the NRA and WFSA positions. Indeed, Bolton reportedly later stated that firearms groups had played a decisive role: "NRA representatives keeping close watch on international gun-ban groups sounded the alarm that brought outrageous gun-ban proposals to the attention of the Bush administration."[59]

IANSA attacked the redlines and the forces behind them, but the gun network had played its trump card. In a setting ruled by consensus, one powerful state's adamant stand forced the UN to trim its sails (although other governments privately cheered). In the end, the 2001 Programme of Action (PoA) included only nonbinding agreements on substantive matters the U.S. delegation approved. The only give in the U.S. redlines was allowing a follow-up conference in 2006.[60]

Control proponents then faced another strategic choice: demote or promote this zombie policy. Some among the control groups leveled devastating critiques. Aaron Karp carped that "the Conference brought international small-arms diplomacy to a near halt . . . repudiat[ing] the global process it was conceived to establish." Human Rights Watch shuttered its small-arms program. IANSA too lamented that the PoA "provides no international mechanism for monitoring compliance, and the UN's role

---

[58] Rachel Stohl, "United States Weakens Outcome of UN Small Arms and Light Weapons," *Arms Control Today*, Sept. 2001, http://www.armscontrol.org/act/2001_09/stohlsepto1.

[59] United States of America, Statement by John R. Bolton, July 9, 2001, http://www.grip.org/bdg/g1894.html; Bolton statement reported in 2007 NRA Annual Meetings and Exhibits, http://www.nraam.org/pastmeetings/2007_pastmeeting.asp. See also Small Arms Working Group, "Small Arms Working Group Condemns Bolton Statement at UN," press release, July 9, 2001.

[60] UN, Programme of Action, 2001, A/CONF.192/15, http://www.poa-iss.org/PoA/poahtml.aspx.

has been limited to compiling information submitted by states on a voluntary basis." Stricken from the draft program were measures relating to human rights, transfers to nonstate actors, public health, and the "gendered nature" of gun misuse and injury.[61]

Yet the control network opted to jerk the zombie into motion. IANSA endorsed it as the best that could be achieved, and the PoA lurched off UN Plaza. Countries promoting arms control adopted its nonbinding guidelines. An army of government officials, UN bureaucrats, and NGO staff drafted upbeat reports. The UN also took steps to fight the gun network directly, for instance initiating the special rapporteur's report on human rights abuses from small arms. In all this, IANSA made the best of what it saw as a poor outcome. The apparent hope was that the PoA might resuscitate itself, its normative web entrapping states in ever-tighter controls.[62]

WFSA remained wary, too, despite having torn the soul out of the PoA. Small arms control was not dead, and the zombie might somehow revive. Therefore, gun groups puffed up the 2006 RevCon as the latest offensive in *The Global War on Your Guns*, as Wayne LaPierre's book – available as an NRA membership gift – was titled. More belligerently, they sought to drive a stake through the heart of this "second attempt to destroy the freedoms that are as American as apple pie."[63]

In these clashing efforts, the two sides again deployed parallel tactics, many of which I have already described. In addition, both published lengthy reports assessing the PoA – in different lights. In these, there was a clash of demonstration effects, each side selecting and interpreting past events for its own purposes.

---

[61] Karp, "Small Arms: Back to the Future," 180; HRW, "U.N.: 'Program of Inaction'"; IANSA, "United Nations Biennial Meeting of States on Small Arms and the Programme of Action: July 7–11, 2003," press release, http://www.iansa.org/media/bms.htm; IANSA, "UN Programme of Action on Small Arms and Light Weapons," http://www.iansa.org/un/programme-of-action.htm.

[62] See, e.g., Rachel Stohl, "UN Conference on Small Arms Concludes with Consensus," Center for Defense Information, July 26, 2001, http://www.cdi.org/program/document.cfm?documentid=631&programID=23; IANSA, "How To Use These Documents."

[63] LaPierre, *Global War*, xxv. See also GOA, "Are Members of Congress Lying."

The control side's report emphasized the beneficent results of the PoA, urged other countries to adopt it, and argued for its strengthening. By contrast, the gun groups played up its evils, denouncing efforts to expand the PoA.[64]

Whether or not the PoA had been beneficial, the Review Conference ended in failure: no agreement, no PoA extension, and no plans for another meeting. Poignant pleas, such as one from a Sierra Leonean advocate whose people had "suffered appallingly from the effects of the uncontrolled arms trade," did not change that outcome. The gun network's activism, particularly its ability to influence the American delegation, again played a key role. Summing up, IANSA director Peters was cutting: "It is to their lasting shame that governments let...a small number of states...hold them all hostage and to derail any plans which might have brought improvement in this global crisis."[65] But the United States and the gun network could not be shamed – they believed they were doing the right thing.

Arms Trade Treaty

So control proponents shifted to a new process to hobble the gun network: a legally binding Arms Trade Treaty (ATT). In December 2006, the UN General Assembly voted to begin work on the ATT, over U.S. opposition and abstentions from major producers such as Russia, China, and Israel. As planned, this would have been negotiated by majority vote of states participating, not by consensus. It would also have taken force with ratification by only the states favoring it. Of course, that would have meant a treaty that was far from global and that would have left much of the problem unsolved. Encouraging this approach nonetheless was the Control Arms campaign, "represent[ing] millions of campaigners around the world." It orchestrated dozens of "People's Consultations" demanding "governments take action

---

[64] IANSA and Biting the Bullet, *Reviewing Action on Small Arms 2006: Assessing the First Five Years of the Programme of Action*, 2006, http://www.iansa.org/un/review2006/redbook2006/index.htm; LaPierre, *Global War*, 91–104.

[65] Florella Hazeley, Sierra Leone Action Network on Small Arms, and Peters quoted in IANSA, "UN Arms Talks Meltdown."

for tough international arms controls." For their part, gun groups such as the British Shooting Sports Council fretted that the ATT process involves "fora less procedurally friendly to us" than the PoA.[66]

With the coming of the Obama administration – viewed by the NRA as a dire threat to the Second Amendment – the United States reversed course. It offered to participate in the ATT negotiations but with major stipulations meant to assuage domestic gun interests aligned with the Democratic Party: use of consensus rules in negotiations and of existing U.S. arms export laws as an ATT model. In 2009, the UN accepted this offer – and, notwithstanding the caveats, American and other gun groups attacked. As NRA leader Bob Barr had earlier claimed, the ATT "necessarily will come to involve at some point domestic laws and policies regarding firearms." Members of the Control Arms campaign such as Oxfam International were of two minds, viewing the U.S. decision as a "major breakthrough" given the country's heft and its strong export policies. They also worried, however, that consensus rules would allow recalcitrant states to "fatally weaken a final deal." Negotiations are ongoing as of 2011.[67]

Firearms Protocol

The UN's disarmament bureaucracy promoted both the ATT and the PoA. Until 2001, ECOSOC also continued its separate crime prevention process, and both the gun groups and IANSA maintained strong interest. In 2001, governments agreed to a binding international agreement, the Firearms Protocol to the existing Transnational Organized Crime Convention. This came

---

[66] UN, First Committee, "Towards an Arms Trade Treaty: Establishing Common International Standards for the Import, Export and Transfer of Conventional Arms," 2006, A/C.1/61/L.55 (A/RES/61/89); IANSA, "Control Arms: The People's Consultation on an ATT," press release, http://www.iansa.org/campaigns_events/PeoplesConsultation.htm; BSSC, Annual Report, 17.

[67] Barr quoted in Charles J. Hanley, "Global Gun Treaty 'Urgent', U.N. Told," *Toronto Globe and Mail*, Sept. 30, 2007; Oxfam and Amnesty International, "US Joins Arms Trade Treaty Talks, But at High Price," press release, Oct. 15, 2009, http://www.oxfam.org/en/pressroom/pressrelease/2009–10–15/us-joins-arms-trade-treaty-talks-high-price.

into force in 2005, and about 100 countries had signed or ratified it by 2010.

On one hand, the Protocol could be considered a success. Real policy was established, although many countries have not ratified it. The Protocol, however, was a far cry from the expansive measures against civilian gun possession long promoted by the Japanese and other countries in the wake of Yoshihiro Hattori's killing. None of the restrictions on civilian gun possession that the NRA and WFSA had earlier decried as radical were included. The Protocol required that manufacturers mark firearms with unique serial numbers, enhancing traceability. This was an important change for some countries. It had been required in the United States for decades, however – and its presence had not saved Hattori's life. Moreover, it had been approved by the Organization of American States (OAS) as part of the Inter-American Convention against the Illicit Manufacture of and Trafficking in Firearms (CIFTA) in 1997. During both sets of negotiations, American gun groups and WFSA had in fact promoted marking to State Department negotiators unfamiliar with domestic firearms issues. According to OAS chief negotiator Jonathan Winer, "We actually had [the NRA] give us language which said, this shall not apply to, or affect, the legitimate rights of hunters and sportsmen."[68]

On the other hand, the Firearms Protocol also suggests limits to gun groups' influence. Although promoting the general marking concept, the NRA and WFSA ultimately opposed ratification because the finalized Protocol included two "hypocritical," "galling," and "scandal[ous]" loopholes. First, it exempted marking on governmental transfers made for ill-defined "national security" reasons. Gun groups had this interpretation: "[I]t is a lot easier to regulate legal firearms owners than it is to control rogue states dumping arms across borders." The second

[68] Winer quoted in Mary Beth Sheridan, "Despite Obama Pledge, Democrats Show Little Enthusiasm for CIFTA Treaty on Gun Trafficking," *Washington Post*, Oct. 21, 2010, http://www.washingtonpost.com/wp-dyn/content/article/2010/10/21/AR2010102107266_pf.html.

loophole allows China, but no other country, to continue nonunique markings on its huge weapons exports. In the NRA's view, this put paid to the "pious...hokum" about the control network's caring about "sav[ing] lives in the Third World." IANSA called these outcomes "unfortunate" but nonetheless urged the Protocol's ratification. China eagerly signed on.[69]

The NRA's explanation for the China loophole is instructive. The American delegate supposedly met with her Chinese counterparts after days of negotiations, late at night, and "without her advisors who usually dealt with firearms matters." Whether or not accurate, this account suggests how gun – and control – groups sway governments: educating them about the implications of proposed ideas; writing key language for negotiators; urging them to stand tough against compromises; and lobbying against ratification of agreements that do not meet their standards. Indeed, the United States has not signed or ratified the Firearms Protocol or CIFTA, in large part because of NRA opposition. The upshot is that both conventions are only partial successes, with large gaps in coverage and major producers omitted.[70]

Conclusion

The contentiousness of the small arms issue might seem surprising. After all, in the early 1990s, scientific communities, advocacy NGOs, and the UN worked together to define what they saw as an important global problem and to devise a detailed set of solutions. From the beginning, however, they faced daunting foes. Center stage was deep disagreement over the most basic issues – indeed two conflicting world views. As a result, the process itself was marked by bitter infighting among the primary NGO and

---

[69] LaPierre, *Global War*, 33–35; IANSA, "The World's First Global Gun Treaty Enters into Force," n.d. 2004, http://www.iansa.org/un/global-gun-treaty.htm.

[70] LaPierre, *Global War*, 35–37. See also Sheridan, "Despite Obama Pledge"; Antonio Maria Costa, "Stop the Flow of Guns," *New York Times*, Apr. 14, 2009, http://www.nytimes.com/2009/04/15/opinion/15iht-edcosta.html.

state combatants. The contending groups lobbied states both at the UN conferences and, more importantly, at home. Although using the UN as an institution, both networks were comfortable abandoning it when this served their purposes. The NRA in particular questioned the UN's legitimacy, stating what other WFSA members believed but seldom expressed.[71] IANSA has been reticent to attack the UN process, but its actions speak volumes. With the Programme of Action a zombie and the RevCon failing to revive it, top members began promoting other mechanisms, with the ATT the chosen vehicle.

More broadly and on an ongoing basis, the contending networks shape one another's strategies and behavior. Obviously, this is not the only basis on which the groups act. There is little question, however, that in understanding small arms policy, it is essential to analyze not just the NGOs claiming a crisis, but also those denying it – and their recurring clashes with one another.

[71] Andrew Arulanandam quoted in Sheridan, "Despite Obama Pledge."

6

Battlefield Brazil

National Disarmament and International Activism

Nelson Mandela was furious. Without permission, his picture had appeared in a Brazilian television commercial attacking the country's latest proposal to fight gun crime – a citizen referendum to ban firearms sales. The nationally broadcast advertisement warned that Brazilians would put their liberties at risk by supporting "disarmament" in the October 2005 vote. But the South African freedom fighter was having none of it. With apartheid's end, Mandela had become a staunch gun control proponent – although in 1961 he had founded the African National Congress's armed wing. In conjunction with Brazil's internationally supported "Yes campaign" for disarmament, his lawyers denounced the "outrageous cooptation of Nelson Mandela's image." They threatened to sue Brazil's pro-gun/anti-referendum campaigners, attacking the ad as "incorrect, improper and illegal."[1]

The "No campaign" had its own overseas muscle, however, America's National Rifle Association (NRA), Canada's National Firearms Association (NFA), and other members of the World Forum on the Future of Sport Shooting Activities (WFSA). They

---

[1] IANSA, "Dirty Tricks as Brazilian Gun Referendum Approaches," press release. Oct. 19, 2005, http://www.iansa.org/regions/samerica/dirty-tricks.htm.

supplied the nation's small gun rights movement with strategies, ideas, and messages. Most powerfully, they urged the activists to stress a human rights argument: that Brazilians must preserve their rights to self-defense and to possess firearms. At the beginning of the referendum fight, the disarmament side had high hopes. The country's president, legislature, major media, and Catholic Church all backed it. IANSA provided aid and encouragement. In the summer of 2005, polls estimated about 80 percent popular support. In the campaign's final weeks, however, the tide shifted as advertisements such as the Mandela one reached the electorate. The result was resounding and pervasive. Both urban and rural areas voted against the proposal, with the No campaign winning by 64 percent to 36 percent.

In the years before the vote, gun control had become a national concern in Brazil. Beginning in 1998, two newly formed coalitions squared off in the National Congress, the courts, and the media battling over a proposed disarmament law. The fight lasted years, until Luiz Inácio Lula da Silva swept to the Brazilian presidency in 2003, then signed the bill into law. Restricting civilian gun ownership, the Statute of Disarmament required registration of all firearms, increased fees to a level significantly higher than previously, raised the purchase age from twenty-one to twenty-five, and banned civilians from carrying weapons. In addition, the law called for a national referendum: Should the sale of firearms and ammunition be prohibited in Brazil? After months of struggle over its scheduling, the referendum came before the Brazilian people.

The conflict transcended the Amazon, however, with activists on both sides drawing assistance from the world's opposing gun and control networks. In fact, Brazilians might not have come to believe they had a "gun crisis" and disarmament might not have become a burning national issue without foreign influences and an inviting international climate. In turn, the global networks showcased Brazil as a bellwether for other countries. The case therefore illustrates how rival transnational forces expand their wars onto domestic fronts, as well as the logic and limits to their doing so.

Skeptics might retort that Brazil is too unique for broader lessons. True, no country had previously brought private arms sales to popular vote, although Californians had turned down a handgun freeze referendum in 1982. Brazil is also one of the world's largest countries by population, area, and economy. For that reason, however, Brazil would seem a most likely case for autonomous development of contending interests. If, nonetheless, international influences played key roles, this suggests that their effect would be even greater elsewhere. For social scientists, Brazil makes a good case study. Although the 2005 referendum fell short, other control efforts succeeded – the mix of achievement and failure reducing potential biases.

I start by discussing the construction – and deconstruction – of Brazil's "gun crisis," highlighting the influence of transnational networks. I then reverse the crosshairs to show how foreign interests used the Brazilian gun battle in their larger policy war. Before beginning the analysis, it is noteworthy that Brazil has long had one of the world's highest rates of gun-related crime. According to a UNESCO report, in 2003 Brazil suffered almost 40,000 gun deaths, second highest per capita worldwide among countries at peace. On the other hand, relatively few Brazilians own guns, legally or illegally. The Small Arms Survey estimated 15.3 million guns in civilian hands in 2007, approximately 8.8 guns for every 100 Brazilians, less than in many other nations of the western hemisphere. The country has no analogue to America's Second Amendment, although its laws recognize the right to self-defense in criminal proceedings. Of further note, Brazil has a large gun industry led by Forjas Taurus, one of the world's major civilian weapons producers.[2]

---

[2] UNESCO, *Mortes Matadas por Armas de Fogo no Brasil: 1979–2003* [*Deaths by Firearms in Brazil: 1979–2003*] (Brasília: Edições UNESCO, 2005), 23; Small Arms Survey, *Survey 2007*, 47. The SAS's Brazilian figures are based on another work funded by Brazilian and international gun control advocates, Rubem César Fernandes, ed., *Brazil: The Arms and the Victims* (Rio de Janeiro: Instituto de Estudos da Religião, 2005). Brazilian gun supporters have questioned these studies, however, and the NRA has denounced the SAS report as "self-serving." LaPierre, *The Global War on Your Guns*, 198.

Constructing Brazil's Gun Crisis

In the 1980s, as Brazil slowly democratized and social controls loosened, crime skyrocketed. The firearms death rate tripled from 1979 to 1990, and then doubled again in the 1990s, giving Brazil one of the worst rates among countries at peace, according to UNESCO. By 1997, São Paulo's murder rate was about thirteen people per day, 90 percent from guns – more than double New York City's on a per capita basis. Early in the transition period, the government unleashed lethal firepower against the criminal gangs blamed for much of the killing. Abusive police had little effect, however.[3]

By the early 1990s, the growing criminal and state violence had spurred citizen protest. Notably, however, this did not target firearms or demand gun control. Rather, its focus was public insecurity caused by both criminals and police. The movement began to highlight firearms only in late 1997, when prominent politicians and activists, influenced by the emerging international control movement, diagnosed the country as suffering an "epidemic" of gun violence.

Consider Viva Rio, often seen as Brazil's premiere control NGO. In fact, Viva Rio came late to gun issues. The group has its origins in 1993 when Rio de Janeiro activists called for two minutes of citywide silence against public insecurity. Months later, they founded Viva Rio, headed by Rubem Fernandes, a Rio-based anthropology professor. The group demanded that the city reform the thuggish police force and reduce inequality – but did not advocate firearms control. As long-time campaigner Antônio Rangel Bandeira recalled, "the issue of guns did not exist" in the group's first years. To have advocated restrictions would have left only the authorities in legal possession. In the early 1990s, however, Viva Rio viewed the city force with revulsion and the federal government with suspicion. Viva Rio's leaders – "veterans from the Cold War years, hard skinned from so much 'class

---

[3] UNESCO, *Mortes Matadas por Armas de Fogo*, 23; Larry Rohter, "Brazil, High in Shootings, Is Proposing to Ban Guns," *New York Times*, June 13, 1999, p. 19.

struggle' talk and . . . clandestine armed actions," as Fernandes described them – did not talk of citizens surrendering weapons to a recently authoritarian, still brutal state.[4]

Only in 1997 did this begin to change under the influence of President Fernando Henrique Cardoso. In February, the legislature created a new agency, the National Firearms System (SINARM), in an early, small effort to control guns. The law centralized local ownership records, registered purchases, and required licenses to carry weapons. SINARM, however, exempted government officials and did not require arms collectors, hunters, or professional shooters to comply with the law. Brazilian gun owners remained sanguine. By contrast, in later years control advocates criticized SINARM as "timid" because of the "shocking" privileges accorded a "separate class" of "hobb[yists]."[5]

SINARM was in fact only a wan opening shot in a withering new volley of gun control. This had two main sources, both Brazilian but both influenced by international forces: a São Paulo-based civic campaign, Sou da Paz pelo Desarmamento (I'm for Peace Disarmament campaign); and, more powerfully if less colorfully, the Cardoso government. Sou da Paz started in mid-1997 as a project of the University of São Paulo's law student

---

[4] Bandeira quoted in Adèle Kirsten, "The Role of Social Movements in Gun Control: An International Comparison between South Africa, Brazil and Australia," Research Report No. 21 (Durban, South Africa: Centre for Civil Society, 2004), 6–7; Fernandes, "The Art of Breaking the Gun," in *A Nation without Guns? The Story of Gun Free South Africa*, ed. Adèle Kirsten (Scottsville, South Africa: University of KwaZulu-Natal Press, 2008), ix. See also Reese Erlich, "Brazilian Capital Beefs Up Efforts to Fight Crime against Tourists," *Christian Science Monitor*, Sept. 12, 1994, p. 4; Rubem César Fernandes, "Urban Violence and Civic Action: The Experience of Viva Rio," Sept. 1998, http://religiondatabases.georgetown.edu/berkley/religiondev.php?sortColumn=Author&direction=DESC#tag2492; George Yúdice, *The Expediency of Culture: Uses of Culture in the Global Era* (Durham, NC: Duke University Press, 2003), 133–59.

[5] Carolina Iootty Dias, "Small Arms Control Legislation in Brazil: From Vargas to Lula," in *Brazil: The Arms and the Victims*, ed. Fernandes, 26–49, 37. For their part, gun owners believed that SINARM maintained "windows for the right to self-defense" and legal gun ownership. Jairo Paes de Lira, Brazilian Coalition for Self Defense (Coalizão Brasileira Pela Legítima Defesa [PLD]), personal interview with author, Nov. 7, 2007, São Paulo (audiotape).

association. For months beforehand, its leader, Denis Mizne, had worked for Tulio Kahn, head of the São Paulo branch of ECOSOC's Commission on Crime Prevention and Criminal Justice. By 1997, the Commission, at Japan's prompting, had been working on gun control for years (see Chapter 5). Kahn was part of the ECOSOC panel evaluating gun laws around the world. Mizne therefore became "connected, at least on the research level, with what was being debated on the issue of small arms," meeting many members of what would soon become IANSA. Exposed to these influences, he urged his student group to choose disarmament as its focus.[6]

For the first time in Brazil, Sou da Paz stressed gun crime and deaths as major problems, in addition to violence and insecurity more generally. The solution as Mizne expressed it? "Don't buy a gun, don't rely on a gun, don't think that guns can protect you." Sou da Paz, following international mentors, called for civilian disarmament, gun buybacks, and firearms destruction. The students counseled peace-building and "disarmament of the soul." They expected the campaign to be small and to last only one year. Instead, it resonated strongly, winning support from civic leaders, the bar association, the Catholic Church, and the media. Even the two teams in the wildly popular national soccer championship entered the stadium wearing Sou da Paz T-shirts. Within months, the campaign had collected and destroyed thousands of firearms.[7]

This unexpected success dovetailed with President Cardoso's prior interests. These were reinforced in late 1997, when the ECOSOC panel held a workshop in São Paulo and more importantly when Cardoso paid a state visit to Great Britain.

---

[6] Denis Mizne, Executive Director, Instituto Sou da Paz, telephone interview with author, Oct. 11, 2007 (audiotape). See also Rohter, "Brazil, High in Shootings."

[7] Mizne telephone interview. See also Instituto Sou da Paz, "Brazil: Changing a History of Violence," 2006, http://www.iansa.org/regions/samerica/documents/Brazil-gun-referendum-analysis-SoudaPaz-2006.pdf; Stuart Elliott, "Public-Service Campaigns in Brazil and Australia Boast a Sophistication Regular Ads Might Envy," *New York Times*, Dec. 24, 1997, D4.

He returned, according to Tulio Kahn, "impressed by the rigorous system of gun control" there, instituted after the 1996 Dunblane, Scotland mass shooting. All this helped convince Cardoso that Brazil too had a major gun problem requiring a robust solution: a fast-track bill banning private ownership. As Justice Minister Renan Calheiros put it: "We want to offer an example to the entire world[,]...a radical measure that shows we are serious about confronting the issue."[8]

In turn, the belief that Brazil had a gun crisis mushroomed in civil society. In 1999, Mizne founded Instituto Sou da Paz, an organization focusing on firearms control. In 1999–2000, he worked as Justice Ministry chief of staff, promoting disarmament. More unexpectedly, Viva Rio converted to control too, in what its leader Fernandes called "almost a second foundation" binding itself to a state it had long distrusted. Both NGOs then began receiving government contracts and grants. In 1999, the two mounted a petition campaign for disarmament with more than 1 million signatures. They organized gun buyback and destruction days, providing legitimacy and publicity to the gun crisis and the government's proposals. By early in the new century, disarmament had become a major issue nationwide, with TV networks not only reporting on it in news programs, but also weaving it into soap opera plots.[9]

Global connections fortified Sou da Paz and Viva Rio as gun control advocates. As discussed in Chapter 5, in 1998 IANSA's predecessor, Project PrepCom, was scrambling to add NGOs, particularly in the developing world, to authenticate the budding small arms network. PrepCom leaders such as Edward Laurance knew of Brazilian developments and saw the country as a

---

[8] Kahn and Calheiros quoted in Rohter, "Brazil, High in Shootings."

[9] Fernandes quoted in Kirsten, "Role of Social Movements in Gun Control," 10; Instituto Sou da Paz, "Brazil: Changing a History of Violence"; IANSA, "Gun Free Marches Boom in Brazil," 2003, http://www.iansa.org/regions/samerica/brazil_marches.htm; IANSA, "New Gun Laws in Brazil: A Victory for Civil Society" (interview with Antônio Rangel Bandeira, coordinator, Arms Control project, Viva Rio), 2003, http://www.iansa.org/regions/samerica/rangel_interview.htm.

trendsetter. They therefore tapped Sou da Paz and Viva Rio, with both becoming early IANSA members and receiving overseas financial support. In turn, the two groups redoubled their focus on guns in Brazil, Latin America, and the globe. Before the UN's 2001 Small Arms conference, Viva Rio campaigned with IANSA to have the UN declare July 9 Small Arms Destruction Day, then worked with the government to prepare public gun bulldozings.[10]

It is impossible to know whether the construction of Brazil's gun crisis – and the turn to radical solutions – would have occurred without Cardoso's British visit, Mizne's UN link, the Sou da Paz campaign, or the international small arms movement. Global developments, however, had significant influence on recognition and promotion of the crisis.

Constructing Brazil's Rights Crisis

As disarmament proponents constructed the crisis, a small but sinuous firearms movement arose, influenced by international and especially American sources. Before then it barely existed. Although owners had participated in hunting clubs, shooting associations, or collectors' groups, only a handful worried about gun politics. But with Sou da Paz's campaign and especially Cardoso's disarmament proposal, arms manufacturers and citizen gunners mobilized. Motivated by varied concerns, these groups united in denying that Brazil had a gun crisis. On the contrary: the solutions proposed for this nonproblem would themselves create a crisis of rights and security in Brazil.

A cornerstone of this network is Brazil's large arms industry. Key companies have multinational operations and are familiar with overseas gun issues. Taurus proclaims its thriving American subsidiary as the first company to offer a free NRA membership with every firearms purchase. The manufacturers have played a powerful, if backstage, role, bankrolling the referendum campaign and influencing politics particularly in rural areas

[10] Laurance interview.

and in the southern state of Rio Grande do Sul, site of many gun factories.

Playing a more public role are legislators from those regions and three civil society organizations that focus on gun issues. The National Association of Gun Owners and Merchants (ANPCA) was founded in 1999 by Leonardo Arruda, a gun collector and businessman. With his zeal for firearms, Arruda had been an NRA member for decades: "If you are a gun nut, you have to know the NRA." (When I interviewed him in a Rio bistro, Arruda still carried the business card of NRA director and *Soldier of Fortune* magazine editor Robert K. Brown, who had visited months earlier.) Unsurprisingly then, the Rio-based ANPCA modeled itself on the NRA's powerful Institute for Legislative Action. As Arruda told a reporter after the ANPCA's formation in 1999, "In the style of the United States, we plan to help candidates who help us." From the beginning, its leaders contacted overseas gun organizations such as the NRA and the Sporting Shooters' Association of Australia. The ANPCA today claims 1,200 members but has no paid staff and only a small budget. To finance operations, its Web site includes a plea for individual donations: "Get real, give a reale" (the Brazilian currency), a slogan suggested by Canada's National Firearms Association, with its own "Give One Lousy Loonie" fundraising drive.[11]

A second small organization is the Viva Brazil Movement (MVB), founded by Bene Barbosa, a São Paulo technical school teacher. After purchasing a revolver to defend his family, Barbosa became interested in the ideas of University of Chicago economist John Lott, who argued in a controversial academic

[11] Except where noted, information and quotations in this paragraph come from Leonardo Arruda, Public Relations Director, National Association of Firearms Owners and Merchants (Associaçáo Nacional dos Proprietários e Comerciantes de Armas), personal interview, Rio de Janeiro, Nov. 12, 2007 (audiotape); Arruda quoted in Katherine Ellison, "Under Fire from Gun-Control Advocates, Brazilian Exporter Fights Back," Knight Ridder Washington Bureau, Aug. 20, 1999; Leo Arruda, "ANPCA Formed to Fight Gun Ban Plan (NEW!)", email message to Sporting Shooters' Association of Australia, July 7, 1999, http://www.afn.org/~afn18566/brazil2.html; Armaria, http://www.armaria.com.br/.

book that jurisdictions with more guns have less crime. In the late 1990s, Barbosa opened a Web site stressing that honest Brazilians needed more guns to protect themselves from crime. In 2004, this became Viva Brazil, which portrays the country as menaced by plots to disarm citizens, restrict press freedom, and create a "dictatorship of political correctness." Choosing its name to deauthenticate and trump Viva Rio's, Viva Brazil aims to show that gun owners too are "for Brazil; we want Brazil to live."[12]

International influences are even stronger in the Brazilian Society for the Defense of Tradition, Family, and Property (TFP). A lay Roman Catholic organization, TFP was founded in 1960 by Brazilian theologian, Plinio Corrêa de Oliveira. Its goal is the "restoration of order" in the Catholic Church and in broader society: "Christian civilization, austere and hierarchical, fundamentally sacral, antiegalitarian, and antiliberal." TFP opposes abortion, pornography, land redistribution, and the "number one enemy of the family" – homosexuality. Outside Brazil, TFP sprouted offshoots in Europe and the Americas, with more than a dozen communicating electronically, meeting annually, and coordinating transnationally. One recent target was Dan Brown's worldwide bestseller and movie, *The Da Vinci Code*, condemned as blasphemous.[13]

Corrêa de Oliveira died in 1995, before the Brazilian government and NGOs took up strict gun control. His death led to conflict between TFP members desiring to turn the group into a religious order and those who wanted it to remain political. The growing firearms issue deepened this division, changing the

[12] Information and quotations in this paragraph come from Bene Barbosa, President, Movimento Viva Brasil (MVB), personal interview, Nov. 7, 2007, São Paulo (audiotape; translation by Jairo Paes de Lira). See also http://www.mvb.org.br/.

[13] Corrêa de Oliveira, *Revolution and Counter-Revolution* (1959; 1977), reprinted and translated by American Society for the Defense of Tradition, Family and Property (American TFP), http://www.tfp.org/books/rcr.pdf 52, 96; Corrêa de Oliveira, "Homosexual Union is the Opposite of the Family" (interview) *O Globo*, Oct. 29, 1992, reprinted and translated by American TFP, http://www.tfp.org/index.php?option=com_content&task=view&id=154&Itemid=3; PLD.

group's identity and leading to the Brazilian TFP's split after lengthy litigation. Members interested in activism formed the Association of Founders in 2006. Religious principles undergird their beliefs about owning guns – notwithstanding the fact that Brazil's Catholic Bishop's organization backs disarmament. One TFP leader, Jairo Paes de Lira, a retired colonel in Rio's police force and an elected Christian Workers Party (PTC) deputy to Brazil's lower house, cites St. Augustine and other theologians as upholding the need for weapons. In addition, the group opposed disarmament because they saw firearms as the last line of citizen defense against criminals – and, as another leader Diogo Waki put it, against the "leftists, the communists, the Marxists, and the dictator government." In this view, the right to self-defense – through arms, if necessary – is a natural and necessary right for all people.[14]

TFP members began mobilizing against President Cardoso's disarmament bill in August 2000. That month, a delegation led by Waki journeyed to the American TFP's Washington, DC bureau looking for advice and assistance. Tapping the office's extensive and long-standing contacts with other American conservatives, the delegation visited the NRA, the Second Amendment Foundation, the Citizens Committee for the Right to Keep and Bear Arms, and the Leadership Institute. The goal, according to Paes de Lira, was "to know something about the specific activism related to the right to keep and bear arms – and to utilize that knowledge here in Brazil."[15]

The Brazilians won a sympathetic response, as reported by Paul Weyrich, a Heritage Foundation leader. Writing for a

---

[14] Paes de Lira interview; Diogo C. Waki, Brazilian Coalition for Self Defense (PLD), personal interview, Nov. 7, 2007, São Paulo, Brazil (audiotape). See also Pela Legitima Defesa (PLD), http://www.pelalegitimadefesa.org.br/.

[15] Paes de Lira interview. Ties between the Brazilian TFP and its U.S. branch are tight. In 2003, days after leftist President Lula's inauguration, the American TFP opened a special Web page, "LulaWatch" to focus on Latin America's new "axis of evil." American TFP, "TFP Launches LulaWatch," press release, Jan. 16, 2003, http://www.tfp.org/current-campaigns/2003/tfp-launches-lulawatch.html.

Canadian Web site, "Enter Stage Right," he described TFP officials "learning the ropes from the gun lobbies in the USA." Weyrich urged his North American audience to help fight Brazil's "gun grabbers anyway (sic) we can." After all, disarming Brazil could bring communism "roaring back" all across Latin America, "in our backyard." He and the NRA worried too that control groups might flaunt a restrictive Brazilian statute as a precedent in other countries, including the United States: "Policies . . . adopted in one developed nation will end up spilling over into other developed and even developing nations as well."[16]

For TFP leaders, the information gleaned from the Americans had great influence. As Waki remarked, "the most important point for us in terms of knowledge was how to put together . . . a national coalition" to block disarmament. The Brazilians knew that the United States, with its Second Amendment and powerful NRA, presented a different context. As Paes de Lira stated, however, his group found it possible to "transpose the general idea for our case, [to make] the necessary adaptations to put together our coalition, [and to] put together the [American] experience [with] the mobilization experience of the TFP."[17]

In late 2000, TFP formed a coalition, Pro Legítima Defesa (after 2006, Pela Legítima Defesa) (PLD). As spokesperson Paes de Lira emphasized, one of the NRA's key points was that "we should not permit internal differences to influence our work." Although the "way of thinking of a hunter is a little bit different from the way of thinking of a person who believes in the right of legitimate self defense, we decided that we would not show any difference in our opinions because this would be a flank exposure to our opponents." PLD soon became the main civil society network fighting the disarmament statute and referendum. It included the ANPCA, sport shooting groups, hunters' associations, and organizations promoting individual rights. In 2007,

---

[16] Paul M. Weyrich, "Brazil: Will It Be the Next Cuba?" Enter Stage Right.com, Aug. 7, 2000, http://www.enterstageright.com/archive/articles/0800brazil .htm.

[17] Waki interview; Paes de Lira interview.

PLD claimed about 500 individual members, each of whom contributed an average of $R30–100 ($15–50) per month, as well as about 10,000 noncontributing supporters.[18]

To summarize, PLD and its member organizations mobilized in reaction to the growing national alarm about a gun crisis and the sweeping disarmament proposed to solve it. They acknowledged that Brazil suffered a public security problem but denied that the country had a gun crisis. Indeed, they believed that more guns in the right hands were the answer – and that disarmament would itself create a crisis of rights and security. Like their foes, they reached out to experienced foreigners who strengthened their unity, sharpened their arguments, and raised their capacities. None of this is to say that Brazil's contest over guns is an overseas transplant. Its primary sources are national. However, key players on both sides are coached, aided, and cheered by rival transnational networks.

Girding for Combat

As the two sides skirmished, first over the Statute of Disarmament, then over the referendum, and still later over court challenges and legislative rollbacks, they deployed both affirmative and negative strategies. Rather than chronologically detailing this multiyear war, I highlight the two sides' recurrent approaches – and international actors' influences on them.

Building Networks

First, disarmament groups made a major effort to build a national network spanning NGOs, churches, and the media. Contributing to this, foreign sources supplied monetary and strategic support. For Viva Rio, international sources accounted for about

---

[18] Paes de Lira interview. PLD members included the Brazilian branch of the ANPCA, Safari Club International, a hunting group, Associação Brasileira dos Atiradores de Rifle (ABAR), Associação Paulista de Defesa dos Direitos e Liberdades Individuais (APADDI), Federação Paulista de Tiro Prático (FPTP), and Ram Clube de Silhuetas Metálicas (RCSM). PLD, Quem Somos, http://www.pelalegitimadefesa.org.br/.

49 percent of its R$14 million budget in 2004. Much of this came from European donors led by the United Kingdom's Department for International Development (DFID), which provided almost 20 percent. Sou da Paz's overseas funding started in 2004. By 2007, it had reached about 25 percent, with UNESCO its single largest contributor and the U.S.-based Ford, EMpower, and Tinker Foundations providing significant backing.[19]

In a more focused effort in March 2005, the Ford Foundation and UNESCO granted Viva Rio $75,000 to "facilitate communications – via the media, electronic networking, and regular meetings . . . with an eye toward the National Gun Ban referendum." Overseas activists joined the disarmament campaign, with a member of IANSA's international board, Daniel Luz, basing himself at Viva Rio for long periods. They strategized with local NGOs, wrote and translated documents, and spoke to the press.[20]

For their part, the self-defense groups gained further foreign support too. Although no money or personnel appears to have changed hands, the PLD energized and educated its troops by inviting two Americans to Brazil: Morton Blackwell, founder of the Leadership Institute, an organization that has trained activists since 1979; and Charles Cunningham, a top NRA lobbyist active in its 1982 defeat of California's handgun freeze referendum. TFP leader Paes de Lira hoped the visits, in August 2002 and August 2003, respectively, would provide Brazilian audiences

---

[19] Instituto Sou da Paz, "Histórico," http://www.soudapaz.org/instituto/texto.asp?id=1; Viva Rio, *Annual Report 2004*, http://www.vivario.org.br/relatorio/2004/en/pages/Slide01.htm; Rubem Cesar Fernandes, "NGO Presentation to the OEWG, 17 June 2004," http://64.233.169.104/search?q=cache:BzbKRsHdeSMJ:www.iansa.org/issues/documents/presentation_rubem_cesar_fernandes.doc+unifem+%22viva+rio%22&hl=en&ct=clnk&cd=2&gl=us&client=firefox-a.

[20] UNESCO, "New Projects Approved: Part III: Latin America and the Caribbean," IPDC Bureau, forty-eighth meeting, Paris, Mar. 7–9, 2005, 15, http://portal.unesco.org/intranet/fr/ev.php-URL_ID=4561&URL_DO=DO_TOPIC&URL_SECTION=201.html (in author's files); Daniel Luz, Board of Directors, IANSA, personal interview, Nov. 14, 2007, Rio de Janeiro (audiotape).

with a "vision about conservative activism" and "the right to keep and bear arms."[21]

The duo did not disappoint, strengthening the PLD's network building and strategic communications. For now, it is worth noting that the Americans provided financial mentorship. As PLD leader Jairo Paes de Lira acknowledged, "Because of our lack of financial means, they counseled us, they gave us advice on developing an internet network campaign," which its members implemented in 2003. Today, their Web sites bristle with electronic contribution menus, complete with secure credit card links.[22]

Unbuilding Networks

Even as the contending coalitions grabbed overseas aid, they assailed their foes – for doing the same. Tarring opponents as stalking horses for foreign interlopers, they commended themselves as representing authentic Brazilians. In this, they hoped both to sway Brazilian citizens in their favor – and against their foes – and to attract more foreign aid.

Disarmament groups fingered the firearms industry and the NRA as the gun coalition's paymaster and puppeteer. As one NGO strategist stated: "We know that the new 'globalised' gun lobby will play tough, and we will need more than ever the support of IANSA." To stir activism, Viva Rio invoked "efforts of the rich and powerful to protect the financial interests of arms producers – in spite of great human cost." It raised the specter of "the famous gun lobbyist Charlton Heston... com[ing] to Brazil to support these efforts." In fact the NRA president and actor, renowned for such performances as astronaut George Taylor in the 1966 film *Planet of the Apes*, did not land in Brazil.[23]

---

[21] Paes de Lira interview. See also Oscar Vidal, "Legitimate Defense" (Legítima Defesa), Pela Legítima Defesa, Oct. 2003, http://www.pelalegitimadefesa.org .br/materias/encontros/2003/; Diogo Waki, "Morton Blackwell, American Conservative Leader, Comes to Brazil and Suggests How to Succeed against Leftist Laws, Such as the Law of Disarmament, TFP, 2002, http://www .pelalegitimadefesa.org.br/ (author's files);

[22] Paes de Lira interview.

[23] Bandeira quoted in IANSA, "New Gun Laws in Brazil: A Victory for Civil Society," n.d., 2003, http://www.iansa.org/regions/samerica/rangel

Meanwhile, the PLD returned fire, smearing Viva Rio and Sou da Paz as tools of alien governments, NGOs, and corporations. The Soros and Ford foundations took top dishonors in this rogues' list – just as they do for the NRA and WFSA. Less predictably, American gun manufacturers came under nationalist attack during the final days of the referendum campaign. Widely circulated anonymous e-mails claimed the companies as the disarmament side's secret wellspring, out to undermine Brazil's firearms industry and steal the country's jobs.[24]

How much impact did these attacks have? As tools of tarring, the effects are unclear among ordinary Brazilians. General innuendoes about foreign meddling might have affected some. But Soros, Ford, the NRA, and even Heston have low Brazilian profiles, except among those versed in American politics (or Hollywood camp). No matter: just as important an audience for these slurs were the dueling campaigns' foreign friends, most of whom already knew and loathed the NRA or Soros. Such familiar bête noires signal the gravity of distant clashes – and underline the need for more help.

Setting and Unsetting Agendas

If coalition building and unbuilding are central to mobilization, activating institutions and setting agendas are necessary for winning policy battles. Doing so, however, is not simply a matter of affirmative tactics by policy proponents. Rivals deactivate institutions and unset agendas, requiring scholars to analyze not only the good tactics, but also the bad and the ugly.

interview.htm; Viva Rio, "Message from Viva Rio," http://www2.wcc-coe .org/dov.nsf/f4f5a8b3b4d0f25fc1256c83004f1a28/c23f58010877af17c1257 08f0058e550?OpenDocument. In *Planet of the Apes*, apes are the "superior beings" who "control the guns that hunt the race of lowly, terrified humans." Heston's character is shot, caged, and threatened with gelding, perhaps contributing to his stiff defense of firearms rights, at least for people. "Planet of the Apes," 1968, http://www.youtube.com/watch?v=uAH-Tw2hue8.

24 Bernardo Sorj, "Internet, Public Sphere and Political Marketing: Between the Promotion of Communication and Moralist Solipsism," Edelstein Center for Social Research, Working Paper 2, March, 2006, http://www.bernardosorj. com.br/pdf/wp2_english.pdf.

In the battle over the Statute of Disarmament, control groups held a cardinal institutional advantage. The country's executive and much of his party in the bicameral national legislature were on their side. For years, however, champions of the statute could not pass it – or land a knockout blow against its detractors. The gun industry and firearms movement fought rearguard actions, disrupting the law's passage and picking off what provisions they could. Describing the infighting, Viva Rio activist Antônio Rangel Bandeira observed, "What we saw in Congress and in the media was a war of information," with data provided by the two camps "nearly always different, contradictory." In the first round, the statute that emerged after Lula's election as President was stringent, a major success for disarmament groups. Because of their rivals' resistance, however, an outright ban on gun sales had to be made contingent on a referendum. Disarmament forces nonetheless painted this as "the main victory . . . to make sure that [the population's] will is heard, in spite of continuing pressure on government by the gun lobby."[25]

As for the self-defense groups, when Lula signed the law, they pivoted to less hostile terrain: the judiciary. From that institutional redoubt, they sallied forth, lawsuit upon lawsuit, sniping away at provisions of the statute. (Their main legal thrust, however, to overturn the entire disarmament law as unconstitutional, fell short in a May 2007 Federal Supreme Court decision). At the same time, they remained in Congress, angling to prevent or postpone the next round in the conflict, the referendum vote.

Meanwhile, confident control forces, eager for battle, pressured the legislature to schedule the referendum on the earliest possible date. In this protracted skirmish, international actors again played key roles. On the disarmament side, they cultivated Brazilian journalists, turning watchdogs into lapdogs and pit bulls. Consider the UNESCO/Ford Foundation grant to Viva

[25] Bandeira quoted in IANSA, "New Gun Laws in Brazil: A Victory for Civil Society." See also IANSA, "Brazilian Gun Referendum Approaches: A Historic Opportunity to Make People Safer from Gun Violence," press release, n.d., 2005, http://www.iansa.org/regions/samerica/brazil-referendum.htm.

Rio. It called for the NGO, as "one of its high priorities," to train reporters "to express a unified message and . . . increas[e] the quality and quantity of coverage on . . . armed violence, human security, and development in the lead-up to the 2005 gun ban referendum." Under the grant, Viva Rio tracked press reports and compiled a database of contacts, "identify[ing] gaps and potential allies." The goal was to "influence policy-makers, in Brazil and internationally, by increasing public pressure and accountability." At least regarding the media, these goals may have been achieved. Major outlets, with the exception of the influential news magazine *Veja*, barked for disarmament.[26]

Intervention took more targeted forms too. On March 16–18, 2005, the Switzerland-based Centre for Humanitarian Dialogue (CHD), a major backer of the global movement, held a conference on civilian arms in Rio de Janeiro. Orchestrating the meeting, Sou da Paz, Viva Rio, and the Brazilian government portrayed the world as trending toward the disarmament position, particularly on the crucial Brazilian issue of self-defense. Headlining the speakers' list was Barbara Frey, UN special rapporteur on prevention of human rights violations committed with small arms. She spoke about her study finding, contrary to the NRA, WFSA, and PLD, that international law provides no right to self-defense. Further to assure uniform views, conference sponsors denied the NRA's repeated requests to participate, claiming that the conclave concerned international, not American, issues. As Frey acknowledged in an interview, however, "no question [the conference] was helping Brazil at the time of the referendum." In that context, the gun group's discordant views were unwelcome. An angry NRA was reduced to holding a rival conference in the United States where it inveighed against the disarmament network's silencing "representatives of the hundreds of millions of legal firearms owners" worldwide.[27]

---

[26] UNESCO, New Projects Approved, 14–16.
[27] Center for Humanitarian Dialogue (CHD), "Small Arms Meeting in Rio De Janeiro." *Small Arms and Human Security Bulletin* 5, Apr. 2005, 3, http://www.iansa.org/documents/2005/Bul5English.pdf; Barbara Frey, UN Special

In May 2005, the intervention was more overt: UNESCO's Brazil director Jorge Werthein met with the president of the Chamber of Deputies – Brazil's lower house – urging Congress to certify the referendum so that Brazilians could "protect society" and "serve as an example for the world." Bolstering this advocacy, UNESCO released a report showing a 461.8 percent increase in Brazilian gun deaths between 1979 and 2003.[28] Two months later, Congress certified the October date for the vote, and the sides joined battle, naming themselves the Parliamentary Front for the Right to Legitimate Self-Defense (the No campaign) and the Parliamentary Front for the Right to Life (the Yes).

Still the pro-gun groups exploited institutional rules to unset their rivals' agendas and drive them from the field. Under Brazilian law, organizations receiving foreign funds are barred from participating in elections. On this basis, the firearms network used lawsuits to eject Sou da Paz and Viva Rio from the referendum campaign. Staff of both NGOs still played key roles but could do so only in individual capacities. Unsurprisingly, the disarmament network tried to turn the tables and exclude the firearms groups. The gunners, however, had apparently received no overseas money (not for lack of soliciting, as discussed later in this chapter), and financing from Brazilian arms companies was an insufficient basis. Nonetheless, disarmament lawyers kept busy too, harrying the gun groups for using Nelson Mandela's image and distorting facts in their advertisements.

Persuading and Dissuading Brazilians

Although institutional activation and agenda setting are necessary for policy making, in the end, decision makers must . . .

Rapporteur on the Prevention of Human Rights Violations Committed with Small Arms and Light Weapons; Director, Human Rights Program, University of Minnesota, telephone interview, May 30, 2007 (audiotape); LaPierre, *Global War on Your Guns*, 13.

[28] Werthein quoted in Paraiba.com.br, "Brasil é o 2° em mortes por arma de fogo segundo, Unesco," May 6, 2005, http://www.paraiba.com.br/noticia .shtml?12524; UNESCO, *Deaths by Firearms*, 12.

decide. To understand how they do so, scholars have focused on persuasion. To look only at the bright side of these tactics is misleading, however. Even while one side is persuading, the other is dissuading – and in most cases, they are attacking one another. Of course, certain targets are more convincible than others. In many cases, politicians and bureaucrats are best seen as themselves members of policy networks – meaning that they are not very persuadable. However, when a huge country holds a national referendum – and when voting is required by national law – tens of millions of ordinary people, most of whom have not thought much about an issue beforehand, become decision makers. In that unusual circumstance, persuasion – and dissuasion – matter.

In this battle, both sides' rhetoric reflected overseas influences. Not that Brazilian advocates were puppets, mouthing the words of foreign ventriloquists – although each side accused the other of being that. Savvy and autonomous, they selected their own approaches. However, the Brazilians are also internationally linked and in some cases reliant on distant patrons. The broader currents in which they swim move them, shaping their views of the most persuasive arguments. Similarities in rhetoric are predictable too, because, for any issue, there are a limited number of credible claims, even in different societies. In sum, although overseas influences on the framing of the Brazilian gun battle should not be overstated, they cannot be overlooked.

Disease Deployed and Denied
Disarmament activists portrayed Brazil as suffering from a gun violence "epidemic" leading to untold heartache – much the same framing as used by IANSA worldwide. Viva Rio grafted its gun work to public health themes. The broader campaign took the formal name, "Right to Life" – a move denounced as misleading by the TFP, which had run a similarly labeled anti-abortion campaign. Throughout, advocates backed their views with wrenching advertisements about the risks of guns in the home, the perils of self-defense, and the dangers of an armed society.

In this view, disarmament and peace building were the best cures.[29]

To certify these beliefs, campaigners turned to scientific authorities, many international, such as the Small Arms Survey. As Viva Rio activist Bandeira stated, "We used research carried out in Brazil as well as data from other countries in the IANSA network ... in helping convince those who believe that disarmament is a utopian impossibility." Of course, campaigners knew that Brazilians cared most about Brazil. Even here, overseas supporters played a key role, generating and publicizing studies such as the June 2005 UNESCO report – issued to much hoopla in Brazil. The study makes little secret of its politics, starting with its preface by Brazilian Senate President Renan Calheiros, a top control proponent. He acknowledged the imprecision of data on guns, nonetheless asserting that Brazil has "too many" and urging that "now, more than ever, the country needs disarmament." The study's author, sociologist Julio Waiselfisz, echoed the Yes campaign's mantra, albeit turgidly: disarmament is an "indispensable, fundamental, primordial requirement for limiting and restricting the conditions and opportunities for manifestations of lethal violence."[30]

The Brazilian gun groups, however, derided the disease analogy and smashed the medical frame using their own foreign-laced data and arguments. They severed the purported link between firearms ownership and crime rates using scientific and legal articles published in the United States, Canada, and other countries. The gun groups' American "Bible," John Lott's *More Guns,*

[29] Jessica Galeria and Luciana Phebo, "Using Public Health Information to Inform, Build Support and Implement Policies for Gun Violence Prevention: A Case Study from the Gun Ban Referendum," *African Security Review* 15, no. 2 (2006): 16–37, 23; Waki interview. See also, e.g., Sou da Paz, "Celebration of 3,234 Lives Saved: 3,234 Reasons for Brazilians to Vote YES on the Refendum to Ban Gun Comerce (sic), press release, Sept. 9, 2005, http://www.iansa .org/regions/samerica/documents/Celebration-of-gun-death-decline.pdf.

[30] Bandeira quoted in IANSA, "New Gun Laws in Brazil"; Calheiros and Waiselfisz quoted in UNESCO, *Deaths by Firearms*, 7, 30. See also Paraiba .com.br, "Brasil é o 2° em mortes por arma."

Less Crime, was translated into Portuguese and was "useful for our cause." The No campaign's Web site featured an international "Statistics" section studded with links to foreign, especially American, Web sites. These simultaneously certified the gun groups' scientific arguments – and decertified the control groups' epistemic community.[31]

As for peace building, here the No appeared in rare agreement with the Yes. Then again, who is not for peace? The sticking point is how to achieve it, and the self-defense network could not have disagreed more on method. According to the MVB's Barbosa, "We are also for peace . . . if necessary by means of firearms in the hands of good persons. . . . We are able to fight for peace. We don't like to put on white clothes and beg for peace."[32]

Celebrities Feted and Flayed

On another front, disarmament activists unleashed a horde of moral megastars. Peace Prize Nobelist Desmond Tutu posted an electronic video and "Dear Friends" letter to the Brazilian people. Seize this "wonderful opportunity" to "take the guns out of your homes," to "help to make our world a safer place," and to "show [South Africa] the way." Other Nobelists joined the chorus, with Jody Williams, leader of the International Campaign to Ban Landmines, making a special plea to Brazil's women: a Yes vote would "reverberate around the world" and "make a significant contribution to the prevention of armed violence globally." Adding panache to the laureates' gravitas, the disarmament campaign flashed a galaxy of glittering entertainment figures. The

---

[31] Paes de Lira interview. See also IBOPE, "Corruption in Politics: Voter, Victim or Accomplice?" ("Corrupção na Política: Eleitor Vítima ou Cúmplice?"), paper presented at 2nd Brazilian Congress on Research – ABEP 2006, 2 (in author's files); Sorj, "Internet, Public Sphere and Political Marketing"; Associação Nacional das Indústrias de Armas e Munições (ANIAM), *Dossiê: Armas de Fogo Legais versus Crimes* (Porto Alegre: Nova Prova Editora, 2003). For more on the continuing statistical battle, see Marina Lemle, "The Controversy around Gun Deaths in Brazil," Comunidade Segura, Sept. 15, 2010, http://www.comunidadesegura.org/en/node/45569#.

[32] Barbosa interview.

television industry had long provided space for anti-gun messages. Now, with the stars aligned in their favor, Yes campaigners such as Heather Sutton predicted that "well-known actresses and singers, and... ten Nobel Peace Prize Laureates [would leave] 'No' campaigners... scrabbling to make up supporters."[33]

Far from scrabbling, however, the gun groups performed celebrity jujitsu, stoking a populist backlash against the glitterati. Their message, as disarmament advocate Pablo Dreyfus ruefully admitted: referendum proponents "have soap opera stars with private security... telling you who do not have the money for bodyguards that you have to renounce your right to have a gun." True, the No campaign had no pet Nobels. So they snatched images of Nelson Mandela to make their points. Turning from fame to infamy, the No tapped a moral monster, Adolph Hitler. An ANPCA print ad showed him, arm lifted in *sieg heil* salute, with a caption stating: "Whoever is for Disarmament, raise your right hand! Before he issued orders to kill Jews... Hitler did what was logical: disarmed the populace. Without arms, tyranny can't be resisted." Facing the photograph, a second page listed countries in which disarmament preceded tyranny, massacre, and genocide. The NRA has long made similar arguments in America.[34]

---

[33] Tutu, "Message from Desmond Tutu to the Brazilian People on the National Gun Referendum," Sept. 8, 2005, http://www.iansa.org/regions/samerica/tutu-message.htm; Williams, "YES, a More Peaceful Brazil Is Possible," n.d. 2005, http://www.iansa.org/regions/samerica/jody-williams.htm; Sutton quoted in IANSA, "Dirty Tricks as Brazilian Gun Referendum Approaches," press release, Oct. 19, 2005, http://www.iansa.org/regions/samerica/dirty-tricks.htm. See also IANSA, "International Day of Support for the Brazil Gun Referendum (16 October)," press release, n.d. 2005 http://www.iansa.org/regions/samerica/brazil-support.htm.

[34] Pablo Dreyfus, Research Manager, Small Arms Control Project, Viva Rio, personal interview, July 6, 2006, New York, NY (audiotape); ANPCA, "Whoever Is for Disarmament, Raise Your Right Hand!" advertisement, n.d. 2005, http://www.armaria.com.br/folheto%20hitler.pdf; Stephen P. Halbrook, "Registration: The Nazi Paradigm," Sept. 11, 2001, http://www.nraila.org//Issues/Articles/Read.aspx?ID=67. See also IBOPE, "Corruption in Politics," 4; ANPCA, "Enough Hypocrisy," advertisement, 2005,

Rights Raised and Resisted

The Hitler ad hints at a broader point. The No did not simply problematize the Yes's solution, smash its frames, decertify its authorities, and blemish its celebrities. It stressed the referendum's threat to law-abiding Brazilians, using its own, contrary frames. For the Yes, disarmament meant social peace; for the No, it portended personal vulnerability. In this view, gun ownership was both a human right and a matter of individual security.

These entwined frames have few indigenous roots, and foreign influences played a major role in their rise. With his hoary NRA membership, ANPCA leader Arruda appreciated the rights argument early on. TFP leaders' pilgrimage to the United States in 2000 contributed to its incorporation. So did NRA official Charles Cunningham's August 2003 mission to Brazil, near the climax of the legislative battle over the statute of disarmament. The visit included strategy sessions with top activists, as well as public appearances to sellout crowds in Rio and São Paulo. At the latter's elegant National Club, Cunningham spoke to 300 guests on "Effective Pro-Gun Strategies in an Anti-Gun Culture." He stressed the need to battle the "anti-gun people" and their media henchmen who took advantage of tragedies to spread misinformation. More important, he urged Brazilians to "preserve your rights:" firearms control is about "more than just guns, it is about freedom."[35]

The American-inspired rights frame shot to prominence in the referendum. Using it, gun groups portrayed themselves as upholding fundamental freedoms. Conversely, they vilified disarmament advocates for depriving the people of "a democratically conquered right," as Viva Rio staff member Bandeira lamented. In this way too, the No could appeal not only to the small minority of Brazilians who legally owned guns (only about

http://Armaria.com.br/guardacostas.pdf; Armaria, "The Jews and Disarmament" (Os judeus e o desarmamento), http://www.armaria.com.br/JudeusBrasil.pdf, June 28, 2005.

[35] Cunningham quoted in Vidal, "Legitimate Defense"; Cunningham quoted in Thomas McKenna, "Crime Control Not Gun Control in Brazil," American TFP, Aug. 13, 2003, http://www.tfp.org/current-campaigns/2003/crime-control-not-gun-control-in-brazil.html.

10 percent), but also to the vast majority who did not. Campaign commercials featured ordinary Brazilians acknowledging that they did not possess a firearm but expressing concern about the referendum's prohibition. The ads raised a troubling question: Even for nonowners, was it wise to forever deprive themselves and others of the possibility of purchase? In raising this, the No campaign stressed rights, particularly the right to self-defense, alluding to firearms only "when it was clearly necessary," as the TFP's Paes de Lira confided.[36]

For its part, the disarmament campaign fought back, always associating the No with guns and destruction. Aware of the rights argument's power, the disarmament campaign framejacked – from the start adopting the Right to Life title. This fell flat, however. Yes activists could devise no effective riposte to the imported rights argument, despite anxious consultations with IANSA. A nitpicking legal analysis as voiced by Viva Rio's Jessica Galeria – that Brazilians "don't even have a pseudo right to bear arms. It's not in their Constitution" – did not catch fire. Similarly futile were last-ditch efforts to tar the No as "merchants of death," not defenders of rights. In the campaign's waning days, the Yes changed its main advertising agency and released television commercials contrasting gun industry profits to the cost of firearms injuries – all against a backdrop of a spinning revolver cylinder, the sound of a cash register, and heartrending interviews with victims. Even this did not displace the rights argument, however.[37]

Security Framed and Smashed

Just as potent and internationally influenced was a second frame: guns as the ultimate protector of personal security. Echoing decades of American bumper stickers – "If guns are outlawed,

---

[36] Bandeira quoted in Mario Osava, "Brazil: Sudden Shift in Public Opinion Could Torpedo Gun Ban," Oct. 24, 2005, http://www.redorbit.com/news/politics/282608/brazil_sudden_shift_in_public_opinion_could_torpedo_gun_ban/; Paes de Lira interview.

[37] Galeria quoted in Associated Press, "Violence-Plagued Brazil Holds Referendum on Gun Sales," *USA Today*, Oct. 23, 2005, http://www.usatoday.com/news/world/2005-10-23-brazilguns_x.htm; Dreyfus interview.

only outlaws will have guns" – the No campaign contended that only law-abiding citizens, not criminals, would adhere to the referendum's ban. In response, disarmament advocates frame-jacked the security argument: "it's the police who provide security, not the people themselves having [guns]," as Viva Rio's Dreyfus put it. The No, however, played on citizens' fears that the country's notoriously unreliable police might arrive late, be in cahoots with felons, or display general ineptness. (Viva Rio had itself expounded these critiques through the mid-1990s.) Statistics about the dangers of handguns in homes proved fruitless. As Dreyfus lamented, "Logically and rationally it was a very persuasive argument. But people were angry . . . they were scared – people are afraid, of getting killed, robbed."[38]

To strengthen the security argument, self-defense groups highlighted women as a vulnerable population. They aimed to show "the human side of No," as the campaign's public relations agency, IBOPE, put it. In this the gunners adhered to the strategic advice and even the advertising patter of their overseas allies. For control proponents, this move was galling, given their belief that women were a natural constituency for disarmament. (In 2001, Viva Rio had itself milked the feminine for its "Choose Gun Free! It's Your Weapon or Me" campaign, launched on Mother's Day by a throng of sultry soap opera stars.) To Viva Rio official Dreyfus, the No groups' use of women seemed a prime example of its "cutting and pasting NRA messages." As he noted, "In their outdoor banners, the No would put a woman with a shotgun saying, 'I want to defend my home,' while in Brazil women are completely against any kind of violence. . . . Women do not like guns."[39]

Whether or not an accurate view of women – and the 64 percent vote against the referendum suggests its error – Dreyfus was right about a WFSA member prompting the ad. However,

---

[38] Dreyfus interview.
[39] IBOPE, "Corruption in Politics," 5; Dreyfus interview. See also Carien du Plessis, "Putting a Hold on Bullets," *This Day* (South Africa), Mar. 8, 2004, http://www.iansa.org/women/hold_on_bullets.htm.

it was not the NRA but Canada's National Firearms Association (NFA) that lent its "fighting techniques." As the NFA's president David Tomlinson recalled about e-mail exchanges initiated by the ANPCA's Leonardo Arruda:

I injected a few suggestions about ways in which they could pull in different groups.... For example, firearms groups have a tendency to ignore women, which is really stupid because that's 50% of the population. You have to get them in on it, you have to get them to realize that the government is asking them to make themselves even more defenseless than they normally are.

Whether or not an accurate view of women – and the NFA's promotion of an unarmed rape-defense technique, "The Lioness," suggests its error – Tomlinson's ideas inspired the No's ad campaign.[40]

As for the woman's photograph in the Brazilian billboards, Dreyfus was right about its foreign origins, but wrong again about its being the NRA. Tennessee photographer and gun enthusiast Oleg Volk was the source. His intervention occurred at the ANPCA's e-mailed initiative. When Brazilian photographers refused to help the gun groups – apparently fearing business losses if they furnished No activists with snapshots of gun-wielding Amazons – Arruda turned to the World Wide Web. There he found a trove of pictures at Volk's "Girls with Guns" Web site: dozens of respectful, even artistic photos of women (in various states of dress and undress) cradling rifles, semiautomatics, and pistols. Volk encouraged the ANPCA to use any of his work, gratis, "help[ing the No campaign] very much," according to Arruda.[41]

---

[40] David Tomlinson, National President, NFA, personal interview, June 30, 2006, New York, NY (audiotape). "The Lioness," freely available on the Internet as the "NFA's contribution to the safety of women," presents techniques that go well beyond "the 'knee in the groin' [which] does not work, because men spend their entire lives being protective of their testicles." NFA, "For Women Only–The Lioness Method of Rape Prevention," n.d., http://www.nfa.ca/taxonomy/term/37.

[41] Information and quotations in this and the next paragraph are from Arruda interview. See also Girls with Guns, http://www.moviebadgirls.com/olegvolk_

The latter was careful to pick photos appropriate to Brazil, where it would be "strange" to see people holding guns in a political ad. Sorting through the rough, Arruda found a diamond: an attractive young woman – dressed, and in a conservative business suit – shotgun in one hand (but only a small part visible), mobile phone in the other. The ANPCA used the same photo in two-page magazine spreads, captioning it less aggressively. Across from the photo, a full page of text denounced the referendum, even quoting Pope John Paul II on the right to self-defense.[42]

Other ads did have NRA origins. The industrious Arruda studied its past campaigns and used what he could. Explaining his method in one case, he said,

I based this campaign on one the NRA made. It showed situations when it was a good thing to have a gun at hand: . . . A woman coming outside a supermarket with some bags and a little child, and the parking lot completely empty at night. And written below, "There are some times when it is good to have a gun at hand." I could use this. But . . . the woman was too much American, and the parking lot was not what we see here in Brazil. So I needed a Brazilian photographer to help, but I couldn't find one."[43]

Citizens Won and Lost

In the end, the self-defense campaign won the referendum's battle for public opinion. Why is less certain. At the deepest level, there is no question that the No campaign enjoyed a significant monetary advantage. Although the civil society groups have few resources themselves, Brazil's gun industry underwrote the campaign, employing top public relations talent, in addition to scrapping in the legislature and courts before and after. Official filings with the Brazilian electoral commission showed that the

page1.html; Oleg Volk, Creative Advertising Director, Volkstudio, telephone interview, Jan. 28, 2011 (audiotape).

[42] Compare Volk, "Alive," n.d. http://www.moviebadgirls.com/olegvolk_page4 .html to Armaria, "Call 190," 2005, http://Armaria.com.br/disque%20190 .pdf.

[43] Arruda interview.

No campaign outspent the Yes by about 2:1.[44] On the other hand, this monetary advantage was reduced by the Brazilian election law providing equal media time in the referendum's final weeks. The Yes had a raft of powerful domestic supporters, from the Presidency, to the media, to major corporations. Unlike the self-defense NGOs, Viva Rio and Sou da Paz enjoy foreign and government financing, large budgets, and professional staffs.

Leaving money aside, in the referendum vote itself, Brazilians appear to have rejected the idea that disarmament could bring peace – and to have preferred the possibility of owning firearms in the future. As the No campaign's advertising firm IBOPE reported in the waning days of the campaign, the "idea of individual rights" was creating a "strong and instant echo." After the vote, media reports confirmed this anecdotally, and Sou da Paz acknowledged it: "Cleverly, the 'No' campaign ... emphasized that a citizen, by voting for the ban, would lose a fundamental 'right' ... convinc[ing] most of the population of this right."[45]

Promoting and Demoting Brazil

The outcome of the Brazilian gun fight, like that of many policy battles, is multiple and muddled. On one hand, the watershed victory is the strict Statute of Disarmament in 2003. On the other, a core goal, ending private gun sales, died at the hands of the Brazilian people in 2005. We have seen how the warring factions fought the major battles. After the referendum vote, they kept on sparring. Gun groups, fired up by the result, demanded the statute's immediate repeal. Although this has not happened, sympathetic legislators introduced myriad bills whittling away at individual provisions, while their lawyerly counterparts harassed through the courts. For their part, dispirited control advocates

---

[44] Josias De Souza, "Arms Industry Backer of the No Campaign," *Folha de S. Paulo*, Nov. 25, 2005, http://josiasdesouza.folha.blog.uol.com.br/arch2005-11-20_2005-11-26.html.

[45] IBOPE, "Corrpution in Politics," 3; Instituto Sou da Paz, "Brazil: Changing a History of Violence," 6.

nonetheless rallied to the law's defense, pushing for its full implementation. Among other things, they created a Web site, "Eye on the Disarmament Statute," to promote it and fend off attacks.

How did overseas networks respond to this ongoing battle? Answering this question illuminates how transnational networks use local skirmishes in larger wars. Often they do so as demonstrations, both positive and negative, of their own preferences – or their foes' perversity. In addition, analyzing the issue reveals the logic and limits of transnational support. In the Brazilian shootout, there is rough symmetry to the transnational responses. IANSA hailed the statute and the referendum before the vote, when victory seemed likely. Then, in the face of stinging defeat, it distanced itself. The NRA is a study in contrasts – helping the self-defense coalition when the Brazilian congressional brawl over the disarmament statute still seemed winnable, keeping its distance when the referendum campaign seemed lost, and righteously braying when Brazilians voted "Não."

Ballyhooing Brazil: IANSA before the Vote

As we have seen, the control network's interest in Brazil was long-standing because of the country's size and importance. When the disarmament statute passed in 2003, albeit in curtailed form after a grueling battle, Viva Rio activist Bandeira touted the victory in an IANSA publication: "The population has spoken: Brazilians want tighter gun laws." IANSA itself gloated over the "big defeat" for the "Brazilian gun lobby and the NRA."[46] Kicking a sworn enemy when down not only feels good; it may help in the next round, demoralizing the foe, or at least making it appear vulnerable.

To excite its troops before the referendum, IANSA portrayed Brazil as a decisive battleground in a larger war. A few days before the vote, the World Council of Churches and IANSA promoted an International Day of Support for this "historic

---

[46] Bandeira quoted in IANSA, "New Gun Laws in Brazil"; IANSA, "Historic Decision: Disarmament Statute Passed in Congress," 2003, http://www.iansa.org/regions/samerica/campaigners_congress.htm.

opportunity to make people safer from gun violence." With actions in many countries, the day's events included picketing Brazilian consulates to show that the referendum was an "international concern." Leaders of the Control Arms campaign predicted that the referendum would be "ground-breaking globally" and would be a "first step towards support for an international treaty to control the arms trade." In private, IANSA was even more aggressive. According to board member Daniel Luz, Brazil would pioneer a new, populist approach to gun control, with similar referenda projected first for South Africa and then other countries.[47]

Burying Brazil: IANSA after the Vote

After the referendum rout, however, demotion and rationalization took the fore. The control network blamed dark foreign elements and the immaturity of the Brazilian electorate. American Viva Rio staff member Jessica Galeria griped to CNN without irony, "The whole campaign [against the ban] was imported from the United States. They just translated a lot of material from the NRA.... Now, a lot of Brazilians are insisting on their right to bear arms." There is something to this charge, but neither Brazilian activists nor voters blindly embraced foreign influences. Newfound critics also claimed that the vote did not represent Brazilians' real beliefs. Instead, the referendum was "polluted by politics," a "protest vote" against an unpopular federal government, as Viva Rio's Pablo Dreyfus said – although President Lula was handily reelected the following year.[48]

Most strikingly, the control groups delegitimated referendum politics itself. Earlier, activists such as Sou da Paz's Denis Mizne

[47] World Council of Churches, "International Day of Support for the Brazilian Disarmament Referendum," press release, http://www2.wcc-coe.org/dov .nsf/f4f5a8b3b4d0f25fc1256c83004f1a28/c23f58010877af17c125708f0058 e550?OpenDocument; Control Arms Campaign, "Brazilians in London say 'Yes' to a Ban on Gun Sales Back Home," press release, Oct. 16, 2005 (author's files); Luz interview.

[48] Galeria quoted in Associated Press, "Violence-Plagued Brazil"; Dreyfus interview.

had celebrated it for uniting "two of our unalienable (sic) civil rights . . . : democratic participation and the defense of life" – and had planned for more referenda in other countries. Months later, however, at a sober World Council of Churches debriefing led by Viva Rio's Rubem Fernandes, participants "broadly agreed that referendums invite manipulation of values and perceptions, especially when the system staging the vote has limited public confidence and public safety is low." Or, as the NRA's Wayne LaPierre hyped the remarks, using words attributed to Viva Rio's Fernandes: "First lesson is don't trust direct democracy."[49]

Gun-Shy: NRA before the Vote

How did the gun network treat its local counterparts? Early on, of course, the NRA helped the Brazilians, and this had lasting effects. After the disarmament statute's passage, however, the NRA's direct involvement waned. By 2004, Brazil looked to be a lost cause. Cautious with their resources, the NRA and WFSA therefore provided little concrete support in the referendum battle itself.

This was true despite the ANPCA directly and repeatedly seeking help. Days after the Statute of Disarmament's passage, it dispatched written appeals to the NRA, the American Conservative Union, the John Birch Society, the Cato Institute, the Heritage Foundation, and eight other American groups. The letters, individually scripted but from a common English prototype, are paragons of entreaty, salesmanship, and blunt requests for cash. In the NRA letter, a "defeated" ANPCA extols the American organization as the Brazilians' "inspiration source. We have modeled some of our actions based on the success of your strategy.

---

[49] Mizne quoted in Instituto Sou da Paz, "The Campaign for the Brazilian Referendum Starts Today," press release, Aug. 1, 2005, http://www. iansa.org/regions/samerica/documents/soudapaz-pr10805.pdf; World Council of Churches and Ecumenical Network on Small Arms, "Firearms, Politics & Faith: Lessons from the Brazilian Referendum," *Global Action to Stop Gun Violence: PrepCom for the Review Conference 9–20 January 2006*, http://www.iansa.org/un/review2006/documents/PrepCom-report.pdf, 10; LaPierre, *Global War on Your Guns*, 187.

The ANPCA was created to be something similar to your ILA [Institute of Legislative Action]." After detailing the gun groups' gallant but losing fight against the Statute of Disarmament, the letter blames the defeat on Brazil's "leftist" government and on "strong international support" from such right-wing anathemas as the Ford and Soros Foundations. But all was not lost! The Referendum lay ahead, an opportunity "to change this draconian law" and help American gun owners stem a looming threat. Concluding, the ANPCA declared that "we cannot go on without international help" either from the NRA or from "any other conservative institution in the US or abroad that could assist in our figh[t]."[50]

The NRA rejected the pleas, however, according to ANPCA president Antonio Alves: "'Your proposal does not square with programs the NRA sponsors.' Full stop." In addition, the NRA ignored less formal requests for low-cost solidarity:

It was not necessary that the NRA take money from its coffers. It was enough that they mount a campaign to support us. Something like: Help Brazilians stop a gun ban. We are certain numerous NRA members would have aided us spontaneously. The American people have a tradition of solidarity and international aid.[51]

The NRA rejected this plea too, only issuing a self-regarding statement that Brazil could be "a steppingstone for the global gun-ban lobby to inflict its will on law-abiding gun owners in the United States." ANPCA President Alves's view of this rejection appears correct: "The NRA was intimidated by our situation.... The fight was unequal and the chance of victory appeared minute."[52] Only less powerful foreign activists, such as Canada's NFA and the American photographer Oleg Volk, provided small-scale aid at this time. For the NRA, however,

---

[50] ANPCA, letter from Leonardo Arruda to Kayne Robinson, president, National Rifle Association, Jan. 12, 2004, (on file with author).

[51] Antonio Alves, "Should the NRA Care about Brazil?" (Deve a NRA se importar com o Brasil?), ANPCA, Feb. 15, 2006 (on file with author).

[52] Ibid; Chris W. Cox quoted in Kelly Hearn, "As Brazil Votes to Ban Guns, NRA Joins the Fight," *Nation*, Oct. 21, 2005, available online at http://www .csgv.org/news/headlines/thenation_brazil.cfm; Tomlinson interview.

organizational needs appear to have trumped its clear ideological affinity with Brazil's gun groups.

Guns Ablaze: NRA after the Vote

After the unexpected result, however, the NRA and WFSA trumpeted the Brazilian referendum as a global triumph. Within hours, an astonished NRA Radio host interviewed PLD spokesperson Jairo Paes de Lira by telephone. In December 2005, the NRA membership magazine, *America's 1st Freedom*, featured a lengthy interview with a No campaign leader. In early 2006, the NRA Web site posted a Wayne LaPierre story on "Why You Should Care about Brazil" – because the control NGOs want to bring "civil disarmament" to "our shores," fulfilling Rebecca "Peters' and George Soros' ultimate dream." Back in Brazil, however, ANPCA leaders were having none of it. ANPCA President Alves penned a mockingly titled article, "Does the NRA Care about Brazil?" in which he questioned the Americans' real commitment to Brazilian gun owners.[53]

Undeterred, LaPierre dedicated a full chapter of his April 2006 book to the "handful of men and women who have created an obviously effective pro-gun grassroots effort out of whole cloth." Exploiting the referendum for its positive demonstration effects, he urged that the No's "victory, that resonance with ordinary citizens of the world who understood that they possess a basic human right to own firearms, must be studied, amplified, and replicated." Gun Owners of America broadened the outcome, too, albeit more negatively. It linked President Lula and the referendum to other "corrupt, socialist politicians such as Chicago Mayor Richard Daley and New Orleans Mayor Ray Nagin," both gun control supporters.[54]

---

[53] Wayne LaPierre, "Why You Should Care about Brazil," *America's 1st Freedom*, Dec. 2005, reprinted in NRA Political Victory Fund, Feb. 18, 2006. http://www.nrapvf.org/News/Article.aspx?ID=189; Antonio Alves, "Should the NRA Care about Brazil?"

[54] LaPierre, "Why You Should Care about Brazil"; LaPierre, *Global War on Your Guns*, 190; Larry Pratt, "Brazilians Say No to Gun Ban," Gun Owners of America, Oct. 2005, http://gunowners.org/op0547.htm.

PLD spokesperson Jairo Paes de Lira soared to celebrity in the global gun network. Although Brazilian gun groups have not been able to afford WFSA's high dues, he was acclaimed at its yearly meeting in Nuremberg. He spoke, too, under WFSA's umbrella at the 2006 UN Small Arms Review Conference, arguing that the Brazilian vote proved the unpopularity and wrongheadedness of controls. And at the NRA's 2006 annual convention, Paes de Lira was honored as a "remarkable man" for his "service in the cause of freedom."[55]

Despite all the post hoc acclaim, however, the NRA's refusal to help the Brazilian self-defense groups during the campaign is telling. Transnational support is a matter of hard-nosed organizational choice, as much as moral sympathy. Just as critical as whether it will help a client is whether it will help or harm a patron engaged in larger international wars.

Conclusion

Brazil's continuing conflict over disarmament is, first and foremost, a matter of national politics. In everyday skirmishes between control proponents and opponents – in Brazil's Congress, courts, and media – domestic forces predominate. At crucial moments, however, the battle was influenced by the same international antagonists who struggled over small arms at the UN. The very recognition of a gun crisis, as opposed to long-standing public security and policing problems, hinged on the skill of activists and politicians linked to UN agencies and IANSA. An array of tactics and ideas had international sources, even if they were fine-tuned for deployment in the Brazilian theater.

As at the UN, however, the Brazilian control movement sparked opposition, rooted in national and international sources.

---

[55] Paes de Lira, "Mandate from Brazil"; NRA, "2006 Annual Meeting Officers' Speeches: Sandra Froman," http://www.nra.org/speech.aspx?id=6756. See also TFP.org, "How to Say No to Gun Control," June 29, 2006, http://www.tfp.org/current-campaigns/2006/how-to-say-no-to-gun-control.html.

Foes questioned the very existence of the problem and excoriated the disarmament solution. The conflict's dynamics and outcomes hinged as much on the transnationally linked domestic actors proposing disarmament as on their equally connected opposite numbers. Nor is Brazil unusual in this regard. Many countries around the globe debate domestic gun measures. In many of them, the battles have important international dimensions, involving both the import of resources and ideas and the export of useful local developments to the larger global war.

7

Conclusion

The Landmines Treaty, the International Criminal Court (ICC), the Responsibility to Protect (R2P): recent decades have seen a host of new international initiatives celebrated as triumphs of civil society. As the activists involved well know, however, these were hard-fought accomplishments, achieved after years of bruising battles against recalcitrant states and broader networks. Each policy emerged diminished from the original dream: the Landmines Treaty, unratified by the world's biggest mine producers and users; the ICC, similarly partial; and R2P, simply a contested idea.

Nor has conflict over these institutions and norms ended. With the ICC's passage, sovereigntist NGOs and the U.S. government, which did not ratify the Rome Statute, demanded Article 98 agreements from other states, further insulating American officials from the already small possibility of prosecution. A key practitioner of universal jurisdiction, Spanish judge Baltazar Garzon, found himself indicted by a national court – for pursuing such foreigners as Chilean President Augusto Pinochet – much to the delight of conservative legal lights overseas. The Landmines Treaty faces continued attack from those who doubt its effectiveness and sensibility. For its part, R2P has been denounced by both left and right.

None of this is to say that these developments are pointless or weak. Indeed, the post hoc potshots may indicate their potential. Placing these accomplishments in broader context, however, demonstrates two things: abiding controversy over global issues, even those touted as major wins for civil society; and consequent need for analysts to devote equal attention to policy making and unmaking. The clash of networks, spanning states and NGOs, is central. Confrontation runs deep, to the very existence of supposed global problems. It plays out in their denial, as well as in the construction/deconstruction of solutions, the building/unbuilding of networks, the dynamics of combat, and the contingent and temporary outcomes that result. To examine only one side in one institution – and to neglect the way contenders bash one another even as they seek to influence decision makers across domestic and international arenas – is to miss the turbulent core of transnational politics.

The analytic approach proposed in this book highlights these critical clashes. Rooted in recognition that activists have both moral and material motivations, it emphasizes the strategic dilemmas they face. These have no easy or certain answers. Opponents' anticipated reactions play a major role in decisions, even if internal network dynamics, institutional rules, and broader political opportunities matter too. The book's main hypothesis highlights an important, seemingly obvious, but overlooked point: resistance makes new policy harder to achieve. The model draws attention to reasons this is so, identifying how rival networks undermine one another as an integral part of promoting their own agendas. Using this approach and taking a panoramic view, analysts will gain a more realistic understanding of policy making/unmaking.

International Norms and Domestic Politics

The international cases in this book, focusing on the UN and the broader global stage, show how rival networks confront one another at every turn. In the gun control and gay rights cases, proponents succeeded in constructing problems and mobilizing networks, galvanizing media and popular attention. Opponents did the same, however, with both sides deploying affirmative and negative tactics to advance their causes and batter their foes. UN advocacy, however, does not appear to have changed diplomats' minds or states' policies, let alone the rivals' views. The real action occurs in domestic politics, where states formulate their stances on international issues.[1]

National battle lines parallel those at the international level, and influences among them are mutual. However, a country's support for a disputed norm is contingent primarily on domestic forces. Claims about what is internationally appropriate remain at odds. Nor is there anything obvious about how a state should maintain its reputation. Has Sweden's adoption of homophobic hate speech laws raised its standing by making it more friendly to sexual minorities – or hurt it by making it more hostile to free speech? That is a political question. People of different beliefs will answer it in different ways, frequently with strategic ends in mind.

Consider too the United States, where recent shifts in ruling coalitions have resulted in changes to America's position on international gun and gay issues. In 2009, the Obama administration, in a bow to the political import of the American gay movement, opted to sign the General Assembly joint resolution on gay rights, whereas the Bush administration had refused. On the gun issue, President Obama, already fingered by domestic gun groups as enemy number one, warmed to the Arms Trade Treaty (ATT), whereas President Bush had given it a cold shoulder. Days after taking office, he also reversed the Mexico City policy barring government-supported family planning groups from promoting abortion overseas – a flip-flop that has occurred after every change in party control of the presidency since 1984. In an earlier and well-known example, Bush, moved by a strong sovereigntist current in his coalition, unsigned the Rome Statute of the ICC.

---

[1] Daniel W. Drezner, *All Politics Is Global: Explaining International Regulatory Regimes* (Princeton, N.J.: Princeton University Press, 2008).

Further back in history, Congress's rejection of Woodrow Wilson's League of Nations makes a similar point.

In these cases, especially the latter two, state preferences shifted in directions contrary to what many considered an emerging international norm. They did so in the wake of sharp conflict and because of the power of the ruling domestic coalition. Even in the first three cases, it would be difficult to say that the international norm itself had an effect, given the limited nature of the shift in U.S. policy. And it seems likely, at least in the case of the ATT and the Mexico City policy, that the return of a Republican administration backed by a coalition similar to President Bush's will lead to another reversal. In short, shifts in national political control result in changes to state policy, even when the international normative climate remains unchanged or shifts in opposite ways.

If this is correct, what is international combat all about? For one thing, domestic activists import overseas ideas and approaches to fight about national laws. Brazil's Disarmament Statute, encouraged by transnational networks, illustrates this, even if domestic politics was still central to its eventual passage. Romania's marriage laws had a similar mix of foreign and indigenous roots. As both cases show, however, transnationally linked domestic activism faces resistance: rival networks deploy other international developments and contrary soft law to make polar points. If one side insists that its favored norms are modern or even civilized, foes will deny the assertion or discount it as posturing. All sides fabricate echo chambers reverberating with their ideas, hoping that shouting them will make them so. Likewise, they revel in reports that their norms are cascading, splashing the news hither and yon to extend their success. They float soft law to lift their prospects. And they urge states to enhance their reputations by adopting pet policies. Persuasion is always challenged, however, not least by civil society rivals. There are multiple echo chambers and cascades – or, more accurately, claims to them. For example, even against the recent tide of European institutions accepting gay unions, most Romanians have deplored the supposed error and immorality of this move.

In such combat, contenders use the gamut of democratic procedures to further their goals. This was what Sweden's gay activists did in criminalizing homophobic hate speech – and what their Romanian opposite numbers did in preserving traditional marriage later in the decade. In all this, overseas allies supplied ideas, tactics, and resources. Strategists met with local leaders and helped them mold approaches used elsewhere to specific domestic contexts. In some cases, foreigners took prominent symbolic roles, as Desmond Tutu and Nelson Mandela did in Brazil's referendum. Even among the U.S. right, such support occurs. Witness Åke Green's California visitation at the height of the Proposition 8 campaign – or the NRA's trumpeting of Brazil's surprising referendum result in the United States and beyond. Even in defeat, activists use local outcomes to influence events elsewhere. With Green's stinging acquittal, Swedish and European gay groups redoubled efforts to restrict hate speech.

Scope

How representative are the issues I examined here, guns and gays? Skeptics might argue they are unrepresentative, involving activists moved by the "lurid glow of strong convictions."[2] In what issues are fervent policy entrepreneurs not critical, however? Even in matters of war and peace, where some might imagine differences would be submerged in the joint quest for survival, partisans rear their heads – albeit shrouding themselves in anesthetizing billows of national security rhetoric. America's 2003 Iraq invasion proves the power of neoconservative networks operating at the pinnacles of high politics. This is only one episode among numerous others, demonstrating the pervasiveness of conflict and activism.

Critics might claim that by choosing notorious culture-war issues, I stacked the deck in favor of finding contention. As noted

[2] Joseph Conrad, *Nostromo: A Tale of the Seaboard* (London: Harper & Bros., 1904), 164.

in Chapter 1, my primary reason for doing so was methodological – choosing cases typical in that they have not resulted in major new policy, at least at the international level. In addition, such cases provided the best research site for finding recurrent but neglected strategies central to transnational clashes. No doubt the cases elicit strong emotions. By contrast, some would argue, economic issues do not raise such deep-seated feelings, do not have such black-and-white solutions, and are therefore more negotiable.

The distinction between moral and material is overdrawn, however. The gun case is a good example. For some, it might seem material, simply a matter of the number or caliber of firearms one may possess. For gun owners, however, it is much more – a moral, if not sacral, issue. Much the same goes even for "pure" economic issues, such as wages. The figures can be compromised, at least temporarily, but even labor disputes elicit rival ethical claims – about a living wage or a right to contract, whether they erupt in Indonesia or Indiana.

The question remains: do certain issues elicit more contention than others? Although this book was not designed to find an answer, I have suggested throughout that conflict is endemic to politics. Hardly an original observation, it is true by definition. Nor is strife confined to the left-right axis. The analytic model developed here applies beyond that divide. Nonetheless, it is obvious that certain issues generate more or less friction than the norm. To determine the model's scope, several hypotheses are worth exploring.

First, the less an issue affects the basic interests or beliefs of an organized segment of society, the less likely it will spark conflict. This triviality hypothesis seems plausible, given the human condition of scarce time and resources. It is worth noting, however, that advocacy groups have internal, organizational reasons for hyping even small threats. A second and more interesting hypothesis comes from game theory. Issues in which groups desire to cooperate will be more tractable than those in which they do not. Trade is an example. If the goal of different interests is to exchange with one another, they have strong incentive to reach agreement. That does not foreclose hard bargaining and forceful efforts to attain the best possible deal. In trade policy, however, there is a clear incentive to . . . trade. By contrast, for issues in which such incentives are not present, conflict is more likely to be deep and abiding. Of course in such cases, those who style a problem as international claim that it must be solved through cooperation. That claim is disputed, however, by those who reject the problem's pervasiveness or existence. Climate change is an important example, with many defining its solution as necessarily global, whereas others oppose such responses or reject the problem entirely.

Third, lack of conflict around important issues may mean that powerful forces are stifling mobilization. At the extreme, absence of controversy may indicate the sway of hegemonic beliefs backed by commanding interests or force. Of course, in democratic or diverse settings, such as the international system, dominance is difficult to maintain. Rivals nonetheless seek supremacy. They wrest institutions from one another, guarding them against ideological enemies. They squelch the merest whisper of debate, hounding those who dare speak out against the consensus. They proclaim their own position as beyond politics or as unequivocally in the public interest, hoping that this will quell resistance, at least for a while.[3]

Finally, technical issues are less likely to spark conflict, whereas political issues – those linked to varying ideological or moral visions – are more likely to do so. Standard setting about Internet protocols or, in the more distant past, about electrical currents epitomize such matters. Of course, the very question of what is political and what technical is contested. Indeed, a redoubtable gambit involves slipping an issue from the first to the second category, engaging authorities to solemnize the shift. If that works, conflicts may be reduced or avoided. As we have seen, however, rivals spit in the face of one another's sages. They politicize what others claim is "for experts only." Nonetheless,

---

[3] See, e.g., John Gaventa, *Power and Powerlessness: Quiescence and Rebellion in an Appalachian Valley* (Urbana: University of Illinois Press, 1980).

once an issue has been relegated to the technical realm, it is less likely to elicit controversy. Challenging it becomes harder once the policy is locked in by routine behavior or protected by potent new interests.[4]

Extensions

These and other hypotheses are worth exploring and potentially explain variation in conflict levels. I nonetheless maintain that contention is central to international policy making/unmaking and should be the focus of analysis. To signal this throughout the book, I have illustrated key arguments, strategies, and ideas with diverse examples beyond guns and gay rights. In addition, consider other issues, several transcending the left-right divide.

Human trafficking has gained significant attention in recent years as a violation of rights, especially women's rights. Mainstream activists have documented the problem's scope, particularly in Southeast Asia and Eastern Europe. Others have taken a more vigorous tack, rescuing women and girls from slave-like conditions. At the same time, however, a rival network argues that significant parts of "trafficking" are "sex work" – a hard choice made by women in unfavorable circumstances. The sides differ on numerous points, attacking one another for misconception, misconduct, and immorality.[5]

Poverty and its solutions have spawned enduring controversy. Some decry the selfishness of Northern countries in making

---

[4] See generally Tim Buthe, "The Power of Norms; The Norms of Power: Who Governs International Electrical and Electronic Technology," in *Who Governs the Globe?* ed. Deborah D. Avant, Martha Finnemore, and Susan K Sell (Cambridge: Cambridge University Press, 2010), 292–332.

[5] Aaron Cohen with Christine Buckley, *Slave Hunter: One Man's Global Quest to Free Victims of Human Trafficking* (New York: Simon & Schuster, 2009); Global Network of Sex Work Projects, "Making Sex Work Safe: A Practical Guide for Programme Managers, Policy-Makers and Field Workers," http://www.nswp.org/makesexsafe/; Terrence McKeegan, "UN Promotes Prostitution as Harm Reduction," Friday Fax, C-FAM, Feb. 24, 2011, http://www.c-fam.org/publications/id.1793/pub_detail.asp.

too little foreign assistance available. An enormous development industry has sprung up to feed the apparent need, replete with NGOs, think tanks, and celebrities. Aid, however, has been condemned by a powerful network featuring Africans such as Kenya's James Shikwati, whose interview in a major international magazine was titled, "'For God's Sake, Please Stop the Aid.'" Shikwati received his initial infusion of resources from the Mackinac Center for Public Policy, a free-market think tank located in Midland, Michigan. In turn, Mackinac is part of a larger international network anchored by the Atlas Economic Research Foundation that aims at "exporting the [free market] revolution" to the world.[6]

Consider too the controversy over genetically modified (GM) foods. The primary policy division is regional, with the European Union and the United States adopting contradictory standards for cultivation and consumption. This is not a culture-war issue, and in some ways it crosscuts left-right divisions. Nonetheless, it has sparked protracted and deep conflict. As new technologies made these foods available in the 1990s, food and environmental activists criticized their safety and ecological impacts. For some, the existence of these organisms raises profound moral questions about tampering with nature. Simultaneously, however, a global network denounced opponents as Luddites. It lobbied for change in restrictive national policies. It unearthed allies in the developing world. It urged the United Nations to solve world hunger not with donated food aid but with cultivable GM seeds sold to farmers. As in the other cases noted in this book, contention

---

[6] "'For God's Sake, Please Stop the Aid': *Spiegel* interview with African Economics Expert," *Der Spiegel Online*, http://www.spiegel.de/international/spiegel/0,1518,363663,00.html; personal interview, Josephat Juma, Managing Editor, *African Executive*, Inter Region Economic Network (IREN), July 21, 2008, Nairobi, Kenya (notes); personal interview, Lawrence Reed, President, Mackinac Center for Public Policy, Midland, MI, July 26, 2007, Midland, MI (audiotape). See also Dambisa Moyo, *Dead Aid: Why Aid Is Not Working and How There Is a Better Way for Africa* (New York: Farrar, Straus and Giroux, 2009); Gerald Frost, *Antony Fisher: Champion of Liberty* (London: Profile Books, 2002).

envelops the issue. The warring sides have their own rival epistemic communities, and the combatants deploy the full range of affirmative and negative tactics against one another. The upshot has been lasting conflict that has spilled into international institutions and countries. Resolution may be possible through the slow development of scientific consensus. Given the powerful interests that have taken arms on both sides, however, this seems likely only in the long term, after much more vituperation, and with aspects of the issue remaining disputed.[7]

Implications

Right Wing in World Politics

If the approach developed here is broadly applicable, what are the implications? Some of these relate to right-wing groups; others to conflict's centrality in transnational politics. Regarding the first, if this book shows anything, it is that the right has entered global politics in force and with sophistication – despite, in many cases, fearing, opposing, and detesting internationalism. The NRA, often derided as parochial – as a bunch of red-blooded, redneck, red-state Americans – is in fact anything but: it is a seasoned, cosmopolitan actor. The World Congress of Family's "Petition in Support of Romania's Defense of Marriage" makes the same point in a different way: an international appeal emphasizing the virtues of national culture. This is not to say that

---

7 Mark A. Pollack and Gregory C. Shaffer, *When Cooperation Fails: The International Law and Politics of Genetically Modified Foods* (Oxford: Oxford University Press, 2009); Robert Paarlberg, *Starved for Science: How Biotechnology Is Being Kept Out of Africa* (Cambridge, MA: Harvard University Press, 2008); Ronald J. Herring, *Transgenics and the Poor: Biotechnology in Development Studies* (New York: Routledge, 2007); Lovemore Simwanda, President, Zambia National Farmers Union, personal interview, July 24, 2008, Lusaka, Zambia (audiotape); Mwananyanda Mbikusita Lewanika, Executive Director, National Institute for Scientific and Industrial Research, Lusaka, Zambia. Personal interview, July 22, 2008, Lusaka (audiotape); Margaret Karembu, Director, International Service for the Acquisition of Agri-Biotech Applications (ISAAA) AfriCenter, Nairobi, Kenya. Personal interview, July 22, 2008, Nairobi, Kenya (audiotape).

there is a vast, right-wing conspiracy working across borders. In fact, there are sharp divisions within what is too easily seen as a cohesive wing, just as there are on the left.

Beyond particular issues, right-wing activists are sharp critics of global institutions writ large. In this book, I alluded to these views, such as attacks on the UN by the NRA and C-FAM. Recent years have seen the rise of groups broadly antagonistic to transnational politics. These have long been present in the United States, the John Birch Society being a prime example. Today, they have become more active and widespread. Examples include not only the Atlas Foundation, but also the American Enterprise Institute's NGO Watch, the United Kingdom's Institute of Economic Affairs, Israel's NGO Monitor, and Australia's Institute of Public Affairs. Behind the scenes, their wide-ranging critiques provide rich fodder for more narrowly gauged organizations. The assaults center on the alleged inaccuracy, hyperbole, and bias of NGOs, at least those of the left. They extend to opacity, unaccountability, and arrogance – the same accusations NGOs hurl at corporations and international financial institutions. In addition, there are more fundamental charges: that NGO activism undermines democracy, capitalism, and national sovereignty. These views may seem extreme, even histrionic. The accusers' close ties to corporate, governmental, and academic institutions mean that NGOs cannot ignore the attacks, however.[8]

These broad developments and the cases in this book raise questions about the role of the international in progressive dreams. Although world government has few fans today, global governance is touted to solve crises that states, limited by parochial views, cannot. As this book has shown, however, the left cannot be sanguine that global governance will meet its

---

[8] AEI and Federalist Society, NGO Watch, http://www.globalgovernancewatch .org/ngo_watch/; Michael Edwards, *Civil Society* (Cambridge: Polity Press, 2004); Global Accountability Project, "Pathways to Accountability: The GAP Framework," One World Trust, 2005, http://www.oneworldtrust.org/pages/ download.cfm?did=314. See generally John Fonte, "Liberal Democracy vs. Transnational Progressivism: The Ideological War Within the West," *Orbis* 46, no. 3 (2002), 449–67.

hopes. The right uses international institutions to advance its aims and frustrate its foes. This is most obvious in the economic realm, where powerful corporations, governments, foundations, and think tanks support market arrangements against which global movements have formed. The sharp conflicts surrounding neoliberalism demonstrate that transnational processes in themselves are neutral.[9]

The situation resembles that facing American liberals, who once saw the judicial branch as a countermajoritarian means of attaining progressive ends not achievable through legislative politics. Opponents quickly caught on. They trained their own cause lawyers. They built their own legal action networks. When they could, they packed the bench with stalwarts. As a result, the left's expectations that the courts would solve pressing social problems have faded. The judiciary is again recognized for what it in fact always was: another political battleground. A similar fate has already befallen the transnational, with the right matching the left network for network.[10]

Conflict in Policy Making/Unmaking

If we are far from general deference to the UN or other international institutions, the conflicts this book highlights raise larger questions. For one, what is the role of rhetorical techniques such as persuading, framing, and grafting? If policy is unmade as much as it is made, dissuasion – smashing, severing, tarring, and more – merits equal attention. So do nonrhetorical strategies such as intimidating, stripping, blocking, and excluding. These can thwart a network's formation, distort its identity, muffle its voice, or shut it out of key institutions. In such cases, persuasive and dissuasive rhetoric stand little chance. Given the power of the negative, the venerable battle of ideas metaphor takes on new depth and meaning.

---

[9] Smith, *Social Movements for Global Democracy.*
[10] Brian Z. Tamanaha, *Law as a Means to an End: Threat to the Rule of Law* (Cambridge: Cambridge University Press, 2006). Teles, *Rise of the Conservative Legal Movement.*

In addition, this book calls into issue the larger effects of persuasion – and dissuasion. Of course, if one side's arguments and denunciations can be voiced, they have meaning, if only to each conflicting network. In confirming deep-seated beliefs about "our" side's rectitude and "their" side's treachery, the rhetoric energizes the troops for another assault on the institutions and the enemy. As I showed in this book, however, few minds were changed on either guns or gay rights at the UN, in Sweden, or in Romania. Only in the Brazilian referendum, where many voters probably resembled a tabula rasa condition, is something resembling persuasion likely to have occurred. Of course, there is no question that political change happens over long periods of time, with public attitudes evolving on numerous issues. The widening acceptance of gay lifestyles exemplifies this. However, the mechanisms by which this occurs are more conflictual – and the results more fragile – than often assumed. Recent studies suggest that people confronted with contrary ideas often become more set in their beliefs, no matter how compelling the evidence against them. This is an important area for future research that should go beyond glib paeans to the powers of persuasion.[11]

For the more normatively inclined, this book raises additional questions. No doubt citizens, at least in democracies, yearn for an end to wrangling, even imagining that politics was once polite, or bemoaning our current age of antagonism. Fanning that desire, theorists promote constructive dialogue and deliberative democracy as alternatives to bickering, besmirching, and brawling. After all, there is an objective reality out there, and at the highest level of abstraction, there may be principles that all can agree to.

---

[11] See e.g., Brian J. Gaines, James H. Kuklinski, and Paul J. Quirk, "Same Facts, Different Interpretations: Partisan Motivation and Opinion on Iraq," *Journal of Politics* 15 (2007): 1–21; Brendan Nyhan and Jason Reifler, "When Corrections Fail: The Persistence of Political Misperceptions," *Political Behavior* 32, no. 2 (2010): 303–30; Brendan Nyhan, "Why the 'Death Panel' Myth Wouldn't Die: Misinformation in the Health Care Reform Debate," *Forum* (Berkeley Electronic Press) 8, no. 1 (2010), art. 5. See generally Diana C. Mutz, *Hearing the Other Side: Deliberative versus Participatory Democracy* (Cambridge: Cambridge University Press, 2006).

Freedom, justice, and security spring to mind – or, at less strato-
spheric heights, human rights and sustainability. Scrape away
the shiny surface of the most unobjectionable principles, however, and one uncovers ugly clashes over practical meanings.
Even when it comes to motherhood and apple pie, feuds break
out: Are the apples genetically modified? Do the crusts contain
transfats? Are the mothers lesbians? Do the women do anything
but bake?

It is true that within networks, civil discourse reigns. Differences, although important, are tactical or strategic. But move
beyond circuits of agreement to clashing networks – and the
persuasive ideal breaks down. Bridges are difficult, if not impossible, to build. Closed communication loops raise the rhetorical heat. The blogs of war deepen distrust. Debates resemble
slanging matches more than respectful dialogues. Often, too,
the controversies serve important purposes for the protagonists:
stoking attention to their issues, mobilizing their base, demonstrating their fighting skills, and securing their organizational
leadership.[12]

In such cases, reason alone is insufficient to convince. IANSA
director Rebecca Peters put it this way when I asked her about
the possibility of deliberating with the NRA:

They are not open to conversion. I think often people in movements
think that if you could just give [the opposition] the right information,
they would see it. That isn't how it's going to work.... There are certain
people you really should not waste one jot of energy attempting to
inform or convert or whatever, because that is a bit of energy you could
be using to save lives in some way.[13]

On this rare point, "certain people" share Peters' view. As Gun
Owners of America's Larry Pratt told me when describing an
exchange with a supporter of small arms control:

I might as well have been talking Chinese.... We were only about 6
feet from each other but actually we were on different planets. You

---

[12] Cf. Pollack and Shaffer, *When Cooperation Fails*, 92–94, 280–83.
[13] Peters interview.

have a clash of worldviews. We start from different premises. We are clearly not going to get to the same place if we are consistent. And they are consistent, and so are we.... This is war without guns – and the opposition wants to take it all. And you behave differently if that is your perception than if you think this is just having a nice meeting at the country club.

Of course, as Pratt states, incompatibility does not mean that "war" with guns is inevitable. In the clash of activisms, groups can persist in nonviolent disagreement indefinitely.[14]

Notably as well, such abiding disputes occur not just in cases of deep value differences. Reasoned debate may be impossible once organizational reputations and personal beliefs become invested in one or another idea. In such cases, actors' positions harden to such an extent that they close themselves off from alternative viewpoints no matter how rational. An important example in the context of international nutrition policy is the dominant – although tenuous – politico-scientific idea that human consumption of fat- and cholesterol-rich foods leads to obesity and heart disease.[15] Belief in a dire terrorist threat is another such hegemonic view. Politicians around the world use fear to sell their campaigns. Voices challenging the orthodoxy court ridicule. Everyone from major corporations to university research centers scrambles to feed at the trough of vast national and international monies available for terrorism-related products and ideas. The combination of monetary, organizational, and reputational investments in this "existential threat" mean that sensible debate about its actual scope is difficult.[16]

In these and other cases, antagonists are not looking for compromise. Dialogue is dismissed as pointless. Each network, backed by its own authorities and rooted in its own values, has

---

[14] Pratt interview.
[15] Gary Taubes, *Good Calories, Bad Calories: Fats, Carbs, and the Controversial Science of Diet and Health* (New York: Alfred A. Knopf, 2007).
[16] Ian S. Lustick, *Trapped in the War on Terror* (Philadelphia: University of Pennsylvania Press, 2006); John Mueller, *Overblown: How Politicians and the Terrorism Industry Inflate National Security Threats, and Why We Believe Them* (New York: Free Press, 2006).

its own "truths" immune to evidence or persuasion.[17] What of the common good – or the global interest? All sides pay it lip service. After all, it is a potent way of packaging anything, even naked self-interest. In fact, however, invoking the public good is seldom just empty words. Many activists are not cynical, even if they must always attend to material and organizational matters. They believe their goals *are* in the public interest. Indeed that may be the case if one takes a minimalist, tautological view – that any policy that staggers battered and bloodied from the political scrum must by definition be in the public interest. Give the term its usual meaning, however, and the contrary ideas of opposing networks cannot be equally for the public good.

Nor is it feasible to exclude extreme advocates, instead leaving policy making to the moderation and good judgment of fair-minded citizens or their political representatives. At the international level, the role of ordinary citizens is tiny, except as they are represented by their elected governments or funded advocates. Even within states, individual voices can seldom be heard above the activist fray. As for political decision makers, they are often members or associates of networks beforehand, and are anything but moderate. As such, many have little interest in accommodation. Of course, because of institutional rules and opposing interests, policy makers are often blocked from achieving maximal ends or forced to compromise. Even then, however, they will keep on striving for what they would prefer, making disputes persist.

In these cases, policy is made – or unmade – through the conflictive processes outlined in this book. From a normative standpoint, open-minded interchange might be preferable, but this is unrealistic. Some may cover their ears and wring their hands at the din, but it is and always will be a hallmark of

---

[17] Bonnie Honig, *Political Theory and the Displacement of Politics* (Ithaca, NY: Cornell University Press, 1993); Chantal Mouffe, *On the Political* (New York, NY: Routledge, 2005). Cf. Archon Fung, "Deliberation before the Revolution: Toward an Ethics of Deliberative Democracy in an Unjust World," *Political Theory* 33, no. 2 (2005), 397–419; Iris Marion Young, "Activist Challenges to Deliberative Democracy," *Political Theory* 29, no. 5 (2001), 670–90.

politics. Those seeking to bolster democracy need to begin from this uncomfortable truth. Does this mean that only zombie policy will lurch across the landscape? No. Some policy does get made, and some of it has life even if little of it satisfies those longing for optimal solutions. What this perspective calls for, however, is clear-eyed appreciation of the process and its outcomes. These can only be conflictive and contingent in the face of the world's divisions.

Appendix

Interviews

Much of the information on which this book is based comes from one- to two-hour interviews I conducted between 2006 and 2011. In the list that follows, these are designated either as "personal interview" or "telephone interview." For shorter and less formal interchanges, I use the term "personal discussion." Most interviews and discussions involved a single person, although a few had multiple participants (as indicated by asterisks in the list). I conducted all interviews in English or Spanish. Although I entered each interview with a set of prewritten questions, I used a dialogic technique – and frequently uncovered new information and insights that I followed up in the exchange.

All interviewees signed a consent form approved by Duquesne University's Institutional Review Board. The form asked interviewees to provide separate consents to audiotaping and to a waiver of anonymity in publications resulting from my research. Most interviewees consented to both requests and are identified in the list below. For those who did not consent to audiotaping, data used in this book is from my handwritten notes. For those not waiving anonymity, I indicate only organizational name and rank. Tapes and notes are filed at Duquesne's archive.

   1. Arruda, Leonardo. Public Relations Director, Associação Nacional dos Proprietários e Comerciantes de Armas,

Rio de Janeiro, Brazil. Personal interview, November 12, 2007, Rio de Janeiro (audiotape).

2. Barbosa, Bene. President, Movimento Viva Brasil, São Paulo. Personal interview, November 7, 2007, São Paulo, Brazil (audiotape) (translation by Jairo Paes de Lira).*

3. Barrios, Adela. Associate, Fundacíon Gamma Idear, Bogotá. Personal interview, April 11, 2008, Bogotá, Colombia (audiotape).*

4. Becket Fund. Senior staff. Telephone interview, June 24, 2009 (anonymity requested; audiotape).

5. Bevan, James. Researcher, Small Arms Survey, Geneva, Switzerland. Personal interview, June 29, 2006, New York, NY (audiotape).

6. Bokanga, Mpoko. Executive Director, African Agricultural Technology Foundation (AATF) Nairobi, Kenya. Personal interview, July 18, 2008, Nairobi, Kenya (audiotape).

7. Bratt, Percy. Attorney, Civil Rights Defenders, Stockholm, Sweden. Personal interview, April 14, 2011, Stockholm, Sweden (audiotape).

8. Bull, Benjamin, Chief Counsel, Alliance Defense Fund, Scottsdale, AZ. Telephone interview, July 22, 2009 (notes).

9. Chileshe, Chilufya. Information Officer, Jesuit Centre for Theological Reflection, Lusaka. Personal interview, July 23, 2008, Lusaka, Zambia (notes).

10. Costea, Peter. President, Association of Romanian Families. Telephone interview, March 11, 2010 (audiotape).

11. De Caris, Ricardo. Senior Programme Officer, Safer Africa, Pretoria. Personal interview, July 5, 2006, New York, NY (audiotape).

12. De Sanctis, José Luiz. Pela Legítima Defesa, São Paulo. Personal interview, November 7, 2007, São Paulo, Brazil (audiotape) (translation by Jairo Paes de Lira).*

13. De Jonge Oudraat, Chantal. United States Institute of Peace; former Senior Research Associated, UN Institute for

Disarmament Research, Geneva, Switzerland. Telephone interview, April 12, 2007 (notes).

14. Dreyfus, Pablo. Research Manager, Small Arms Control Project, Viva Rio, Rio de Janeiro. Personal interview, July 6, 2006, New York, NY (audiotape).

15. Edwards, Michael. Program Officer, Ford Foundation, New York. Personal interview, June 30, 2006, New York, NY (audiotape).*

16. Frey, Barbara. UN Special Rapporteur on the Prevention of Human Rights Violations Committed with Small Arms and Light Weapons, Director, Human Rights Program, University of Minnesota, Minneapolis. Telephone interview, May 30, 2007 (audiotape).

17. Goldring, Natalie. Georgetown University; former staff member, British American Security Institute (BASIC), Washington. Personal interview, May 11, 2006, Washington, DC (audiotape).

18. Goodman, Colby. Advocacy Associate, Amnesty International-USA, Washington. Personal interview, July 5, 2006, New York, NY (audiotape).

19. Green, Robert. National President, Sporting Shooters Association of Australia, Kent Town, South Australia. Personal interview, July 7, 2006, New York, NY (audiotape).

20. Greene, Owen. University of Bradford, UK; former Consultant to the UN Group of Governmental Experts on Small Arms. Personal interview, July 6, 2006, New York, NY (audiotape).

21. Hartung, William. Director, Arms Trade Resource Center, World Policy Institute, New York. Personal interview, October 11, 2007, Pittsburgh, PA (audiotape).

22. Henriot, Peter J. Director, Jesuit Center for Theological Reflection, Lusaka. Personal interview, July 23, 2008, Lusaka, Zambia (audiotape).

23. Hernandez, Juan Pablo. Vida Sagrada de la Secretaría de Gobierno, Alcaldía Mayor de Bogotá D.C., Bogotá. Personal interview, April 11, 2008, Bogotá, Colombia (audiotape).

24. Hobbs, Jeremy. Oxfam International-USA, Washington. Personal discussion, June 29, 2006, New York, NY (notes).

25. Howat, John. Chairman, New Zealand Council of Licensed Firearms Owners Inc., Wellington. Personal interview, July 7, 2006, New York, NY (audiotape).

26. Hurtado Correa, Julio E. President, Sociedad Colombiana Tradicíon y Accíon, Bogotá. Personal interview, April 11, 12, 2008, Bogotá, Colombia (audiotape).**

27. Husbands, Jo. Senior Project Director, National Academy of Sciences, Washington. Telephone interview, May 10, 2007 (audiotape).

28. Jiménez, Abel E. President, Asociacíon Colombiano de Colecionistas de Armas, Bogotá. Personal interview, April 11 and 12, 2008, Bogotá, Colombia (audiotape).**

29. Jordan, Lisa. Program officer, Ford Foundation. Personal interview, July 6, 2006, New York, NY (audiotape).*

30. Juma, Josephat. Managing Editor, *African Executive*, Inter Region Economic Network (IREN). Personal interview, July 21, 2008, Nairobi, Kenya (notes).

31. Kambikambi, Tamala T. Lecturer, Department of Crop Science, University of Zambia. Personal interview, July 24, 2008, Lusaka, Zambia (audiotape).

32. Karembu, Margaret. Director, International Service for the Acquisition of Agri-Biotech Applications (ISAAA) Afri-Center, Nairobi, Kenya. Personal interview, July 22, 2008, Nairobi, Kenya (audiotape).

33. Kirsten, Adele. Research Associate for Arms Management, Institute for Security Studies, Pretoria. Personal interview, July 7, 2006, New York, NY (notes).

34. Laurance, Edward. Dean and Professor, Graduate School of International Policy Studies, Monterey Institute of International Studies, Monterey; former consultant, United Nations Department of Disarmament Affairs. Telephone interview, June 8, 2007 (audiotape).

35. Lewanika, Mwananyanda Mbikusita. Executive Director, National Institute for Scientific and Industrial Research,

Lusaka, Zambia. Personal interview, July 22, 2008, Lusaka, Zambia (audiotape).

36. Lumpe, Lora. Former staff member, Federation of American Scientists, Washington. Telephone interview, May 9, 2007 (audiotape).

37. Lutz, Stephan. Program Consultant, Christian Reformed World Relief Committee, Kenya. Personal interview, July 21, 2008, Nairobi, Kenya.

38. Luz, Daniel. Board of Directors, IANSA, London. Personal interview, November 14, 2007, Rio de Janeiro (audiotape).

39. McDonald, Glenn. Senior Researcher, Small Arms Survey, Geneva, Switzerland. Personal interview, July 6, 2006, New York, NY (audiotape).

40. Mack, Daniel. Arms Control Coordinator, Instituto Sou da Paz, São Paulo. Personal interview, November 7, 2007, São Paulo, Brazil (audiotape).

41. Mantilla de Ardila, Amparo. Director, Fundacíon Gamma Idear; founder ARIANSA (Red Andina de Organizacíones Femeninas Trabajando en Desarme, Seguridad Humana, Salvacíon de Vidas, y Cultura de Paz), Bogotá. Personal interview, April 11, 2008, Bogotá, Colombia (audiotape).*

42. Mizne, Denis. Executive Director, Instituto Sou da Paz, São Paulo. Telephone interview, October 11, 2007 (audiotape).

43. Muhunyu, Samuel. National Coordinator, Network for Ecofarming in Africa (NECOFA) Kenya, Molo, Kenya. Personal interview, July 21, 2008, Nairobi, Kenya (audiotape).

44. Otunge, Daniel. Communication Officer, International Service for the Acquisition of Agri-Biotech Applications (ISAAA) AfriCenter. Personal interview, July 22, 2008, Nairobi, Kenya (audiotape).

45. Paes de Lira, Jairo. Coalizão Brasileira Pela Legítima Defesa, São Paulo. Personal interview, November 7, 2007, São Paulo (audiotape).*

46. Peters, Rebecca. Director, IANSA, London. Personal interview, July 7, 2006, New York, NY (audiotape).

47. Prado Alfaya, Jr., Caio Luiz. Member, Brazilian Safari Club/Pela Legítima Defesa, São Paulo. Personal interview, November 7, 2007, São Paulo, Brazil (audiotape).

48. Pratt, Larry. Executive Director, Gun Owners of America. Personal Interview, April 23, 2009, Pittsburgh, PA (audiotape).

49. Principal, Participatory Ecological Land-Use Management (PELUM) Association. Personal interview, July 24, 2008, Lusaka, Zambia (notes).

50. Ramirez Mejía, Néstor. Retired Major General, Colombian army. Personal interview, April 11, 2008, Bogotá, Colombia (audiotape).**

51. Reed, Lawrence. President, Mackinac Center for Public Policy, Midland, MI. Personal interview, July 26, 2007, Midland, MI (audiotape).

52. Restrepo, Jorge Alberto. Research associate, Centro de Recursos para el Análisis de Conflictos (CERAC); associate professor of economics, Pontifica Universidad Javeriana, Bogotá. Personal interview, April 11, 2008, Bogotá, Colombia (audiotape).

53. Ruse, Austin. President, Catholic Family and Human Rights Institute (C-FAM). Telephone interview, June 29, 2010 (audiotape).*

54. Simwanda, Lovemore. President, Zambia National Farmers Union. Personal interview, July 24, 2008, Lusaka, Zambia (audiotape).

55. Sjödin, Maria, Executive Director, RFSL (Swedish Federation for Lesbian, Gay, Bisexual and Transgender Rights); board member, ILGA (International Lesbian, Gay, Bisexual, Transgender and Intersex Association). Personal interview, April 11, 2011, Stockholm, Sweden (audiotape).

56. Spear, Joanna. Director, Security Studies Program, George Washington University, Washington. Personal interview, March 28, 2007, Washington, DC (audiotape).

57. Stedjan, Scott. Legislative Associate, Friends Committee on National Legislation, Washington. Personal interview, June 28, 2006, New York, NY (audiotape).

58. Stohl, Rachel. Senior Analyst, Center for Defense Information, Washington. Telephone interview, May 10, 2006 (audiotape).
59. Tomlinson, David. National President, National Firearms Association, Edmonton, Canada. Personal interview, June 30, 2006, New York, NY (audiotape).
60. Trujillo Villegas, Eugenio. Executive Director, Sociedad Colombiana Tradicíon y Accíon, Bogotá. Personal interview, April 11 and 12, 2008, Bogotá, Colombia (audiotape).**
61. Tunehag, Mats. President, Swedish Evangelical Alliance; global council Advocates International. Personal interview, April 14, 2011, Stockholm, Sweden (audiotape).
62. Volk, Oleg. Creative Advertising Director, Volkstudio. Telephone interview, January 28, 2011 (audiotape).
63. Wakhungu, Judi. Executive Director, African Centre for Technology Studies. Personal interview, July 19, 2008, Nairobi, Kenya (audiotape).
64. Waki, Diogo C. Pela Legítima Defesa, São Paulo. Personal interview, November 7, 2007, São Paulo, Brazil (audiotape) (translation by Jairo Paes de Lira).*
65. Wiseman, Geoffrey. University of Southern California, Los Angeles; former program officer, Ford Foundation. Telephone interview, August 1, 2007 (notes).
66. World Forum on the Future of Sport Shooting Activities (WFSA) official. Personal discussion, July 5, 2006, New York, NY (anonymity requested).
67. Yoshihara, Susan. Vice President for Research, Catholic Family and Human Rights Institute (C-FAM). Telephone interview, June 29, 2010 (audiotape).*
68. Youngman, D. Allen. Executive Director, Defense Small Arms Advisory Council, Arlington, VA. Personal interview, July 5, 2006, New York, NY (audiotape).

Sources

Copies of primary source materials noted in this book are available at the Duquesne University Archive, Gumberg Library. In addition, a full bibliography is available online through the book's permanent Cambridge University Press Web site and my own personal Web site, https://sites.google.com/site/cliffordbob2/. The bibliography provides active Internet links to primary documents available online. Because many Web pages are not permanent, the bibliography also includes brief excerpts of relevant sections of most primary documents. This will allow other scholars to easily examine my sources, probe my interpretations, and challenge my findings – all with the goal of improving reliability, replicability, and knowledge.

Index

Continue from page iii

Made in the USA
Coppell, TX
08 February 2021

49948033R00134